2004

Gay and Lesbian Aging

Research and
Future Directions

Gilbert Herdt, PhD is Director of the National Sexuality Resource Center, and Professor and Director of Human Sexuality Studies at San Francisco State University.

A Fulbright scholar, Dr. Herdt worked in the Highlands of Papua New Guinea, on which his first book, *Guardians of the Flutes* (nominated for the National Book Award) and a subsequent BBC film were based. Dr. Herdt was previously on the faculty at Stanford University, and was a professor and chair of the Committee on Human Development at the University of Chicago.

The recipient of many awards and honors, including a Guggenheim Fellowship and NIMH Individual Postdoctoral Fellowship, and the Ruth Benedict Prize in Anthropology, Herdt has written and edited more than 25 books and 100 journal articles, chapters, monographs, and reports.

Brian de Vries, PhD, is Professor and Director of Gerontology at San Francisco State University and Adjunct Professor of Gerontology at the University of Texas, School of Public Health, Houston.

Dr. de Vries is a Fellow of the Gerontological Society of America; he is a founding member and former chair of the Interest Group of Death, Dying, Bereavement and Widowhood and a founding member of the Interest Group on Reminiscence and Life Review. He is Associate Editor of *The International Journal of Aging and Human Development* and has served as Guest Editor of two special issues on *Omega: Journal of Death and Dying* (1977) and Guest Co-Editor of *Generations* (2001), the journal of the American Society on Aging.

Dr. de Vries has also edited *Kinship Breavement in Later Life; End of Life Issues: Interdisciplinary and Multidimensional Perspectives* (Springer 1999); and *Narrative Gerontology: Theory, Research and Practice* (co-edited with G. Kenyon and P. Clark, Springer Publishing, 2001).

Gay and Lesbian Aging

Research and
Future Directions

Gilbert Herdt, PhD
Brian de Vries, PhD
Editors

 Springer Publishing Company

Springer Publishing Company, Inc.
536 Broadway
New York, NY 10012-3955

Acquisitions Editor: Helvi Gold
Production Editor: Betsy Day
Cover design by Joanne Honigman

04 05 06 07 08 / 5 4 3 2 1

Library of Congress Cataloging-in-Publication Data

Gay and lesbian aging : research and future directions / Gilbert Herdt, Brian de Vries, editors.
    p. cm.
    "Product of a major research conference at San Francisco State University organized . . . in October 2001, entitled Development, Aging, and Well-being: a Research Agenda for the 21st Century"—Ack.
    Includes bibliographical references and index.
    ISBN 0-8261-2234-5
    1. Middle aged gays—Congresses. 2. Aged gays—Congresses. 3. Aging—Congresses. 4. Gerontology—Congresses. I. Herdt, Gilbert H., 1949–
II. de Vries, B. (Brian)
HQ75.115.G39 2004
305.244–dc22   2003063324

Printed in the United States of America by Integrated Book Technology.

Dedicated to the memory of Andrew M. (Andy) Boxer and Jeanette Gurevitch two cherished departed colleagues and two guiding lights in the field of gay and lesbian aging.

Acknowledgments

This book is the product of a major research conference at San Francisco State University organized by Gilbert Herdt, Brian de Vries, and Todd Rawls in October 2001, entitled "Development, Aging, and Well-Being: A Research Agenda for the 21st Century." We should like to thank the Ford Foundation for its program support and the Social Science Research Council (Dr. Diane DiMauro, in particular) for cosponsorship support. We would also like to thank Dean Joel Kassiola, College of Behavioral and Social Sciences, SFSU, for his kind support of the project. The editors are also grateful to Judith Barker, Doug Kimmel, Todd Rawls, and Caitlin Ryan for their guidance and help. Additionally, the editors wish to thank Paul Hammond for his assistance during the conference. Finally, we wish to thank the capable and supportive staff of Springer Publishing, particularly Helvi Gold, Betsy Day, and Susan Zorn, for their assistance in the development and production of this book.

Contents

Contents

Section 3   Future Directions

List of Contributors

Judith C. Barker, Ph.D.
Professor of Medical
  Anthropology
University of California,
  San Francisco
San Francisco, CA

John A. Blando, Ph.D.
Assistant Professor of
  Counseling
San Francisco State University
San Francisco, CA

Bertram J. Cohler, Ph.D.
The Committee on Human
  Development
University of Chicago
Chicago, IL

Brian de Vries, Ph.D.
Professor, Director of
  Gerontology
San Francisco State University
San Francisco, CA

Curtis Dolezal, Ph.D.
Columbia University
  Department of Psychiatry
The New York State Psychiatric
  Institute
New York, NY

E. Michael Gorman, Ph.D.
Assistant Professor of Social
  Work
San Jose State University
San Jose, CA

Gilbert Herdt, Ph.D.
Professor, Director of Human
  Sexuality Studies
San Francisco State University
San Francisco, CA

Andrew Hostetler, Ph.D.
Assistant Professor of
  Psychology
University of Minnesota
Morris, MN

Robert Kertzner, MD
Associate Clinical Professor of
  Psychiatry
Columbia University
New York, NY

Douglas C. Kimmel, Ph.D.
Professor Emeritus
Department of Psychology,
City College, CUNY,
  New York, NY

Hans W. Kristiansen, Ph.D.
Institute of Criminology and
  Sociology of Law
University of Oslo
Oslo, Norway

Keith Nelson, MSW
Santa Clara Kaiser Permanente
  Medical Center
Santa Clara, CA

Ilan Meyer, Ph.D.
Joseph L. Mailman School of
  Public Health
Columbia University
New York, NY

Todd Rawls, MA
Program in Human Sexuality
San Francisco State University
San Francisco, CA

**Jacqueline S. Weinstock,
  Ph.D.**
Associate Professor of Integrated
  Professional Studies
University of Vermont
Burlington, VT

Introduction

Gilbert Herdt and Brian de Vries

The year 2003 marks the 30th anniversary of the landmark "declassification" of homosexuality as a disease by the American Psychiatric Association in 1973—a watershed in the lives of gays and lesbians in the United States. It seems fitting at this time to examine how the generation of lesbian, gay, bisexual, and transgender (LGBT) people who led this social movement are themselves now moving into midlife and beyond. Moreover, this occasion provides a unique opportunity to examine how the baby boomers and their peers are confronting the prospects and problems of aging in the United States and other countries. We believe that these critical issues in research and policy have only begun to be addressed by gerontology and the social sciences, and we welcome this opportunity to raise a new agenda in research and policy for the 21st century. The authors in this book have considered major theoretical and methodological questions bearing upon the emergence of well-being at midlife and beyond for gay and lesbian seniors, a much ignored population, as Ray Berger (1982) suggested long ago. The book is purposely interdisciplinary; it bring together psychologists, anthropologists, sociologists, gerontologists, and health providers who have sought to enter a dialogue with the reader in framing a broad and inclusive gerontology in this new century.

This book follows upon a major research conference in 2001 that was dedicated to gay and lesbian midlife and aging and its inclusion in social gerontology. The reader should know the background of this emphasis. Because of the resources available and the lack of identifiable authorities on bisexuals and transgender people, the editors decided to focus specifically on gay men and lesbians; however, it is vital that subsequent efforts be directed to the broader social and health concerns of LGBT people more broadly.

The meaning of adult development and aging of sexual minorities is little understood in the United States. For the first time in history, a generation of *self-identified* lesbians, gay men, bisexuals, and transgender individuals are approaching retirement, and yet we know little of the health, mental health, and concomitant special social service needs of this population (as Barker addresses in her chapter). Even less do we understand what well-being and successful development in later life mean in these communities. Moreover, the aging processes among lesbians and gay men who are already in their retirement years, many of whom are still "closeted," remain invisible.

A recent and modest line of research suggests that some aging gay men and lesbians are facing several unique challenges, including limited access to gay-friendly health care, feelings of invisibility and confrontations with ageism within gay and lesbian community contexts, denial of hospital and nursing home visitation rights for their partners, loneliness and social isolation, internalized homophobia, and accelerated aging. A parallel and equally modest line of research suggests, however, that gay men and lesbians age with the advantage of crisis competence and mastery of stigma, having weathered the trials of coming out and having developed positive self-identities within a homophobic society; the chapters by Kertzner et al. and by Rawls address some of these issues.

The complex web formed by these perspectives and the social policy related to such changes is unknown, as in other areas of LGBT life course development. Unprecedented demographic changes in the United States associated with the "elder boom," are placing enormous demands on private and governmental social service agencies and health care providers. These demands are particularly acute for those attempting to address the special needs of sexual minorities, and additional research to guide their efforts is sorely needed. Agencies and policymakers are currently scrambling to meet these special needs. The time is ripe for the development of an agenda of research to address the needs of this population in the 21st century.

The HIV epidemic (addressed by Gorman and Nelson in their chapter) has dominated the attention of researchers in the area of sexual minorities and the gay and lesbian public in general over the past two decades. Most recent issues relate to risk and prevention in gay and lesbian communities (Levine, Gagnon, & Nardi, 1997; Paul et al.,

2002). A youth focus (Boxer & Cohler, 1989; Cohler & Galatzer-Levy, 2000; Herdt & Boxer, 1993) has obscured from view lesbian and gay seniors, many of whom remain in the shadows of the lesbian and gay community (Herdt, Beeler, & Rawls, 1997).

Moreover, the attitudes and beliefs of the surrounding culture and the peers of these generations—youth and seniors—make clear the urgent need to study how midlife and senior gay men and lesbians are aging in America. As a recent report (2002) of the Henry J. Kaiser Foundation on the experiences of lesbians, gay men, and bisexuals suggests, a huge difference in positive attitudes exists between the peers of younger lesbians and gay men and their senior counterparts. As the study shows, a high number of younger people are more open and accepting of LGBT people in their schools, churches, and work-places than ever before. However, individuals age 65 and older are least likely to have accepting attitudes toward LGBT people. Moreover, young people and seniors, according to the report, hold very different views about policy. The great majority of young people aged 18 to 29 support lesbian and gay unions, marriage, and adoptions for LGBT people, while for people over 65 only about 25% support these poli-cies—a huge gulf that defines the problems of each cohort as it adapts to society and finds a foothold in this new century.

MILESTONES OF GAY AND LESBIAN COMMUNITY EMPOWERMENT

Social scientists and historians over the past two decades have docu-mented the roots of the gay and lesbian social movement in the United States (D'Emilio, 1983; Herdt, 1997; Kimmel & Sang, 1995; Levine et al., 1997). Institutional forces of discrimination, homophobia, and anti-gay/lesbian violence in the 1960s provided the context for police brutality and harassment, blackmail, hate crimes, and religious perse-cution directed against homosexuals (Herek, 1995; Herrell, 1992) and ultimately the rise of social movements as a consequence.

San Francisco was the scene in the mid-1960s of the first resistance to this prejudice, as activists were supported by heterosexual allies in fighting back against police harassment (Stryker & van Buskirk, 1996). The Stonewall Tavern riots in New York City in 1969, and the emer-gence of the AIDS epidemic in the early to mid-1980s approximately 15 years later, frame the most critical social history of midlife and senior gays and lesbians. Gay and lesbian organizing across North American cities was boosted in the 1970s through the momentous APA "declassification" of homosexuality as a disease, which led to the mobilization of bars, clubs, and social venues to become more openly gay-friendly. Soon thereafter, the mobilization of the women's health movement was to provide a necessary model for subsequent HIV care and a bridge between the lesbian and gay communities (Rubin, 1997).

Of course, it will not go unnoticed that the cohort of those who experienced these dramatic events is now in midlife or beyond. As so-called baby boomers, many of these people have been engaged in the gay and lesbian social movement which has led the way to significant social changes over the past 30 years: first in their late teens and young adult years during the sexual revolution of the 1960s, when new norms and sexual values were advanced following upon the black power and feminist movements; and then in the 1970s in the formation of a public and politically visible gay and lesbian community in such cities as New York, Chicago, San Francisco, Los Angeles, and others. These communities in turn provided the critical historical and cultural context for the creation of a new developmental cohort of adolescents in the 1980s who, as teens, would self-identify as gay, lesbian, and bisexual youth, some of whom went on to be involved in the gay culture (Herdt & Boxer, 1993).

The HIV epidemic further mobilized and fed this movement: by way of the controversies in the early 1980s and decisions over whether gay bathhouses should be closed (a topic further discussed by Cohler in this volume) and how this would impact the community; through responses to the evolving epidemic and the lack of government and medical support for persons with AIDS; and through more radical movements, such as AIDS ACT UP, in the late 1980s and early 1990s, when the morbidity rate was accelerating in the gay community and as people living with AIDS became distinctly visible (Levine, 1992). The subsequent emphasis upon youth and risk in the late 1980s and 1990s and the increased awareness of people living with HIV gave way to a recognition of the lack of attention to seniors. For example, New York City witnessed the creation of a gay and lesbian seniors group (Senior Action in a Gay Environment: SAGE), as did San Francisco (Gay and Lesbian Outreach to Elders: GLOE, which has since become New Leaf Outreach to Elders), to address issues of aging and care for older members of the gay and lesbian community.

GAY AND LESBIAN BABY BOOMERS
IN THE NEW CENTURY

On January 1, 1996, the first boomers turned 50, signaling a dramatic demographic change that will extend not only the longevity of Americans (Morgan, 1998) but also the influence of this cohort beyond smaller, more traditional generations that came before (e.g., Valliant, 2002). In education, career choices, political beliefs, and consumer behavior, the boomers dominated American culture for a half century. As we know from studies of social movements and sexual change and as intimated above, boomers led the second sexual revolution of this century in the 1960s, following the invention of the Pill and the influence of second-wave feminism and related activities driven by the then college-age boomers (D'Emilio & Freedman, 1988). For example, college boomers began to openly resist the taboo on premarital sexual intercourse in the early 1960s, challenging traditional sex segregation in college dorms, and delaying marriage (Moran, 2000). Only recently has the sexuality of the boomers been studied, and it is our hope that this collection will give a significant new impetus to studies of sexuality and romantic relations in the second half of life, as suggested by de Vries and Blando in Chapter 1.

Uncovering the complexities of these effects and experiences is itself a complex enterprise. Over the past two decades social scientists discovered that individual interviews were insufficient in studying the effects of major events or life-changing experiences, such as the AIDS epidemic (Elder, 1980; Farmer, 1999; Gagnon, 1992). For example, in studying HIV, individuals who self-identified as heterosexual were initially passed by in tracking the epidemic and in prevention efforts; only when ethnographic study was used did researchers discover the critical disconnect between sexual identity and sexual behavior. Then too, the puzzling dissonance between knowledge and sexual action that contributed to risk and infection (Diaz, 1998; Parker, Carballo, & Herdt, 1991) became the focus of intense analysis.

During the years of this transformation, gay men and lesbians have moved from a status of individual pathology to group identity (Kimmel & Sang, 1995). Legal and political barriers have prevented formal recognition of partnership, marriage, family formation, adoption, inheritance, caretaking, and a variety of other forms of normative development and support in society. Religions have often stigmatized or excluded homosexuals from their congregations, and some churches continue to bar their ministers from being homosexual or performing religious ceremonies or functions such as weddings for their lesbian and gay parishioners (Lewin, 1996). Ethnographic studies have shown strong correlations between marginalization, lack of social support, and negative outcomes such as enhanced alcohol abuse (Newton, 1993), increased sexual risk taking (Rubin, 1997), and loss of self-esteem with aging (Herdt et al., 1997). Being without a partner seems to enhance the feeling of loneliness and the use of alcohol as a coping device (Grossman et al., 2000), and further addressed by Hostetler in this volume; Weinstock also addresses the complex issue of social support and network composition in the lives of midlife lesbians). In such respects, a lifetime legacy of sexual prejudice (Herdt, 1995) has plagued the social development of sexual minority people, much as racial prejudice has affected African Americans. The cohort effects upon morale and adjustment have clearly changed with time (Berger, 1982; Kooden & Flowers, 2000; Sang, Warshaw, & Smith, 1991). As this cohort ages and experiences increasing marginalization due to ageism, with concomitant increase in chronic disease, the need for informal care becomes of critical importance.

Sexual citizenship—a construct that describes how citizenship is shaped by and/or denied to those who do not engage in normative and socially accepted sexual behavior and social practices within modern society—has emerged as a significant means of understanding these challenges across societies (Weeks, 1985; Plummer, 1995). This emphasis on sexual citizenship almost always dovetails with a profound emphasis on heterosexuality and reproductive heterosexual marriage with the aim of producing children and grandchildren. As Herdt (1997) has characterized the issue, virtually all cultures known to anthropology have emphasized reproductive heterosexuality in marriage for the production of children and grandchildren as the necessary and desirable aim of social life. Thus the pressure on lesbians and gay men to conform to this norm has profoundly impacted their lives, creating what sociologist/psychoanalyst Nancy Chodorow (1992) has called the "heterosexual compromises" of adapting to our society, even against their own desires and wishes.

More generally this process is known as *heteronormativity* or "social heterosexuality," whereby regardless of someone's actual sexual orientation and sexual practice, one lives by the code of being and acting heterosexual. Thus social heterosexuality is a policy and moral standard that is enforced within the society and that all of society assumes to be operative. It follows that those who do not marry and have children pay a steep price, and those lesbians and gay men who did not marry heterosexually and bear children were the most obvious and the most vulnerable; Kristiansen addresses some of these issues in his chapter. Of course, women in the prior generation who chose to follow professional careers faced this dilemma from the start. However, we would like to speculate that lesbians who resisted the code of social heterosexuality in the last generation were often punished and denied citizenship in fundamental ways that should be investigated in their aftermath.

A template of self-fulfilling prophecies is thus created—what will go wrong, and what will be lost, through becoming gay or lesbian? Indeed, those expected rights and duties that are incumbent on all persons to achieve full personhood might be completely out of the reach of someone who is openly gay or lesbian. Someone who fails to achieve all of these rights and to carry out these duties and responsibilities is thus denied sexual citizenship as well as full personhood. In the vast majority of all contemporary Western societies, and in the United States in particular, full personhood means being socialized in the direction of erotic and emotional attachments to members of the other sex, with the expectation that one will marry heterosexually, rear a family, and eventually become a grandparent (Herdt & Koff, 2000). Here, once more, the impact of living as a gay or lesbian person under the sign of social heterosexuality is profound and oppressive.

Gay men and lesbians in the past accommodated themselves to, and even were invisible within, the general heterosexual population. We observe that those who came out in the 1960s or 1970s as adults did so often for political or personal reasons that inspired their ability to fight against oppression. Conversely, those who were unable or unwilling to disclose their feelings or relationships in public were saddled with the burdens of discrimination and isolation, while never being able to fight back in public. This difference has important implications for the formation of community building, citizenship, and resilience across the life course.

As the baby boomers move into the second half of life, many of them seem to move into and out of gay and lesbian communities; this movement may derive from health and/or relationship status, or from identification with gay and lesbian communities. Those who live on the margins or who are hidden from communities may suffer as a result. Among LGBT seniors, such transformation is compounded by the impact of the AIDS epidemic, the loss of cohort support, the cumulative effect of homophobia and discrimination across a lifetime, and fear of aging and ultimately dying in the absence of social support. A small number of studies have shown that these communities, while resilient, are increasingly shunned or excluded from the mainstream of gay and lesbian social life, perhaps because this mainstream is youth-oriented and centers on bars. The double impact of racism and homophobia in LGBT people of color is particularly worrisome and little known. The social policy related to such changes is unknown, as in other areas of LGBT life course development. The demands are particularly acute for those attempting to address the special needs of sexual minorities, and additional research to guide their efforts is sorely needed.

THE ORGANIZATION OF THIS BOOK

This book marks an interesting coming of age of an area of research; at the same time, it necessarily suffers from some of the same limitations of the general literature on gay and lesbian aging, namely, the modest presentation of issues and research on aging lesbians, bisexuals, and transgender individuals. The absence of research in these areas, both in the literature in general and in this book in particular, makes an important empirical point itself. It also makes an important political statement of voices still unheard. Both should be seen as a call to action.

This book is organized into three areas. The first is intended to set the stage by addressing, broadly and somewhat selectively, issues of aging for lesbians and gay men. In the service of this intention, three chapters are included.

The first chapter of **Section 1** is written by Brian de Vries and John A. Blando, a gerontologist and clinical psychologist, respectively. De Vries and Blando broadly, yet selectively, review what is known about the social context of gay and lesbian aging and the way in which it is studied. This chapter is useful as an assemblage of empirical research of older lesbians and gay men, and its embedded goal is the elucidation of the particular questions posed in the study of gay and lesbian elders that may have relevance for the study of heterosexual elders as well. That is to say, in studying gay and lesbian lives, researchers have quite naturally adopted stances that may be broadly characterized as more attuned to the person-environment fit, more sensitive to the cohort effects in which the experiences of older individuals must be placed, and more mindful of the (related) social conditions marking their development. These stances are not (and should not be) restricted to a gay and lesbian gerontology.

The second chapter is by Judith Barker, an anthropologist, who focuses her writing on the situation of older women, aged 65 and above. Barker points out that, given that 75% of all older persons in society are women, older LGBT persons are likely to be lesbians rather than gay men. Notwithstanding these dramatic differences in number, there exist very few published reports about the experiences of older lesbians. Barker summarizes this literature and offers implications for future work on several dimensions: social support, family relations, health, economics and occupation, housing, and access to services.

The final chapter in this section, by E. Michael Gorman and Keith Nelson, both of whom are social workers and public health scientists, addresses the particular issue of HIV/AIDS for older gay and bisexual men. The lesbian and especially the gay communities have suffered greatly under the impact of AIDS and have shouldered a great deal of the burden of care and the work of advocacy. Gorman and Nelson reflect on some of the current HIV/AIDS challenges facing gay and bisexual men in the middle and later years and offer insight into the strengths and resilience by which this cohort of men may be characterized.

Section 2, the largest of the three sections of this book, presents accounts of empirical research into the myriad issues of aging for lesbians and gay men. There are six chapters in this section, representing ethnographic qualitative research as well as more scalar quantitative research.

The first chapter in this section, authored by Robert Kertzner, Ilan Meyer, and Curtis Dolezal, psychiatrists, adopts the latter of these research approaches in its analysis of the psychological well-being in middle and later life of gay, heterosexual, and bisexual men over the age of 40. The authors draw their data from the National Survey of Midlife Development in the United States and test a multidimensional model of psychological well-being. They find many similarities and some interesting differences considered in the context of sociohistorical developmental differences.

The second chapter of this section is written by Todd Rawls, a sociologist, who similarly adopts a quantitative approach. Rawls uses data from the Urban Men's Health Study, a probabilistic sample of men who have sex with men in the metropolitan communities of San Francisco, Los Angeles, Chicago, and New York City. Those over the age of 50 are the focus of these analyses, which concentrate on degrees of sexual identity disclosure and the relationship of disclosure to indicators of mental health and well-being.

Andrew Hostetler, a developmental psychologist, authors the section's third chapter, on the well-being of middle-aged and older single gay men. Hostetler offers an ecologically grounded analysis of well-being using both quantitative and qualitative research methods. In his analysis, Hostetler considers some of the barriers single men encounter and the resources at their disposal in their efforts to "age successfully." He further examines the meaning and experience of community, particularly in the context of "chosen families," a frequently used term in gay and lesbian studies, and the manifestation of such chosen families in the lives of gay men who may be single by circumstance or by choice.

The fourth chapter of this section is by Jacqueline S. Weinstock, a developmental psychologist. Weinstock elaborates further on a construct entertained by Hostetler, "friends as family," with a sample of midlife lesbians. In her qualitative study, Weinstock draws upon the historical and developmental experiences of lesbians and identifies three patterns of friends as family, each of which reflects a unique valuation of friendship and each of which holds implications for the organization and prioritization of lesbians' other relationships and life choices.

The fifth chapter of this section is written by Bertram Cohler, a life-course psychologist and practicing psychoanalyst, on the topic of sexual desire of middle-aged and older men who seek sex with other men. This ethnographic report, based on several years of participant observation, contrasts both setting and patterns of social interaction of two cohorts of men (older men and younger adults) patronizing bathhouses. Cohler's analyses reveal the culture of the gay bath and the social and sexual spaces of older and younger gay men and their self-definitions and relationship to the "gay community."

Hans Kristiansen, a social anthropologist, contributes the final chapter in this section, exploring the links between relationship history and moral concerns in the lives of older gay men in Norway. Kristiansen situates his research within the broader cultural and historical framework of Norway in the postwar period. Based on participant observation, Kristiansen identifies three patterns of relationship histories and considers within these patterns the differences and similarities of discretion, sexual dignity, and familial ties.

Section 3 of this book comprises a single chapter, the intent of which is to reconsider some of the issues of aging among gay men and lesbians and to suggest future directions in the study of midlife and older sexual minorities.

Douglas Kimmel, a leading psychologist of aging, elaborates on the many reasons it is important to study the processes of aging for midlife and older sexual minorities. Kimmel further reviews central theories and models appropriate for such research, as well as some of the important issues to consider in its conduct—an important series of points on which to conclude the book.

REFERENCES

Berger, R. M. (1982). *Gay and gray: The older homosexual man*. Urbana, IL: University of Illinois Press.

Boxer, A. M., & Cohler, B. (1989). The life course of gay and lesbian youth: An immodest proposal for the study of lives. In G. Herdt (Ed.), *Gay and lesbian youth* (pp. 315–355). New York: Harrington Park Press.

Chodorow, N. J. (1992). Heterosexuality as a compromise formation: Reflections on the psychoanalytic theory of sexual development. *Psychoanalysis and Contemporary Thought, 15*, 267–304.

Cohler, B. J., & Galatzer-Levy, R. M. (2000). *The course of gay and lesbian lives*. Chicago: University of Chicago Press.

D'Emilio, J. (1983). *Sexual identities, sexual communities*. Chicago: University of Chicago Press.

D'Emilio, J., & Freedman, E. (1988). *Intimate matters*. New York: Harper & Row.

Diaz, R. M. (1998). *Latino gay men and HIV*. New York: Routledge.

Elder, G. (1980). Adolescents in historical perspective. In J. Adelson (Ed.), *Handbook of adolescent psychology* (pp. 3–46). New York: Wiley.

Farmer, P. (1999). *Infections and inequalities: The modern plagues*. Berkeley, CA: University of California Press.

Gagnon, J. (1992). Epidemics and researchers: AIDS and the practice of social studies. In G. Herdt & S. Lindenbaum (Eds.), *The time of AIDS* (pp. 27–40). Newbury Park, CA: Sage Publications.

Grossman, A. H., D'Augelli, A. R., & Hershberger, S. L. (2000). Social support networks and lesbian, gay, and bisexual adults 60 years of age and older. *Journal of Gerontology, 55*, 171–179.

Herdt, G. (1997). *Same sex, different cultures*. New York: Westview.

Herdt, G., Beeler, J., & Rawls, T. (1997). Life course diversity among older lesbians and gay men: A study in Chicago. *Journal of Gay, Lesbian, and Bisexual Identities,* 2, 231–247.

Herdt, G., & Boxer, A. (1993). *Children of Horizons.* Boston: Beacon Press.

Herdt, G., & Koff, B. (2000). *Something to tell you: The road families travel when a child is gay.* New York: Columbia University Press.

Herek, G. (1995). Psychological heterosexism in the United States. In A. R. D'Augelli & C. Patterson (Eds.), *Lesbian, gay, and bisexual identities over the life span* (pp. 321–346). New York: Oxford University Press.

Herrell, R. (1992). The symbolic strategies of Chicago's gay and lesbian pride day parade. In G. Herdt (Ed.), *Gay culture in America* (pp. 225–252). Boston: Beacon Press.

Kaiser Foundation. (2002). *A report on the experience of lesbians, gays and bisexuals in America and the public's views on issues and policies related to sexual orientation.* Washington, D.C.

Kimmel, D., & Sang, B. (1995). Lesbians and gay men in mid life. In A. R. D'Augelli & C. Patterson (Eds.), *Lesbian, gay and bisexual identities over the life span* (pp. 517–534). New York: Oxford University Press.

Kooden, H., & Flowers, C. (2000). *Golden men: The power of gay midlife.* New York: Morrow.

Levine, J., Gagnon, J., & Nardi, P. (1997). *In changing times.* Chicago: University of Chicago Press.

Levine, M. (1992). The implications of constructionist theory for social research on the AIDS epidemic among gay men. In G. Herdt & S. Lindenbaum (Eds.), *The time of AIDS* (pp. 185–198). Newbury Park, CA: Sage.

Lewin, E. (Ed.). (1996). *Inventing lesbian cultures in America.* Boston: Beacon Press.

Moran, J. (2000). *Teaching sex: The shaping of adolescence in the 20th century.* Cambridge, MA: Harvard University Press.

Morgan, D. L. (1998). Facts and figures about the baby boom. *Generations 12,* 10–15.

Newton, E. (1993). *Cherry Grove, Fire Island.* Boston: Beacon Press.

Parker, R., Carballo, M., & Herdt, G. (1991). Sexual culture, HIV transmission, and AIDS research. *Journal of Sex Research, 28,* 75–96.

Paul, J., et al. (2002). Suicide attempts among gay and bisexual men: Lifetime prevalence and antecedents. *American Journal of Public Health, 92,* 1338–1345.

Plummer, K. (1995). *Telling sexual stories.* New York: Routledge.

Rubin, G. (1997). Elegy for the valley of kings: AIDS and the leather community in San Francisco, 1981–1996. In M. Levine, J. Gagnon, & P. Nardi (Eds.), *In changing times* (pp. 101–145). Chicago: University of Chicago Press.

Sang, B., Warshaw, J., & Smith, A. J. (Eds.). (1991). *Lesbians at midlife: The creative transition.* San Francisco: Spinsters Book Company.

Stryker, S., & van Buskirk, J. (1996). *Gay by the Bay.* San Francisco: Chronicle Books.

Valliant, G. (2002). *Aging well.* Boston: Little, Brown and Co.

Weeks, J. (1985). *Sexuality and its discontents.* London: Routlege and Kegan Paul.

SECTION 1

Setting the Stage

CHAPTER 1

The Study of Gay and Lesbian Aging: Lessons for Social Gerontology

Brian de Vries and John A. Blando

This book stands as evidence of the emerging interest in gay and lesbian aging. An impressive array of research studies and descriptive reports has emerged since the early work on this topic by Marcy Adelman (1986), Raymond Berger (1982), Monika Kehoe (1988), and Douglas Kimmel (1977). This nascent literature has afforded a glimpse into the lives of older lesbians and gay men, with frequent references to how these individuals differ from the larger, nongay (heterosexual) culture in which they are embedded. Such efforts have been valuable and have provided platforms for the articulation of the special and particular needs of these individuals; however, they also risk creating separate "species" of individuals and minimizing or obscuring those dimensions on which groups are similar.

This chapter is intended to broadly, yet selectively, highlight what is known about the social context of gay and lesbian aging and the way in which it is studied. The goals for doing so are twofold: The first and most obvious content goal is to assemble, in a single source, empirical findings characterizing the social worlds of these older individuals. The second and more programmatic structural goal is to elucidate the particular questions posed in the study of gay and lesbian elders that may have relevance for the study of heterosexual elders as well. In studying gay and lesbian lives, researchers have quite naturally adopted stances that may be broadly characterized as more attuned to the person-environment fit, more sensitive to the cohort effects in which the experiences of older individuals must be placed, and more mindful of the (related) social conditions marking their development. These stances are not (and should not be) restricted to a gay and lesbian gerontology. Notwithstanding those issues separating older gay men and lesbians from comparably aged heterosexuals, these two populations also have much in common, and both can benefit from their mutual consideration.

There are myriad areas in which a gay and lesbian gerontology will increase our appreciation for the social issues characterizing and facing older persons in general. The study of any stigmatized or marginalized group speaks largely to the fact that we tend to study single and personally familiar groups (i.e., people much like ourselves), and we tend to study Caucasian, relatively well-educated, and affluent hetero-sexual older adults.

In the review that follows, we examine the social context of gay and lesbian aging from the standpoint of what is known and how it is known, the latter implicating studies of aging more generally. We selectively define social issues in terms of "family" ties, intimate rela-tionships, friendship, community, generativity, and aging well. These issues were chosen not only to represent the social domain of aging in general, but also to represent the critical gaps and issues for the 21st century in research and policy. We conclude by attempting to make explicit the lessons for social gerontology embedded in our discussions.

"FAMILY" TIES

The study of gay men and lesbians in a family context frequently has adopted a political stance, with the more conservative comments focusing on the apparent mutual exclusivity of homosexuality and family and the more liberal comments on the legal and social right to form legal (e.g., marital) unions (e.g., Dean, 1994). Among the social-psychological analyses have been the charting of family responses, and particularly of parents, to the homosexuality of their (typically late-adolescent) child (e.g., Herdt & Koff, 2000) and the consequences and dynamics of gay men, and especially lesbians, as parents (e.g., Bozett, 1987).

This latter area of research, still in its infancy, has revealed that children reared by lesbian parents develop appropriate psychosocial identities and typically heterosexual orientations with no evidence of increased psychiatric, emotional, or relationship difficulties (see Dundas & Kaufman, 2000, for a review). Centering on the relationship itself, the focus has tended to be on issues such as the transience of the relationship (again, with no noted significant differences) and, more recently, on social supports and motives for pregnancy (Gartrell, Hamilton, Banks, Mosbacher, & Bishop, 1996).

Interestingly, motives for decisions to have children (or not to have children) were of interest to family scientists some time ago. Hoffman and Hoffman (1973), for example, wrote about the values and function of children for adults and included in their analyses the following: realizing adult status and achieving a social identity, expansion of self and the continuation of the family name, morality (e.g., religious beliefs), primary group ties (i.e., creating a family), stimulation (e.g., adventure), creativity and a sense of accomplishment, power and influence, social comparison and competition, and economic utility.

There has been little attention directed to such motives in the more recent family science literature and in public discourse. Herein lies an interesting difference between the prospective and new parental experiences of heterosexual adults and lesbians/gay men: In the case of the former, upon hearing of the pregnancy, congratulations are typically expressed by both family and friends; in the case of the latter, upon hearing of the pregnancy (or adoption), queries about the reasons for such actions are typically posed by both family and friends. Although the congratulatory comments are more socially acceptable, the queries about the decision and the responses generated by the prospective parents are important and informative because they reveal social and personal decision-making issues, independent of sexual orientation.

The dynamics of those families that include a gay or lesbian member are infrequently studied, although they are particularly and poignantly implicated in coming-out stories such as those compiled by Vacha (1985). The disclosure by late-adolescent children to their parents has been met with a wide range of emotions and behaviors, from denial and disbelief, to anger and guilt, to grief and shame, to protection and acceptance (e.g., Herdt & Koff, 2000). In later periods of the life course, the management of this "sensitive" information becomes more salient. Murphy (1989), for example, studied the effect of disclosure by lesbian couples to parents. She commented that a common source of complaint by the couples was maintaining secrecy and the concomitant distance and anxiety that ensued, ultimately associated with awkward communications with family members, decreased family contact, and even conflict within the couple relationship. (Barker, in Chapter 2 of this section, addresses the related issue of estrangement.) The ways in which families negotiate this information and their related roles is part of and informs the conceptually rich literature on family secrets, family scripts, and family folklore.

Connidis (in press) has very recently written about the life course family ties of gay men and lesbians. She notes that not only must the gay or lesbian adult deal with his or her sexual orientation, but that one's sexual orientation influences relationships among other family members as well. This may include a gay or lesbian child and his or her parents, for example, although it may also include the parent's parents (and their attempts to prevent disclosure) or the siblings and their knowledge and attitudes about homosexuality. Furthermore, this may be subdivided along gender lines (e.g., mother/father, sister/ brother). This broader image of influence facilitates a more holistic focus on family relationships (e.g., allows a perspective other than that attributable to family role such as child, sibling, or parent and beyond that of the dyad) and points to the continual negotiation that goes on within families—again, independent of sexual orientation.

INTIMATE RELATIONSHIPS

In conjunction with the mounting evidence describing the psychological, social, and physical health benefits of romantic heterosexual partnerships (e.g., Gove, Style, & Hughes, 1990), researchers have attempted to study the parallel associations with gay men and lesbians (Bell & Weinberg, 1978; Kurdek, 1995; Lee, 1987; Peplau, Veniegas, & Campbell, 1996). This research has focused on a wide range of issues (Cohler & Galatzer-Levy, 2000), ranging from partner selection (e.g., Kurdek & Schmitt, 1987) to issues of power and conflict (e.g., Reilly & Lynch, 1990), and from division of household chores (e.g., Kurdek, 1994) to relationship satisfaction (Kurdek, 1994) and sexuality (e.g., Lee, 1995). Cohler and Galatzer-Levy (2000) report many similarities between older gay and lesbian couples and heterosexual couples; they report that the few differences to emerge include a relatively more egalitarian division of labor among gay male couples and lesbian couples, a higher valuation of affection among lesbian couples, and a relatively higher incidence of sexual nonmonogamy among gay male couples.

Issues of sexuality in general offer an interesting juxtaposition of heterosexuals and gay men and lesbians. Schlesinger (1995) writes that perspectives on sexuality and the elderly have been framed by myths declaring that older persons are sexually undesirable, are not desirous of sexual expression, and are not capable of sexual expression. This view that sex is not for the old has prevented the study of sexuality and aging from attaining a mature status in the gerontological literature. In contrast, the very notion of a gay and lesbian gerontology raises the issue of sexuality directly.

Two apparently mutually inconsistent stereotypes operate in the area of (primarily) gay sexuality. On the one hand, following from the above, older persons are perceived as asexual; on the other hand, older gay men are perceived as sexual perverts and predators (e.g., Kelly, 1977). As Friend (1991) suggests, such contradictions may free individuals from role constraints; such stereotypes, however, continue to operate in how these individuals are perceived, thereby restricting access to prospective sex partners and, by extension, influencing personal beliefs and self-concept. Cohler, in Section 2, Chapter 5, addresses the issue of sexuality and aging among gay men, specifically commenting on the dynamics at play in the expression of sexuality and age.

One strikingly consistent structural or demographic difference between the samples of heterosexuals and homosexuals, however, has been the higher frequency of singlehood among the latter in contrast to the former (see, also, Hostetler, Section 1, Chapter 3). For example, from (nonrepresentative) surveys, estimates are that anywhere from 40% to 60% of gay men and 45% to 80% of lesbians are involved in committed relationships (Cohler & Galatzer-Levy, 2000).

Such findings not only point to differences between heterosexuals and homosexuals, but they also identify the different social realities within which lesbians and gay men live. A point masked in such a statement, however, is one of definition: the lack of an acceptable definition of *same-sex couple* (Berger, 1990). As Nardi (1999) has commented, defining *single* is similarly complicated. A wide array of definitions has been offered, leading authors to call for self-definitions of couplehood. That is, just because two people live together does not mean that they are a "couple"; similarly, just because a person lives alone does not mean that he or she is "single." These are terms that are clearly not restricted to gay men and lesbians.

Huyck (2001) describes nine types of romantic relationships in later adulthood. She includes in her typology traditional *marriage, remarriage, partnership, cohabitation, living apart together (LAT), affairs, abandoned relationships, absent relationships,* and *unrequited romantic relationships.* The first two types, *traditional marriage* and *remarriage,* comprise legal, heterosexual relationships, the latter implying a second or later marriage subsequent to a legal divorce (Moss & Moss, 1996). By *partnership,* Huyck means same-gender relationships that are the functional equivalents of marriage, often recognized socially but not legally (Cabaj & Purcell, 1998, cited in Huyck, 2001). *Cohabitation* suggests two heterosexual adults living together in a sexual-affectional relationship (Brines & Joyner, 1999, cited in Huyck, 2001). *Living apart together (LAT)* relationships would be marked by heterosexual or same-gender relationships in which the individuals, though not living in the same home, share a committed sexual-affectional relationship (Levin & Trost, 1999). *Affairs* suggest not-legally recognized sexual-affectional relationships that coexist within a subset of marriages, remarriages, partnerships, or other more socially or legally sanctioned romantic relationships (Treas & Gieson, 2000, cited in Huyck, 2001). Huyck suggests that *abandoned relationships* are those in which the individuals choose to discard their previous way(s) of relating even if they retain some remnants of the former relationship, while *absent relationships* are those in which one of the partners is deceased, infirm, or unavailable, even though there is no legal or social separation (Gladstone, 1995). *Unrequited romantic relationships* exist where at least one partner desires a romantic relationship that remains unfulfilled. Huyck (2001) notes that each of these possibilities is evident in later life, and individuals may come to later life with experience in several of these options. If researchers are concerned about the variety and quality (rather than the quantity) of intimacy in later life, they must pay attention to all these options. A (partial) model for their consideration exists in the writings on gay and lesbian romantic ties.

FRIENDSHIP

Grossman, D'Augelli, and Hershberger (2000) believe that the positive contributions of friends to individual well-being noted throughout the gerontological literature should be even more powerfully noted in the lives of older gay men and lesbians, given that friends and the support they provide "can serve a unique function in mitigating the impact of stigmatization" (p. 171). Surprisingly little is known, however, about the role and meaning of friends in the lives of older gay men and lesbians. Much of the literature in this nascent area is colloquial and inferential and is presented in compilations of personal narratives of older gay men and lesbians (e.g., Adelman, 1986; Farnham & Marshall, 1989; Vacha, 1985). The few empirical attempts at examining friendship among gay men and lesbians, particularly in later life, include Nardi's (1999) study of gay men representing a broad age range; Dorfman et al.'s (1995) exploration of lesbians and gay men over 60; Quam and Whitford's (1992) study on gay men and lesbians over 50; and Beeler, Rawls, Herdt, and Cohler's (1999) study of mid- and later-life gay men and lesbians. In all of these varied efforts, the importance of friendship for the health and psychological well-being of older gay men and lesbians is dramatically underscored.

Many popular and some scholarly (e.g., Weston, 1991) accounts chronicle the "chosen families" of older gays and lesbians. Manasse and Swallow (1995), for example, in photographs and essays characterizing 24 gay families, report that friendships exist at the core, as reported in the following (p. 153):

> The way a lot of gay men and lesbians come out in the world is very alienating. For many of us, building families of linkage and connection is very healing. It's important for us to feel that love and connection because it's the antithesis of the alienation of homophobia. It's important for us to say, "This is the innermost circle."

Dorrell (1991) also comments on the family "of comradery and caring" she helped to create around caregiving for an 84-year-old, terminally ill lesbian. The presence of such families has been noted in empirical accounts as well; Beeler et al. (1999), for example, report that two-thirds of their sample of middle-aged and older gay men and lesbians held that they had a family of choice. Weinstock (2000) addresses the complexity in the pattern of friends as family by proposing three categories: friends as substitute family members; friends as a challenge to the core structure of the family; and friends as in-laws.

de Vries and Hoctel (in press) report in their in-depth qualitative study of 20 gay men and lesbians over the age of 65 that all but one considered their friends to be their family in some manner. Several categories of description were adopted. Six respondents simply reported, "Our friends are like a family to us," or "This inner circle I call family." Other responses were somewhat more qualified. Three participants felt that their friends were like family, yet different: "I consider them like an alternative family," or "I do consider my friends as family but not in the same way as my blood family; it's like my second family." Five people viewed their friends as family by default. Representative statements of this category include: "They're all I have left" to "I see my friends as my family, because I don't have any connections with my birth family." Finally, five respondents saw their friends as greater than, or superior to, their family. They expressed such sentiments as "I feel closer to them than to my own family," or "To my family of choice, I am a whole person," or "They [friends] provide the sustenance that you ordinarily would want a family to provide."

Relatedly, over half of the respondents believed that friendships were more important to gays and lesbians than they were to heterosexuals. For most of these individuals, consistent with the family-friend discussion above, friendships were important because these friends became family for one or more of the reasons offered above. Implicit in many of the responses was a sense of mutual dependence. For example, one man said that "Gay people have to make their friends their family. If my brother and sister-in-law's friends fell away, they'd still have their family. If my friends fell away, I would have nothing." One woman mentioned that "we need each other in a way that heterosexuals don't. We've led a life of nobody being there."

For those for whom friendships were not seen as more important, several patterns of responses were evident. Some participants, for example, expressed the belief that "although friendships were probably more important to gays and lesbians in the past, when you had to have that certain thing with people to be protected, this was no longer the case because it was so easy to be out." Other responses included sentiments such as "We're all social beings regardless of our sexual orientation," or "Friendships are important to everyone." One respondent thought that friendships were equally crucial to "straight people" because many of them were also estranged from their families: "The gayness has nothing to do with it as far as I can see."

The extent to which such evaluations of friends are restricted to gay men and lesbians remains an open matter given that questions about the relative valuing of family and friends tend not to be asked of heterosexual samples. In fact, these are the sorts of questions that tend not to be asked in social and family gerontological studies. The heteronormative and family-of-origin-centric bias of North American social gerontology precludes the asking of these questions and thereby restricts the range of discovery. Restating the central thesis of this chapter, the study of gay and lesbian aging issues contributes to the understanding not only of the lives of older gays and lesbians but also to aging concepts more generally: It leads to the asking of different questions, to the conceptualization of constructs in different ways, and ultimately to creativity and inclusivity in research.

COMMUNITY

Weston (1991, p. 122) has explored the complexity of the term *community* in the context of gay and lesbian lives, claiming that it is "as multifaceted in meaning as it is ubiquitous"; the psychological experience of this term is reviewed above in the framework of friendship, and its more sociological presentation is considered herein. The use of the term *community* evolved from earlier references to "the gay world" (e.g., Hoffman, 1968), implicating a homogeneous group and providing a political identity comparable to an ethnic subculture (e.g., Epstein, 1987). It defies territorial bounds, although "gay districts" are typically well known in larger metropolitan centers and "community" has been associated with bars, taverns, and some clubs. Weston (1991) proposes that gay community can better be understood as "a category implicated in the ways lesbians and gay men have developed collective identities, organized urban space, and conceptualized their significant relationships" (p. 124).

Evidence of community along these definitional lines appears in several forms, a poignant and dramatic example of which are the rituals around loss, including grief. Several authors have proposed that grief—end-of-life rituals in general—are among the most culturally dense experiences (Kastenbaum, 2001; Matsunami, 1998) and reveal the workings and values of a community. The study of grief in this context provides a unique opportunity to explore the meaning of relationships and the importance of community for gay men and lesbians; after all, grief "is the study of people and their most intimate relationships" (Deck & Folta, 1989, p. 80).

However, all grief is not equal. Society endorses various "classes" of grievers: Doka (1989), for example, discusses disenfranchised grievers and disenfranchised deaths, two constructs within which gay men and lesbians figure prominently—those whose grief occurs in relationships with no recognizable *kin* ties and whose loss is not *socially* defined as significant. Disenfranchised deaths are those that are socially unsanctioned and perhaps shameful (e.g., AIDS, suicide); the person who died is thought to be complicit in his or her own death and therefore unworthy of being mourned. Those who are disenfranchised from the grief and death systems of North America are left without the support and tools through which their grief might be addressed; they also are left without the scripts to recite and roles to enact at the time of death.

As a consequence, new languages and systems may be created to attend to this unmet need. The NAMES Project AIDS Memorial Quilt is one such example, in which representations of those individuals who have died of HIV disease are stitched together into a larger whole. The quilt allows for the expression of grief, both individually and as part of a larger community of loss (Corless, 1995). Thus, the exclusion from traditional norms and rituals ultimately is a double-edged sword, as suggested above. On the one hand, disenfranchised grievers are hidden and their losses are minimized or trivialized. The opportunities provided by such exclusion, on the other hand, may lead to the unencumbered expression of grief (i.e., in ways not scripted by norms that may or may not fit) and may lead to the development of rituals and remembrances constructed by grievers themselves to best address their needs. Gay men and lesbians are not the only disenfranchised grievers in North American society; friends, colleagues, and others also fall outside of heteronormative family roles and are lost in the restricted system of grief and bereavement.

Further forms of operating within these restrictions may be seen in the obituaries posted by bereft gay men and lesbians. In a research project surveying partners of gay men who died due to complications associated with AIDS, Richards, Wrubel, and Folkman (2000) found that 38% of the study participants made the death of their partner public through obituary announcements, and these were typically written and published for two audiences. The first was written (often with the aid of friends) for a homosexual audience and was submitted to a San Francisco gay community newspaper. Another, tailored obituary was written for the hometown paper of the kin of the deceased.

The content of the former of these obituaries was examined by Uhlenkott, Blando, and de Vries (in preparation), who found that the obituaries submitted to the gay-identified weekly newspaper (the *Bay Area Reporter* [BAR]) went beyond the demographic description of jobs held, cities lived, and family members survived. Many were written displaying a wide range of emotion. One writer quoted the deceased's last words, "love, love, love" (*BAR*, 1995). Another wrote of his partner's favorite quote, "Like you always used to say, 'The true test of character is the grace with which we accept plan B' " (*BAR*, 1994). And in an obituary dated March 12, 1987, the partner of the deceased warmly and clearly reveals his feelings of loss and sadness: "You never liked to speculate about an afterlife, but there had better be a place where we can be united again some day. This life feels lonely without you. I love you."

Similarly, the obituaries in the *Bay Area Reporter* were not without their humor. One man, who foresaw his approaching death, set aside the necessary money and preparations for a big party to be held in his honor and absence; the get-together was to be called, "Ding, Dong, the Bitch Is Dead" (*BAR*, 1999). Another obituary was written by an acquaintance of the deceased, describing not only his friend's fondness for the great outdoors, but also the often unpleasant logistics behind such an enterprise. "He's now looking for that perfect campsite and someone to set up his tent" (*BAR*, 1987).

The stories told in these obituaries not only reveal information about the deceased; they suggest the voice and developing script of a community in grief and the effect of AIDS on the community. The developing script differs markedly from more traditional obituaries frequently listing occupation, professional accomplishments, community leadership roles, and education (e.g., Maybury, 1995; Moremen & Cradduck, 1998). The collective impact of the death was also frequently noted as in one obituary, dated August of 1987, in which a bereft individual ended the obituary of a friend with the sentence "Our men and women must stop dying!" Embedded in this latter quote is evidence of the magnitude of the loss and the multiple bereavement experience of gay men and lesbians.

Along such lines, Schwartzberg (1992) writes:

"The enormity of loss in the gay community has a secondary, cumulative effect that is greater than the sum total of the various deaths: It creates an unavoidable climate of loss to the community as a whole . . . survivors [grieve] not only for their most personal losses, but also for all the victims, for strangers and for the loss of community and culture" (p. 424).

Martin and Dean (1993) report that almost one-third of their sample of 200 bereaved gay men had experienced 2 or more deaths within the 12 months preceding the interview upon which their study was based. They compare the AIDS experience to "previously studied stressors, such as the experiences of concentration camp survivors and soldiers in combat" (p. 323). Several studies have sought to examine the impact of cumulative grief from multiple losses in gays and lesbians throughout communities in the United States, Great Britain, and Australia (e.g., Biller & Rice, 1990; Carmack, 1992; Martin, 1988; Viney, Henry, Walker, & Crooks, 1992). In general, the research concludes:

> "For gay men, old beliefs about how the world functions, are no longer valid; reality is no longer what it was. A sense of personal vulnerability, a belief that one has control over one's actions, a conception of the world as a place where young men don't regularly die in the prime of their life—these beliefs are no longer viable for gay men to hold" (Schwartzberg, 1992, p. 427).

The vantage point offered by such work further provides a new perspective within which to consider grief and points to the fact that grief is so much more than an emotional, intrapersonal phenomenon; grief is more encompassing, including cognitive and behavioral components, and further may be interpreted as an interpersonal and cultural and sociopolitical phenomenon. Such interpretation is rarely offered. Moreover, grief is not a singular experience; Martin and Dean (1993, p. 323), elaborating on the above comparisons, claim that like "the AIDS epidemic, concentration camps and war combat are lethal enough to kill many individuals in a brief time and are extended in time so that survivors experience unremitting death of fellow companions." With each subsequent loss, each previous loss is reviewed and relived and the world changes as a consequence. These are perspectives not restricted to gay men and lesbians and loss; these perspectives speak to a more inclusive and developmental study of loss in general.

In fairness, some research has addressed these issues with older adults, although it is uncommon. For example, in 1969, Kastenbaum suggested that it is likely that an older individual will experience multiple losses and further that the older adult will show some cumulative effect and be "particularly vulnerable to the psychological effects of loss" (p. 47). He referred to this as "bereavement overload." Along similar lines, Moss and Moss (1989) suggested that the experiences of death over a lifetime form a "personal pool of grief" that persists and intensifies with subsequent losses.

Such statements highlight the odd and unusual pairing between the experiences of gay men and lesbians (of all ages) and the experiences of older individuals in general. For example, entire communities (of friends) of gay men and lesbians have been lost to AIDS. Such numbers are comparable to those reported by researchers studying older adults; de Vries and Johnson (2002) report that an estimated one-third of those over the age of 65 and almost half over the age of 85 (Johnson & Troll, 1994) lose a close friend through death each year.

Further, gay men and lesbians and older adults in general evidence many similar themes in their accounting of these losses. Both groups (homosexuals and heterosexuals) remark on the circumstances of the death with a sort of "there but for the grace of whom or whatever go I"; both groups speak of how they now feel disconnected to previous times and places (de Vries & Johnson, 2002). These are comments not unlike those noted in the reports of and memorials written by those bereft of a loved one who has died with AIDS. Moreover, both groups make explicit reference to the numbers of friends they have lost and place their recent losses in this context. The older adults in the de Vries and Johnson study referred to themselves as survivors—of long lives, of many deaths, of life's hardships. For many, this is represented as an untethered existence, similar to Schwartzberg's quote above.

The consideration of community, from the perspective of gay men and lesbians, shines a fresh light on the broader view of self in relationships, on entitlements to grief, and on the role of rituals. Some efforts in gerontology have adopted similar strategies, but there remains much to be done to fully follow through on the parallels uncovered above.

GENERATIVITY

For Erikson (e.g., 1982), achieving a sense of fidelity (balancing identity with role confusion) and love (balancing intimacy with isolation) prepares an individual for committing to society by way of future generations. This notion of commitment and survivorship in Erikson's thinking on the concept of generativity frequently has been interpreted by researchers, clinicians, and the popular press in terms of child-bearing and child-rearing. However, Erikson never restricted his concept of generativity to parenthood, and he never believed that parenthood and generativity are inseparable. For example, Erikson, Erikson, and Kivnick (1986, p. 50) write:

"In terms of the whole life cycle, however, it is clear that adult libido is destined to reach some maturity in a number of generative ways: from a sexual procreativity to the day's technological productivity and whatever patterns of creativity have developed in the individual in his or her times. Some such combination must assure the vitality of an order of care to those wide areas of adult involvements which, according to Hindu expression, guarantee the 'maintenance of the world.' All this, in short, leads to a participation in areas of involvement in which one can learn to take care of what one truly cares for."

Generativity may be found in a vast variety of life choices, beliefs, and commitments, ranging from child-bearing and child-rearing, certainly, to vocation/occupation, professional activities, volunteer activities, social group memberships, friendships, and even leisure pursuits. These latter areas remain relatively unexplored in the lives of midlife and older heterosexual adults, with the notable exception of some of the work of McAdams and his colleagues (e.g., McAdams, 1993; McAdams & de St. Aubin, 1992; McAdams, Ruetzel, & Foley, 1986).

The multiple manifestations of generativity in the lives of midlife and older gays and lesbians have been entertained by a few authors (e.g., Cohler, Hostetler, & Boxer, 1998; Cornett & Hudson, 1987; de Vries & Herdt, 2000; Isay, 1996). Importantly, child-bearing and child-rearing are activities not restricted to heterosexuals. With increasing frequency, there is evidence of lesbian parents, gay parents, and lesbian coparenting with gay men. These parents are expressing their generativity through their "immortality projects" (Yalom, 1989)—an expression facilitated by changing social norms. Perhaps this tendency to "take care of what one truly cares for" may also be noted in the extensive involvement of humans with animal companions. Recently, for example, it was estimated that 52.9 million dogs and 59.1 million cats are kept as pets in American households (Brooks & Martinez, 1999). Further, over half of all households have at least one companion animal, and many are perceived as family members (Sable, 1995). The bonds between gay men and lesbians and their companion animals have not been explored, to our knowledge, and represent an interesting avenue for research, particularly as informed by a notion of generativity as a motivation for involvement.

Career choices also may be interpreted in terms of generativity. Teaching serves as a notable example in this instance. Mentoring more generally may be similarly understood, which may include group or recreational leadership (e.g., youth groups). A provocative hypothesis to emerge from such observations might be that gays and lesbians might be disproportionately represented among professionals in these categories.

It is a frequently repeated belief that gay men, especially, are overrepresented in artistic pursuits such as dance and theater. These pursuits are works and acts of creativity and generativity. Some of these may be more explicit than others. For example, a dancer performed the story of his life as it was affected by AIDS; these performances were simultaneously videotaped. As the disease progressed, he was unable to endure the entire performance and the videotape was played as he watched. Over time, he watched more and performed less until ultimately he became a member of the audience. This poignant performance was intended to present and serve as a legacy of his life and art (*Singing Myself a Lullaby*, Henry, 2000). Other works of art may include paintings and sculptures and song. They are gifts intended to nurture, engage, and/or provide for others in myriad ways and persist long after the existence of the gift-giver.

Perhaps in companion ways, the same may be said of the restoration and preservation efforts of gays and lesbians. It might be offered that the aptly named "painted ladies" of San Francisco, the hallmark Victorian structures that have won the hearts of residents and visitors alike, have been preserved in large measure by the efforts of gay men and lesbians. Preservation efforts have not been restricted to physical structures, however. In many urban centers across North America, there now exist oral history projects and gay archives to ensure a legacy of developmental markers. The famous lesbian, gay, bisexual, and transgender yearly parades marking the anniversary of the Stonewall riots may be similarly interpreted.

In fact, perhaps political activism in many forms may also been seen as generative; these forms are creating social change to benefit others, including those whose experiences are not yet known to those agents of change. In such ways, the efforts of Oscar Wilde to the Stonewall drag queens to ACT-UP may all be interpreted as changemaking agents in the service of creating for the self and others a better place to be. These are some of the many ways in which generativity may be noted in the lives of gay men and lesbians. These ways are not restricted to gay men and lesbians; these avenues of generativity are equally open to heterosexuals and may have particular applications in the lives of never-married and/or childless (or child-free) couples (e.g., Connidis & McMullin, 1999). The consideration of generativity, however, in this context prompts the broader and fuller consideration of the concept. In fact, the analysis of generativity in the context of gay and lesbian lives prompts the questioning of the heteronormative language used for measuring development and aging and encourages the reconceptualization, or at least the revisiting, of some of the issues currently popular in gerontological scholarship.

AGING WELL

Early gerontological research tended to focus on aging in terms of decline and loss—not an unreasonable focus given that so much research originated in institutional settings with patients as subjects. As the study of aging expanded to include community settings as well, however, so too did the focus expand to include the well elderly. This augmented focus led to comparisons between these two groups (i.e., comparisons of individuals with disease or disability in contrast to those with neither) and further to distinctions among the well elderly, the most notable being the distinction between usual and successful aging (e.g., Rowe & Kahn, 1987, 1997, 1998). This distinction was intended to identify two groups of "nondiseased" older persons—those without pathology but at risk (the usual agers), and those without pathology and not at risk (the successful agers).

The term *successful aging* has enjoyed wide and popular appeal in recent gerontological literature, with applications to physical (e.g., Garfein & Herzog, 1995), cognitive (e.g., Baltes & Baltes, 1990), and psychological and social functioning (e.g., Wong & Watt, 1991). This broader use of the term and its application to a variety of outcome measures have led to deservedly greater scrutiny. Some critics have charged that the adoption of terms like *successful aging* represents the capitalist takeover of aging (Cole, 1984). Certainly, any definition framed in terms of (objective) outcomes may be criticized as bound in a particular historical and cultural period and in a particular gender and class context, without proper recognition of the social construction of old age (e.g., Erikson, Erikson, & Kivnick, 1986; McAdams, 1993).

In contrast, it may be argued that purely subjective definitions of success render the concept ineffectual, echoing the discussion surrounding the measurement of life satisfaction. That is, researchers have questioned the meaning of the life satisfaction concept given that respondents tend to report that they are satisfied with their lives independent of objective life indicators (e.g., Ryff, 1989). Still others have charged that successful aging is an oxymoron in that it implies not aging at all (Baltes & Carstensen, 1996). A variation on this theme is that all aging is successful, given the alternative!

These issues necessarily raise questions concerning the criteria of successful aging. If all criteria from all disciplines are accepted as equally valid, the number of successful agers would be extremely small (Baltes & Carstensen, 1996). In a ranking of possible criteria, Rowe and Kahn (1997, 1998) include three components in their definition: the avoidance of disease, maintenance of high cognitive and physical functioning, and engagement with life. Rowe and Kahn emphasize activity in their definition—more than potential. These criteria are fairly well endorsed, although predictably modified by researchers from differing perspectives. For example, social psychologists in particular have noted the importance of personal meaning in successful aging (e.g., Baltes & Carstensen, 1996; Wong & Watt, 1991), perhaps as a defining characteristic of engagement with life.

Several authors have commented that gay men and lesbians may be more likely than comparably aged heterosexuals to be prepared overall for aging, given their socialization and early experiences with stress (e.g., Brown et al., 2001). Friend (1991) has offered a theory of successful aging as applied to older lesbian and gay men that is primarily based on what has been termed "crisis competence" and that confronts rigid gender roles and ageist assumptions—perhaps specific forms of meaning-making.

Kimmel (1978) proposed "crisis competence" as a consequence of coming out and the potent intrapersonal and interpersonal stresses that are a part of this process. He suggested that dealing with the crises of "family disruption, intensive feelings and sometimes alienation from family . . . will provide a perspective on major life crises . . . that buffers the person against later crises" (p. 117). Crisis competence embodies the development or enhancement of life skills as a result of having to deal with being gay and all that that entails in a heterosexual society. These skills have been interpreted as placing older gay men and lesbians at an advantage, relative to heterosexuals, in confronting the issues and crises of aging. Such predisposing conditions are rarely considered in the gerontological literature on successful aging.

Friend (1991) points to a related process as assisting in the promotion of successful aging. He suggests that the lived experience of having confronted rigid gender roles ultimately serves older lesbians and gay men well. That is, being freed (or forced) from the relative bounds of traditional gender role definitions has afforded gay men and lesbians the opportunity to engage in behaviors throughout their lives that heterosexuals rarely confront until the death of a spouse (e.g., Lund, Caserta, Dimond, & Shaffer, 1989). A similar process is posited to exist about aging stereotypes and myths (Friend, 1991); just as gender is reconstructed, so too is age.

The relationship between gay men and lesbians and aging, however, is probably more complex than is suggested by this process, although nonetheless relevant in the context of judging success. For example, ageism, frequently noted by gerontologists, is perhaps even more dramatically seen in the context of gay and lesbian experiences, as other authors in this volume discuss (e.g., Barker; Hostetler). Weinberg and Williams (1974) have suggested that gay men are particularly youth-oriented. Several authors have proposed that such extreme ageism has led to "accelerated aging" among lesbians and, most prominently, gay men (e.g., Bennett & Thompson, 1991). Accelerated aging was noted among middle-aged gay men in Neugarten, Moore, and Lowe's (1965) classic research study on age norms among gay men; gay men believed they entered midlife earlier than did heterosexual men. Friend (1980) also reported that gay men described themselves as "old" at younger ages than did heterosexual men.

A final comment on the complexity of age merits attention: the pivotal role of cohort. The important role of cohort is not mentioned as frequently in the gerontological literature as it once was, although its impact is no less pronounced. In contrast, the study of gay and lesbian older adults almost uniformly comments on the marked cohort effects in communities of homosexuals and how the lives of gay men and lesbians have been shaped "in important ways by the historical period in which they have grown and developed, lived, and worked" (D'Augelli & Patterson, 1995, p. 217).

On the evening of June 27, 1969, a contingent from the New York City Police Department raided the Stonewall Inn, a gay dance bar in Greenwich Village, New York City. This wasn't the first time it had happened; in fact, it was part of a routine pattern of harassment endured by the occupants of the bar. What stood out on this June evening, however, was that, shockingly, the police raid soon escalated into several nights of street fights and clashes between outraged gay men and a bewildered NYPD that was not accustomed to homosexuals fighting back. The events of these evenings were widely reported in and sensationalized by the media and became known as the Stonewall Rebellion—what many identify as the turning point in the struggle for gay rights in the United States.

Since the time of the Stonewall riots, so much has happened to transform the social and psychological understanding of same-sex relations and lives. AIDS has certainly shaped the experiences of the gay men whose "coming out" and "coming of age" have taken place since Stonewall. AIDS has destroyed communities while simultaneously increasing the visibility of gays and lesbians and facilitating the creation of communities by gays and lesbians themselves. The issue to be underscored here is that large numbers of gay men and lesbians have come out and have come of age and are now facing their third age with little historical experience or cultural expectations to guide them. There exists little literature from which to draw to render comparisons with previous cohorts of older gays and lesbians, and even if such literature existed, the accounts and interpretations of such times are historically broken from the present along the Stonewall lines previously described. The study of gay and lesbian aging is ultimately an attempt to explore these "uncharted lives" (Siegel & Lowe, 1994)—an attempt to examine this unique juncture of history and biography.

These same issues of aging and aging well exist in varying forms in communities of heterosexual older adults. Aging well probably doesn't magically appear at some later life juncture; aging well is at least partially predicated upon the resources individuals bring with them into later life (such as crisis competence or some related sense of resilience and hardiness). Further, aging well is a response to the approaches individuals take in the roles they play in life, gender, and otherwise; aging well is a subjective experience, including how one fits one's own age and the social conditions that have marked its development. These issues of prominence in gay and lesbian gerontology also have a place at the table of gerontology more generally.

CONCLUSION

As revealed in the pages of this chapter—and indeed this book—the lives of older lesbians and gay men are marked, defined, and supported in ways that distinguish them from heterosexual older adults. Their sexual orientation has led to struggles with their families and with

society to justify their "family" connections; their romantic partnerships have similarly been discounted or maligned, ultimately promoting diverse forms of romantic ties. In the context of these struggles
and this disdain, gay men and lesbians have turned to each other
to form friendships and create family and to develop and maintain
communities to honor their lives and contributions. Gay men and
lesbians have sought out ways to express themselves and their creativity and to leave their mark on the world; they have constructed new
ways of, and given new meaning to, aging and aging well.

These social processes of aging are highlighted in the study of gay
and lesbian lives; in many ways, however, these processes are not
restricted to gay men and lesbians. Furthermore, the vantage point
offered by the social constructionist perspective implicit in gay and
lesbian studies has great potential. For example, families of all types
engage in decision-making strategies that could appropriately be the
focus of research; similarly, families of all types operate with various
forms and levels of information and may engage in masking some
aspects of past or present behaviors from other family members, selectively chosen. How do families decide on (choose) caregivers, and how
are caregiving responsibilities allocated, for example? What sorts of
information are disclosed in families (i.e., how do people "out" themselves and/or others in various ways), and what areas form the "demili-
tarized zones" of which Hagestad (1984) spoke?

Gerontology (e.g., Huyck, 2001) is beginning to recognize the diversity of forms romantic relationships take, in line with the vast diversity
evidenced in gay and lesbian relationships. However, the lives of
single, never-married elders mandate attention, as do the lives of
childless (or child-free) elders. How does generativity manifest itself
in such circumstances? How are families constructed outside of traditional norms and legal means? Who is included in the definitions of
families offered by older adults? Even more generally, what role do
friends play in the lives of older women and men? What are the relative
contributions to well-being made by friends and family, and how are
both groups differentially evaluated? Barker and Mitteness (1990) have
begun to explore the particular role of friends as caregivers to the
elderly—a significantly overlooked area in gerontology in general, although frequently identified, at least in theory, in the context of gay
and lesbian research.

Contributions to the study of grief are offered by analyses of loss
in gay and lesbian lives. Certainly, the experience of multiple loss and

bereavement overload applies to lives of older adults. More generally, the context within which the loss takes place merits attention. The ways in which communities, broadly defined, come together in grief is similarly relevant. How do individuals, of all ages, find their voice in grief and share their loss? Several concepts from analyses of successful aging (or aging well) among older lesbians and gay men have significant potential in gerontological research, as previously identified.

The study of gay men and lesbians in later life and across the life course offers much to our understanding of aging in minority communities and under stigmatized conditions. It also offers much to an analysis of aging more generally. It does so in ways that refresh our concepts, stretch our theories, and reshape our ideas. It fosters a more holistic gerontology and a more inclusive view of the human social life course. Gay and lesbian research may be seen to infuse gerontology with the vital concerns of sexuality and aging more broadly, opening hitherto ignored areas of further scholarship and policy for the 21st century.

REFERENCES

Adelman, M. (Ed.). (1986). *Long time passing: Lives of older lesbians*. Boston: Alyson Publications.

Baltes, M. M., & Carstensen, L. L. (1996). The process of successful aging. *Ageing and Society, 16*, 397–422.

Baltes, P. B., & Baltes, M. M. (1990). *Successful aging: Perspectives from the behavioral sciences*. New York: Cambridge University Press.

Barker, J. C., & Mitteness, L. S. (1990). Invisible caregivers in the spotlight: Non-kin caregivers of frail older adults. In J. F. Gubrium & A. Sankar (Eds.), *The home care experience: Ethnography and policy* (pp. 101–127). Newbury Park, CA: Sage.

Beeler, J. A., Rawls, T. D., Herdt, G., & Cohler, B. J. (1999). The needs of older lesbians and gay men in Chicago. *Journal of Gay and Lesbian Social Services, 9*(1), 31–49.

Bell, A., & Weinberg, M. (1978). *Homosexualities: A study of diversity among men and women*. New York: Simon and Schuster.

Bennett, K. C., & Thompson, N. L. (1991). Accelerated aging and male homosexuality: Australian evidence in a continuing debate. In J. A. Lee (Ed.), *Gay midlife and maturity* (pp. 65–75). New York: Haworth Press.

Berger, R. M. (1982). *Gay and gray: The older homosexual man*. Boston: Alyson Publications.

Berger, R. M. (1990). Men together: Understanding the gay couple. *Journal of Homosexuality, 19,* 31–49.

Biller, R., & Rice, S. (1990). Experiencing multiple losses of persons with AIDS: Grief and bereavement. *Health and Social Work, 15*(4), 283–290.

Bozett, F. W. (Ed.). (1987). *Gay and lesbian parents.* New York: Praeger.

Brines, J., & Joyner, K. (1999). The ties that bind: Principles of cohesion in cohabitation and marriage. *American Sociological Review, 64*(3), 964–980.

Brooks, J. D., & Martinez, C. (1999). Animals as neglected members of the family in studies of death and dying. In B. de Vries (Ed.), *End of life issues: Interdisciplinary and multidimensional perspectives* (pp. 167–181). New York: Springer.

Brown, L. B., Alley, G. R., Sarosy, S., Quarto, G., & Cook, T. (2001). Gay men: Aging well! *Journal of Gay and Lesbian Social Services, 13*(4), 41–54.

Cabaj, R., & Purcell, D. (1998; Eds.). *On the road to same-sex marriage: A supportive guide to psychological, political, and legal issues.* San Francisco: Jossey-Bass.

Carmack, B. (1992). Balancing engagement/detachment in AIDS-related multiple losses. *Image: Journal of Nursing Scholarship, 24*(1), 9–14.

Cohler, B. J., & Galatzer-Levy, R. (2000). *The course of gay and lesbian lives: Social and psychoanalytic perspectives.* Chicago: University of Chicago Press.

Cohler, B. J., Hostetler, A., & Boxer, A. (1998). Generativity, social context and lived experience: Narratives of gay men in middle adulthood. In D. McAdams & E. de St. Aubin (Eds.), *Generativity and adult development: How and why we care for the next generation* (pp. 265–309). Washington, DC: American Psychological Association Press.

Cole, T. R. (1984). Aging, meaning, and well-being: Musings of a cultural historian. *International Journal of Aging and Human Development, 19,* 329–336.

Connidis, I. (in press). Bringing outsiders in: Gay and lesbian family ties over the life course.

Connidis, I., & McMullin, J. (1999). Permanent childlessness: Perceived advantages and disadvantages among older persons. *Canadian Journal on Aging, 18*(4), 447–465.

Corless, I. B. (1995). Saying good-bye to tomorrow. In J. Kauffman (Ed.), *Awareness of mortality* (pp. 171–184). Amityville, NY: Baywood.

Cornett, C., & Hudson, R. (1987). Middle adulthood and the theories of Erikson, Gould, and Vaillant: Where does the gay man fit? *Journal of Gerontological Social Work, 10,* 61–73.

D'Augelli, A. R., & Patterson, C. J. (1995). *Lesbian, gay, and bisexual identities over the lifespan. Psychological perspective.* New York: Oxford University Press.

de Vries, B., & Herdt, G. (2000, May). *Rethinking generativity for the aging LGBT communities: Cultural and psychological perspectives.* Symposium conducted at the meeting of SAGE: Mid-life and Aging in Gay America, New York.

de Vries, B., & Hoctel, P. (in press). The family-friends of older gay men and lesbians. In N. Teunis (Ed.), *Sexual inequalities: Case studies from the field.*

de Vries, B., & Johnson, C. L. (2002). Multidimensional reactions to the death of a friend in the later years. *Advances in Life-Course Research: New Frontiers in Socialization, 7,* 299–324.

Dean, C. R. (1994). Gay marriage: A civil right. *Journal of Homosexuality, 27*(3), 111–115.

Deck, E. S., & Folta, J. R. (1989). The friend-griever. In J. K. Doka (Ed.), *Disenfranchised grief: Recognizing hidden sorrow* (p. 77–89). Lexington, MA: Lexington Books.

Doka, J. K. (Ed.). (1989). *Disenfranchised grief: Recognizing hidden sorrow.* Lexington, MA: Lexington Books.

Dorfman, R., Walters, K., Burke, P., Hardin, L., Karanik, T., Raphael, J., & Silverstein, E. (1995). Old, sad and alone: The myth of the aging homosexual. *Journal of Gerontological Social Work, 24*(1/2), 29–44.

Dorrell, B. (1991). Being there: A support network of lesbian women. In J. A. Lee (Ed.), *Gay midlife and maturity* (pp. 89–98). Binghamton, NY: Harrington Park Press.

Dundas, S., & Kaufman, M. (2000). The Toronto lesbian family study. *Journal of Homosexuality, 40*(2), 65–79.

Epstein, S. (1987). Gay politics, ethnic identity: The limits of social constructivism. *Socialist Review, 93,* 9–54.

Erikson, E. (1982). *The life-cycle completed.* New York: Norton.

Erikson, E., Erikson, J., & Kivnick, H. (1986). *Vital involvement in old age: The experience of old age in our time.* New York: Norton.

Farnham, M., & Marshall, P. (Eds.). (1989). *Walking after midnight: Gay men's life stories* (pp. 56–74). New York: Routledge.

Friend, R. A. (1980). GAYaging: Adjustment and the older gay male. *Alternative Lifestyles, 3,* 231–248.

Friend, R. A. (1991). Older lesbian and gay people: A theory of successful aging. *Journal of Homosexuality, 20,* 99–118.

Garfein, A. J., & Herzog, A. R. (1995). Robust aging among the young-old, old-old, and oldest-old. *Journal of Gerontology: Social Sciences, 50B,* S77–S87.

Gartrell, N., Hamilton, J., Banks, A., Mosbacher, D., & Bishop, H. (1996). The national lesbian family study. I: Interview with prospective mothers. *American Journal of Orthopsychiatry, 66*(2), 272–281.

Gladstone, J. W. (1995). The marital perceptions of elderly persons living or having a spouse living in a long-term care institution in Canada. *The Gerontologist, 35*(1), 52–60.

Gove, W. R., Style, C. B., & Hughes, M. (1990). The effect of marriage on the well-being of adults: A theoretical analysis. *Journal of Family Issues, 11,* 4–35.

Grossman, A. H., D'Augelli, A. R., & Hershberger, S. L. (2000). Social support networks of lesbian, gay, and bisexual adults 60 years of age and older. *Journal of Gerontology, 55B*(3), 171–179.

Hagestad, G. (1984). The continuous bond: A dynamic, multigenerational perspective on parent-child relations between adults. In M. Perlmutter (Ed.), *Minnesota symposium on child psychology.* Hillsdale, NJ: Erlbaum.

Herdt, G., & Koff, B. (2000). *Something to tell you: The road families travel when a child is gay.* New York: Columbia University Press.

Hoffman, L. W., & Hoffman, M. L. (1973). The value of children to parents. In J. T. Fawcett (Ed.), *Psychological perspective on population* (pp. 19–76). New York: Basic Books.

Hoffman, M. (1968). *The gay world: Male homosexuality and the social creation of evil*. New York: Basic Books.

Huyck, M. H. (2001). Romantic relationships in later life. *Generations*, 25(2), 9–17.

Isay, R. (1996). *Becoming gay: The journey to self-acceptance*. New York: Pantheon Books.

Johnson, C. L., & Troll, L. E. (1994). Constraints and facilitators to friendship in late late life. *The Gerontologist*, 34, 79–87.

Kastenbaum, R. (1969). Death and bereavement in later life. In A. J. Kutscher (Ed.), *Death and bereavement* (pp. 28–54). Springfield, IL: Charles C. Thomas.

Kastenbaum, R. (2001). *Death, society, and human experience*. Boston: Allyn and Bacon.

Kehoe, M. (1988). *Lesbians over 60 speak for themselves*. New York: Harrington Park Press.

Kelly, J. (1977). The aging male homosexual. *The Gerontologist*, 17, 328–332.

Kimmel, D. C. (1977). Psychotherapy and the older gay man. *Psychotherapy: Theory, Research, and Practice*, 14, 386–393.

Kimmel, D. C. (1978). Adult development and aging: A gay perspective. *Journal of Social Issues*, 34, 113–130.

Kurdek, L. (1994). The nature and correlates of relationship quality in gay, lesbian, and heterosexual cohabiting couples: A test of the contextual, investment, and discrepancy models. In B. Greene & G. Herek (Eds.), *Lesbian and gay psychology: Theory, research and clinical applications* (pp. 135–155). Thousand Oaks, CA: Sage.

Kurdek, L. (1995). Lesbian and gay couples. In A. R. D'Augelli & C. Patterson (Eds.), *Lesbian, gay and bisexual identities over the lifespan: Psychological perspectives* (pp. 243–261). New York: Oxford University Press.

Kurdek, L., & Schmitt, J. P. (1987). Partner homogamy in married, heterosexual cohabiting, gay, and lesbian couples. *Journal of Sex Research*, 23, 212–232.

Lee, J. A. (1987). The invisible lives of Canada's gray gays. In V. Marshall (Ed.), *Aging in Canada: Social perspectives* (pp. 138–155). Toronto: Fitzhenry and Whiteside.

Lee, J. A. (1995). Can we talk? Can we really talk? Communication as a key factor in the maturing homosexual couple. In R. Neugebaurer-Visano (Ed.), *Seniors and sexuality: Experiencing intimacy in later life* (pp. 81–104). Toronto: Canadian Scholar's Press.

Levin, I., & Trost, J. (1999). Living apart together. *Community, Work and Family*, 2(3), 279–294.

Lund, D. A., Caserta, M. S., Dimond, M. F., & Shaffer, S. K. (1989). Competencies: Tasks of daily living and adjustments to spousal bereavement in later life. In D. A. Lund (Ed.), *Older bereaved spouses: Research with practical applications* (pp. 135–156). Washington, DC: Taylor-Francis.

Manasse, G., & Swallow, J. (Eds.). (1995). *Making love visible: In celebration of gay and lesbian families*. Freedom, CA: The Crossing Press.

Martin, J. L. (1988). Psychological consequences of AIDS-related bereavement among gay men. *Journal of Consulting and Clinical Psychology*, 56(6), 856–862.

Martin, J. L., & Dean, L. (1993). Bereavement following death from AIDS: Unique problems, reactions, and special needs. In M. S. Stroebe, W. Stroebe, & R. O. Hansson (Eds.), *Handbook of bereavement: Theory, research, and intervention* (pp. 315–330). New York: Cambridge University Press.

Matsunami, K. (1998). *International handbook of funeral customs*. Westport, CT: Greenwood.

Maybury, K. (1995). Invisible lives: Women, men and obituaries. *Omega: Journal of Death and Dying, 32,* 27–38.

McAdams, D. (1993). *Stories we live by: Personal myths and the making of the self.* New York: William Morrow and Company.

McAdams, D., & de St. Aubin, E. (1992). A theory of generativity and its assessment through self-report, behavioral acts and narrative themes in autobiography. *Journal of Personality and Social Psychology, 62,* 1003–1015.

McAdams, D., Ruetzel, K., & Foley, J. (1986). Complexity and generativity at mid-life: Relations among social motives, ego development, and adults' plans for the future. *Journal of Personality and Social Psychology, 50,* 800–807.

Moremen, R., & Cradduck, C. (1998). "How will you be remembered after you die?" Gender discrimination after death twenty years later. *Omega: Journal of Death and Dying, 38,* 241–254.

Moss, M., & Moss, S. (1989). The impact of death of elderly sibling: Some considerations of a normative loss. *American Behavioral Scientist, 33,* 94–106.

Moss, M., & Moss, S. (1996). Remarriage of widowed persons: A triadic relationship. In D. Klass, P. Silverman, & S. Nickman (Eds.), *Continuing bonds: New understandings of grief* (pp. 163–178). Washington, DC: Taylor and Francis.

Murphy, B. (1989). Lesbian couples and their parents: The effects of perceived parental attitudes on the couple. *Journal of Counseling and Development, 68,* 46–51.

Nardi, P. (1999). *Gay men's friendships: Invincible communities.* Chicago: University of Chicago Press.

Neugarten, B. L., Moore, J. W., & Lowe, J. C. (1965). Age norms, age constraints, and adult socialization. *American Journal of Sociology, 70,* 710–717.

Peplau, L., Veniegas, R., & Campbell, S. (1996). Gay and lesbian relationships. In R. Savin-Williams & K. C. Cohen (Eds.), *The lives of lesbians, gays, and bisexuals: Children to adults* (pp. 250–273). New York: Harcourt Brace.

Quam, J. K., & Whitford, G. S. (1992). Adaptation and age-related expectations of older gay and lesbian adults. *The Gerontologist, 32,* 367–374.

Reilly, M. E., & Lynch, J. (1990). Power-sharing in lesbian partnerships. *Journal of Homosexuality, 19,* 1–30.

Richards, T. A., Wrubel, J., & Folkman, S. (2000). Death rites in the San Francisco gay community: Cultural developments of the AIDS epidemic. *Omega, 40*(2), 335–350.

Rowe, J. W., & Kahn, R. L. (1987). Human aging: Usual and successful. *Science, 237,* 143–149.

Rowe, J. W., & Kahn, R. L. (1997). Successful aging. *The Gerontologist, 37,* 433–440.

Rowe, J. W., & Kahn, R. L. (1997). *Successful aging.* New York: Pantheon Books.

Ryff, C. D. (1989). In the eye of the beholder: Views of psychological well-being among middle-aged and older adults. *Psychology and Aging, 4,* 195–210.

Sable, P. (1995). Pets, attachment, and well-being across the life cycle. *Social Work, 40,* 334–341.

Schlesinger, B. (1995). The sexless years or sex rediscovered. In R. Neugebauer-Visano (Ed.), *Seniors and sexuality: Experiencing intimacy in later life* (pp. 5–16). Toronto: Canadian Scholars Press.

Schwartzberg, S. (1992). AIDS-related bereavement among gay men: The inadequacy of current theories of grief. *Psychotherapy, 29,* 422–429.

Siegel, S., & Lowe, E. (1994). *Uncharted lives: Understanding the life passages of gay men.* New York: Plume.

Treas, J., & Giesen, D. (2000). Sexual infidelity among married and cohabiting Americans. *Journal of Marriage and the Family, 62*(1), 48–60.

Uhlenkott, R., Blando, J. A., & de Vries, B. (in preparation). *Obituaries in the San Francisco gay community during the AIDS crisis.*

Vacha, K. (1985). *Quiet fire: Memoirs of older gay men.* Trumansburg, NY: The Crossing Press.

Viney, L., Henry, R., Walker, B., & Crooks, L. (1992). The psychosocial impact of multiple deaths from AIDS. *Omega, Journal of Death and Dying, 24*(2), 151–163.

Weinberg, M. S., & Williams, C. J. (1974). *Male homosexuals: Their problems and adaptations.* New York: Oxford University Press.

Weinstock, J. S. (2000). Lesbian friendships at midlife: Patterns and possibilities for the 21st century. *Journal of Gay and Lesbian Social Services, 11*(2/3), 1–32.

Weston, K. (1991). *Families we choose: Lesbians, gays, kinship.* New York: Columbia University Press.

Wong, P. T., & Watt, L. M. (1991). What types of reminiscence are associated with successful aging? *Psychology and Aging, 6,* 272–279.

Yalom, I. (1989). *Love's executioner and other tales of psychotherapy.* New York: Basic Books.

CHAPTER 2

Lesbian Aging: An Agenda for Social Research

Judith C. Barker

S exual minorities, whether described as lesbian, gay, bisexual, or transgender, have become more visible and recognized in recent years. Among the signal events and changes over the last few decades responsible for this increase in public awareness are the Stonewall riots, the American Psychological Association's declaration that homosexuality is not pathological, civil rights and feminist movements, identity politics, the advent of "pride" parades and celebrations, unisex fashion in clothing and body decoration, the devastation wrought by the HIV/AIDS epidemic, increased reporting of sexual minority issues by mainstream media, including violence against homosexuals, and the success of conventional film, drama, and art with "gay" themes. Politicians, law courts, social service agents, and policymakers have all taken note and responded—albeit, not always positively—to this increased openness and activism.

In 1982, some 3.5 million people in the United States were reported to be lesbians or gay men aged 60 or more (Friend, 1990, p. 103). With the general aging of the population in recent times, this number not only grew in the last 20 years but will continue to do so over the next decades. Given the already sizeable population and the increasing public visibility of sexual minorities, it is surprising—even startling— how infrequently the literature discusses older sexual-minority individuals. Before 1990, standard texts and handbooks on aging made no mention of homosexuality, and studies of sexuality routinely lacked a focus on people aged 60 years or more (Cruikshank, 1990, p. 77). Kinsey and colleagues' two landmark reports, published in 1948 and 1953, totaled 1,700 pages, yet only three pages were devoted to commentary on older people (Daniluk, 1998). Hite's 1976 report on female sexuality dealt with over 1,000 subjects but included just 20 over the age of 60 (Cruikshank, 1990). This erasure of older people occurs not just with respect to mainstream scholarship but also within the lesbian, gay, bisexual, and transgender community itself. Informal examination of 542 pages from five recently published major magazines aimed at a sexual minority audience reveals only two articles that briefly mention older people, and among the abundant visual images, none represented people aged 60 or above (Kimmel & Martin, 2001, p. 8).

Paralleling the greater presence of negative stereotypes and overt concerns in society in general, when research and scholarly discussion on sexual minorities have occurred, they have tended to focus on gay men rather than lesbians. This has prompted some authors to describe older lesbians as "triply invisible" (Kehoe, 1986, 1988, p. 64)—they are not only old and female but also sexually deviant. This chapter, then, brings the invisible population of older lesbians into the spotlight. It reviews and comments on present literature and issues an invitation to address an agenda for urgently needed social research into the lives of aging lesbians.

SETTING THE SCENE

Before venturing further, central concepts and assumptions underpinning this chapter are first discussed. This is followed by an assessment of the present state of knowledge about older lesbians, in the context of comparison and contrast with their heteronormative age peers. Consideration of demographic and social aspects of older women's lives concludes with a brief examination of health and health-related concerns, especially those that impinge on social issues, such as informal caregiving. The chapter ends with an evaluation of societal institutions and policies that form the context of lesbian life and reiteration of calls throughout the chapter for more detailed, rigorous research and theorizing into the social worlds of aging lesbians.

Definitions and Caveats

Traditionally, gerontology and social science have taken age 65 as the chronological marker for being "old,"[1] although it is increasingly recognized that many people live well beyond this age, even into advanced old age, 85 years or beyond. Indeed, centenarians are the fastest growing population group. While recognizing the arbitrariness and the often inappropriateness of applying this traditional 65+ years definition to contemporary populations, this chapter conforms to that convention in order to present meaningful summaries of current knowledge and to suggest useful comparisons and points of departure for a research agenda focused on aging and older lesbians.

This decision to use 65 as the chronological marker for the beginning of old age also marks a departure from the scant literature on gay men and lesbians, where the majority of research publications and general commentaries most often use the terms *old* or *older* to refer to people aged 40 or above (Berger, 1982; Kehoe, 1988; Kimmel & Martin, 2001; Quam, 1997). While this practice certainly highlights the "youth culture" that so permeates sexual minority populations, especially that of gay men, it leaves a quite misleading—and erroneous—impression that there is no traditionally elderly segment in sexual minority population. In this chapter, *old* and *older* encompass the range from 65 to 105.

A tension exists around the term *aging*. The study of aging as a process over time often gets elided, becoming simply a designation for interest in a particular segment of society, namely "the elderly" or "the old." While emphasis in this chapter is certainly on this previously ignored age/population group, it does not mean the aging process is unimportant or irrelevant for this group, just that data are at present inadequate for building a solid and dynamic understanding of their aging.

Consistent with the broader literature, the term *sex* is used in this chapter to denote biological, chromosomal, genital, or reproductive

---

[1]This is an arbitrary marker. It is based on a decision by Chancellor Bismarck and Kaiser Wilhelm of Germany in the late 19th century to make 65 the age at which a worker could receive a pension, this being at that time an age that relatively few people (5% or less) reached. In most developed or industrial countries since, 65 has remained the "standard" retirement age or marker of old age despite great increases in the proportion of the population (now nearly 15% in the U.S.) living to this age or beyond.

status, while *gender* refers to social, cultural, and psychological phenomena ascribed to individuals. Herein, too, the category *lesbian* is
used as if it were a unitary and unproblematic term, easily and mean-
ingfully contrasted to heteronormative women or people with other
sexual identities. Of course, identity as a lesbian is multiple, contested,
debated, and nuanced (Adelman, 1987, 1990; Cruikshank, 1990;
Kehoe, 1988). The term encompasses a broad range of sentiment and
behavior, from, for example, the heteronormative "political lesbians"
who allied with an oppressed sexual sisterhood especially during the
feminist movements in the 1970s and 1980s, through to "lace curtain
lesbians" (Martin & Lyon, 1970), women who do not reveal their
orientation outside their home, thus denying while living the life of
a sexual minority. Neither should the term *lesbian*—or *dyke* or *gay* or
homosexual or *butch* or *femme* or any other such term—be taken to
simply or even necessarily imply sexual activity. Rather, it designates
an intense and enduring emotional attachment to other women and
a life constructed around those attributes and interests, a life that
might or might not include sexual acts with women (Terry, 1999, p.
131). Until a great deal more research is done that will allow a more
complex understanding of lesbian identities and lesbian lives, the
somewhat pedestrian and undifferentiated label *lesbian* remains appropriate, and is used herein.

In broad agreement with Turner and Troll (1994, p. 1), who declare
that it is time to "turn the study of adult development and aging
away from its prevailing definition of an older person as an urban
heterosexual White non-Latino man," this chapter focuses on older
nonheterosexual women. Older lesbians of color, however, comprise
a "quadruply invisible minority," as do rural women, being virtually
absent in the literature. Because of this, they receive no specific mention in this chapter except for an exhortation to begin a serious study
of their lives and experiences.

Social Theories of Age and Aging

In general, the entire arena of social gerontology is seriously under-
theorized (Bengtson & Schaie, 1999). Health concerns and biomedical
interests dominated the field early and continue to hold considerable
sway, as researchers and practitioners grapple with the unshakeable
fact that as people grow old their body systems and capabilities change

and eventually decline (Hendricks & Achenbaum, 1999). The most pressing needs of older people often are health-related and require fairly immediate solutions. In focusing thus, gerontologists have applied their knowledge and helped improve the lives of many older people, but this has not furthered the discipline as a scholarly, scientific enterprise. Social issues heavily influencing gerontology to date have been access to (health) care and other services, social support and caregiving, and retirement planning and finances, with far less focus being given to religion, politics, law, kinship, or family beyond relations with a spouse or immediate descendants, and so forth—in other words, general social life. Largely missing until recently are works examining diversity by socioeconomic class, minority status, and even gender (Turner & Troll, 1994). Indeed, it is ironic to note, along with Cruikshank (1990, p. 85), that feminists have tackled every kind of oppression except aging.

The overwhelming theoretical influences in social gerontology come from psycho-analytic and social-psychological perspectives centering on morale, cognition, memory, personality, and attachment, bolstered by quantitative approaches to data-gathering (Bengston & Schaie, 1999). Here, the individual is the unit of analysis. From a sociological or anthropological perspective, the predominant social theory underpinning population, group, or macrolevel study is a more or less elaborated structural-functional position, sometimes masquerading at a more microlevel of analysis as family systems or family development theory. Qualitative methods and humanist studies have recently begun to move the field beyond positivist frameworks, as has the political-economic focus of researchers interested in the intersection of social policy and aging (Bengston & Schaie, 1999). Over the last three decades in particular, social gerontology has begun to mature as other styles of social theory have been incorporated, for example, social constructivist and more recently narrative approaches (Gubrium & Holstein, 1999; Marshall, 1999). Feminist, deconstructionist, discourse, and interpretive postmodern analyses derived from the works of Foucault, Bourdieu, Giddens, or other contemporary theorists are rare but are beginning to make an appearance in the social gerontological repertoire.

In noting that theory has been "disinherited" in gerontology, Bengston, Rice, and Johnson (1999, p. 9, emphasis in original) comment that "while we have developed many empirical generalizations *describing* aging, relatively few of these have been deployed in the more fundamental task of *understanding and explaining* aging." The research agenda laid out around lesbian aging acknowledges the importance of explanation and theory but recognizes the futility of attempting to theorize prematurely, in the absence of empirical data. Hence, in this chapter, theory is largely absent, and discussion is empirically driven.

While explanation might lag behind description in social gerontology, empirical investigation has nevertheless resulted in the development of several key concepts and tenets, pivotal among these being the concept of "life course" or lifespan development (Bengston & Schaie, 1999; Settersten, 1999, 2003). *Life course* can be defined as the individual process of moving through time while connecting individual with social changes within specified contexts and population reference groups or cohorts. *Life course* accounts for both individual aging and use of age as a principle of social organization and permits the disentangling of age (a characteristic of an individual), aging (a sociocultural process), and the aged (a specific cohort or population group). As will become evident as this chapter progresses, from this perspective a person's situation in old age is a reflection of the advantages and disadvantages accrued throughout life. Chief among several important assumptions underlying a lifespan approach to aging (Kertzer & Keith, 1984, p. 8) are the following:

- Individual aging consists of a complex interplay among biological aging, psychological aging, and interactions with the changing social and cultural environment.
- Aging can be understood only within the framework of the total life course. People do not begin to age at any specific point in life. Rather, aging occurs from birth (or earlier) up until death. Within any particular society, people of all ages are interdependent.
- Aging is a dynamic process. Aging cannot be separated from the social, cultural, and historical changes surrounding it. It is important to learn how different cohorts age and how society itself is changed by these differences.
- Aging is not a singular process. It can be understood only from the perspective of its socioculturally patterned variability, both within a single society and across societies.

All these underpinning aspects of lifespan development make multiple appearances in this discussion of older lesbians aging. Biological, demographic, psychological, historical, sociocultural, and policy factors all impinge on the lives of older lesbians, creating diversity among them and shaping, driving, and constraining what they have been able to achieve in their past, the circumstances they face presently, as well as their expectations and fears for the future. Attention to older lesbians and other sexually diverse populations is an important way to understand aging as a human phenomenon in general in all its assorted varieties.

OLDER LESBIANS

Adelman (2000, p. xvi) cogently notes that whereas " 'lesbian' was previously a sexual identity with an outlaw sensibility," now lesbians see themselves as "an oppressed sexual minority." Historical changes occurring over the past 30 years have helped create this and other shifts in lesbian perceptions and behaviors. While enduring and significant cohort differences always make it difficult to generalize and predict outcomes from one generation to another, the issues each lesbian cohort confronts nonetheless stem from the same physical, sociocultural, and psychological sources. It is the responses of each cohort that will be different.

Much work that purports to be about older lesbians is in fact firmly focused on lesbians in midlife, i.e., aged 45–64 years (Adelman, 2000; Lee, 1990; Sang, Warshow, & Smith, 1991). Lesbians now at midlife comprise the largest number of "out" lesbians ever (Adelman, 2000, p. xvi), and this openness has enormous implications for the ways in which this cohort will think and behave as they move into old age. Midlife lesbians helped change the world in which they and others presently live. Their activism and advocacy for social reform over the past two decades opened up new possibilities for all lesbians, young and old. But their visibility and accomplishments have not allayed the fears of some older lesbians, many of whom continue to be closeted, remembering past discrimination and hurts. Fear of reprisal is ever present (Genevay, 1982, p. 87). Reluctance to disclose sexual identity remains common in old age (Quam, 1997, p. 2). It has been a major factor influencing the recruitment of older participants into studies and, as a consequence, of limiting what is known currently about lesbian aging.

In many important ways, lesbians aged 65 or more are the success stories, the survivors who grappled with, lived through, fought against, and overcame prejudice and discrimination without succumbing to self-destruction. There is a compelling need to learn much more about what led to this success.

A Composite Profile

Older lesbians have been reticent research subjects. Early studies that intended to examine the lives of lesbians as well as gay men often received too few responses to be analyzed. Berger's (1982) research, for example, garnered only eight interviews and 18 questionnaire responses from women. Through their tireless and persistent efforts at research and writing sustained over many years, however, two authors have made crucial contributions that dominate the sparse literature on aging lesbians: Marcy Adelman (1987, 1990, 2000) and Monica Kehoe (1988). Much of what is presently known about midlife and older lesbians comes from their seminal work, which was based on mail questionnaires and surveys supplemented by interviews, both research and clinical in nature. Their empirical findings and insights are scattered throughout this chapter.

Data from these pioneer studies have been broadly substantiated by a recent national study by Grossman, D'Augelli, and O'Connell (2001), from whose findings the following composite profile has been created. Older lesbians range in age from 65 to over 90, with the greatest proportion being in their 60s. Most identify themselves as lesbian, but up to 10% claim to be bisexual. Though well educated, half being college graduates, in 1997–1998 they had only a modest income, $35,000 or less, due primarily to the fact that the majority (75%) were retired and had been for nearly a decade. Over 90% are white, and 80% live in metropolitan, urban, or suburban locations. Half have a partner and have been in this relationship for a decade or longer, but only one-third live in the same household as their partner. Half belong to one or more community groups that they regularly attend. The majority are psychologically well adjusted with good self-esteem, although a sizeable proportion (25%) experience loneliness, and around 10% have at some point in their life been depressed about their sexual orientation and expressed suicidal thoughts. Three-fourths report their physical health now to be good and not interfering with things they wish to do. Those with higher incomes and fewer feelings of victimization throughout life are in better physical and mental health. Over their lifetimes, 67% suffered verbal abuse because of their sexual orientation, 40% have been physically assaulted, and another 30% were threatened with violence. One-fifth experienced discrimination with respect to employment or housing. Older lesbians report six to eight key members in their friendship circles, which include people of both sexes who range widely in age from the teenage years to the late 90s. Frequently mentioned members of these social networks, in order, are partners, relatives and siblings, friends (including former lovers), and other social acquaintances, not all of whom are lesbian or gay. Most network members know of the older lesbian's sexual orientation. Emotional support is the major function of the network, followed by practical help and advice. The more supportive networks are perceived as being, the less lonely people feel and the more active and healthy they are.

Limitations of the Present Literature

Important as the existing major works on older lesbians are, they suffer from the same drawbacks and limitations in research design that Berger (1982, pp. 122–123) identified with respect to studies of gay men. They have small sample sizes (usually fewer than 200 in number), rely on nonrandom recruitment techniques of convenience samples (posting of flyers, snowball or chain referrals), display limited diversity by ethnicity or socioeconomic class (usually being white, middle class, and well educated), recruit through "gay" organizations and so miss the more marginal, less centrally connected members of the population, and have limited regional or geographic focus (usually central city or metropolitan locations on the East or West Coast). Poorly defined subject populations and eligibility criteria are additional serious constraints.

Resort to such research techniques is not only common but appropriate when investigating populations about whom little is known or who have good reason to remain hidden. The question of representativeness perpetually plagues studies of "hard to find" populations, such as sexual minorities, drug users, child abusers, or people engaged in stigmatized or illegal activities. This is likely to remain an issue until large national datasets, such as the census, health and nutrition surveys, or household surveys, are designed to include questions on sexual orientation, or until government agencies and policymakers are able to fund expensive but necessary research designs (such as random digit dialing) that can overcome many of the present limitations.

Extant major works frequently also suffer from having a truncated set of interests, focusing on topics like life satisfaction, morale, adjustment, loneliness, social isolation, and, particularly, sexual habits and desires. This has resulted in large part because of the authors' sincere wish to examine and dispel harmful myths and stereotypes about sexual minorities. Because of this, they are important contributions to the literature, but unfortunately, they also overlook a broad range of other salient topics and reduce people's lives to a very narrow range of (primarily psychological) concerns. A general and serious problem with the literature is that very little is known about the work, family, leisure, economic, religious, political, or social life of lesbians of any age, let alone older ones, and thus little is known about the impact of these circumstances on sexual identity and aging in late life. There is poor understanding, too, of how these factors affect exposure to or risk for disease or disability, issues that come to special prominence in old age.

Full-scale ethnographic studies of the lives of older lesbians have yet to appear, although these are vital to the development of a richly nuanced, complex, and contextualized understanding. Knowledge about and sensitivity to the social world of lesbians is essential for the success of any study. Many lesbians, young and old, for example, use a roundabout phraseology or euphemisms to describe themselves, sometimes eschewing entirely the label *lesbian*. "Special friend," "girlfriend," "companion," "partner," or "roommate" are all ways of indicating the situation to others able to interpret the situation correctly while not lying or confronting or offending those who know only the surface meaning of these words.

A handful of published pieces providing provocative insight into salient issues are but case studies or commentaries about the experiences of very small samples. Deevey's (1990) case presentation of how an older lesbian couple fared in a nursing home setting is one instance; another is Dorrell's (1990) observations about a group of seven women who took turns providing care to an 84-year-old lesbian in her home (see also Quam, 1997, pp. 8, 97–107). Valuable as these case studies are, in the absence of larger works substantiating and extending their findings or suggestions, they remain unconvincing to policymakers, legislators, and politicians.

The dominance of psychological topics in gerontology generally as well as in previous studies of sexual minorities has resulted in little attention being given to social aspects. This chapter leaves aside the usual list of topics, concentrating instead on social issues and the accompanying cultural meanings that affect the lives of older lesbians, such as having a partner, being a parent, raising children, being poor, having a job, or being frail and needing care. It accomplishes this task through systematic comparison and contrast of the lives of older lesbians with lives of their heteronormative age peers.

OLDER WOMEN IN SOCIETY

The "aging of the population" has enormous implications for the future well-being of all older women, including lesbian women, as well as for the development of social policy and delivery of services. Among other issues, it will affect the need for and training of the "helping professions" such as nursing, medicine, and social work; access to health care and welfare services; taxation and financial security; housing; educational, arts, and civic organizations dependant on the voluntary labor of older docents; the nature and function of charitable, community, and religious organizations; and families and social support. The demographic shifts that will occur over the next decades, combined with the greater political activism and visibility of (younger) lesbians, will make the presence of lesbians among older women more obvious in the future. Differences between heteronormative and lesbian women, in terms of past experiences and of present and continuing needs, will become more obvious too. To ensure more equitable access to services and to diminish health disparities (Solarz, 1999), it is imperative that attention be focused on documenting the specific needs of aging lesbians and how they match or differ from their heteronormative age peers.

Demography

Females comprise half the total population, but with each succeeding decade after age 50, they make up an increasingly greater proportion of the population. Thus, most of the elderly—at least two-thirds, rising to four-fifths in the ninth decade of life—are women. This is because women outlive men at every age, but especially in old age. Despite the predominance of women in old age, until recently most knowledge about the biological, social, and psychological processes of aging and development in later life came from the study of older men, or from rather limited comparisons of men with women. There has been relatively little sustained examination of the lives of older women with respect to experiential or phenomenological aspects of life, and a particular paucity of theory explicitly aimed at understanding older women and their lives (Turner & Troll, 1994). This is reflected in the call for sustained theory development reiterated by many authors (for example, Bengston & Schaie, 1999) and underpins the empirical research agenda laid out in this chapter.

Close to 20 million women in the United States today are old, aged 65–105. At present, older people comprise 15% of the total population; by 2015, however, it is expected that not only will this age group increase, to around 20% of the population, but their life expectancy will have continued to rise, too. While there are still significant ethnic and socioeconomic class variations in life expectancy at birth (Adams, 1995; Bayne-Smith, 1996; DHHS, 2002), over the course of the 20th century women have experienced an increase in life expectancy of about 30 years, such that they now can expect to reach 80 years of age.

The elderly population is often broken into three cohorts or age categories, broadly represented thus: the "young-old," aged 65–74 years, are still employed or newly retired yet active, healthy, widely engaged in voluntary work or travel, and centrally involved in family and social life; the "old-old," aged 75–84 years, are beginning to slow down, to experience the onset or consequences of common chronic illnesses (such as osteoarthritis, heart disease, or diabetes) but are still fully engaged in family and social activities though often closer to home or of a less vigorous nature; and the "oldest-old," aged 85+ years, most of whom have three or more chronic medical conditions, and half of whom need some assistance on a daily basis, such as help with shopping, cooking, or managing finances. Some oldest-old need greater levels of care, requiring assistance with bathing or walking, and many will be experiencing cognitive or memory losses (Guralnik et al., 1995; Merrill & Verbrugge, 1999).

It is not at all uncommon, however, to find frail, debilitated individuals aged 65 and extremely active people in their 90s. The age span from 65 to 105 is the period of greatest heterogeneity in all human populations, exemplifying the widest variation in capacity and achievement, far greater than for any other age range. This heterogeneity exists along every psychological, medical, or social dimension, making it exceptionally difficult to predict where particular individuals fit.

To note that older women significantly outnumber older men is also to acknowledge an implicit point—namely, that most older members of the sexual minority population will be lesbians rather than gay men, bisexuals, or transgendered people. Granted, this assumes an approximately equal number of lesbians and gay men, something that is not known for sure. It is often claimed that lesbians comprise a smaller proportion of their gender group (perhaps 5%) than do gay men (perhaps about 10%). Compared to men, however, the ease with which women can "pass" as heteronormative, and their greater reluctance to self-disclose or participate in surveys or research, make such estimates unreliable (Berger, 1982; Genevay, 1982; Kehoe, 1988). Certainly, a greater proportion of lesbians than gay men will live to old age, especially to advanced old age. Hence, a research agenda focused on lesbians will actually address the largest proportion of this subpopulation, a citizenry much overlooked to date in the literature on aging and sexuality.

Economic Well-Being: Poverty

In old age, a greater proportion of older women than older men lives in poverty: about one-fifth (20%) of older women live at or below poverty level. Widows and married women are often better off financially than never-married or separated/divorced women because of access to survivor benefits from a husband's pension. An unknown but possibly sizeable proportion of poor older women are lesbians. Poverty or near–poverty could be major reasons why many lesbians experience declining quality of life in old age and face difficulties securing adequate care, including health care (DHHS, 2002).

Women are financially disadvantaged in old age as a result of many factors, including differential access to jobs and income over the life course, as well as low societal expectations about their ability or need to manage money. Among the social and cultural reasons why old women end up being poorer than old men are discriminatory hiring and promotion policies; differential pay practices by gender for the same job; less access to education and high pay within occupation groups; more "checkered" work histories, often due to child-rearing or caregiving needs; and restriction to certain kinds of occupations, such as to the "caring" professions (e.g., nursing, teaching, social work), pink-collar occupations (e.g., secretary, sales clerk), or unskilled menial labor (such as domestic work). The impact of diminished economic resources is greatly exacerbated by the low degree of retirement and financial planning in which lesbians engage (Kimmel & Martin, 2001, p. 85).

Nowadays, more women, including lesbians, are able to access nontraditional jobs, such as the professions (e.g., medicine, engineering) or various skilled trades (e.g., plumbing, electrical work, carpentry), including those with a strong fraternal ethos and powerful unions that were formerly reserved for men (e.g., forestry, fire service, police and military, as other than pink-collar workers). What employment in these occupations will do for women's poverty in old age remains unclear, as does the potential impact on physical and mental health.

For gay men, successful adjustment to their sexual identity is linked to overall life satisfaction and degree of disclosure or "outness." Those for whom work was an important linchpin for life satisfaction often expressed little desire to widely disclose their status as a gay man, whereas men who had low psychological or emotional investment in their job were much more likely to be "out" (Adelman, 1990, p. 29; Kimmel & Martin, 2001). How occupational importance, self-esteem and life satisfaction, and disclosure relate for lesbians, young or old, is unclear at present, nor is it known how work relates to life satisfaction.

Geographic Mobility

The social and regional or geographic mobility of lesbians, especially as young adults (for jobs, education, adventure, escape from discrimination, or other reasons), has not yet been examined. Yet it is well known that gay men, lesbians, and bisexual and transgender people migrate from regions perceived or experienced as indifferent or actively hostile to sexual minorities to urban centers, particularly to those with reputations for tolerance and the existence of large numbers of sexual minorities, such as New York or San Francisco. Hassle, discrimination, persecution, and rejection might not cease upon moving to such settings, but they are most certainly muted and likely to be less distressing, in part because of the existence of large and supportive communities.

Within-the-United States and international migration by adult children is another well-recognized phenomenon, leading to "long-distance" caregiving for frail parents. The extent to which children or grandchildren of older lesbians maintain long-distance ties and the form these ties take have not yet been investigated.

There are also lesbians, both young and old, who migrated to the United States from other nations for a variety of reasons and at different life stages. A substantial proportion of these lesbians will likely be women of color. The number, location, and characteristics of immigrant lesbians are essentially undocumented at this point. This uprooting from homeland and reestablishing of life here will have effects on education, work, economics, and marriage and reproductive life, effects that will persist into their old age.

The short- and long-term impacts of mobility have been unexplored, especially on the opportunities and barriers for care in old age, whether as recipient or provider of care. Nor has mobility been examined in relation to the development, sustenance, or breach of ties with kin or other age peers, be they friends, natal families, families of procreation, or families of choice. A now familiar refrain is true here, too—that ethnic, economic, religious, political, occupational, and other factors have not been examined. The impact of residential proximity and social and regional or geographic mobility needs much further investigation, especially when older lesbians are being asked to provide care to others or are in need of receiving care.

Spouses and Partners

In general, a greater proportion of women than men live alone in old age because they become widowed. By age 80, some two-thirds of older heteronormative women have outlived their husbands by some 10 years or more. Or, they live alone because they are a member of the approximately 10% of older women who have never married. In a recent representative survey, 7% (or 135,051) middle-aged and older women who had never married were found to be living with a partner or roommate (Chalfie, 1995, p. 39). Of midlife and older people living with same-sex partners or roommates in nontraditional households (i.e., in non-nuclear families), just over half (52% or 32,192) were women (Chalfie, 1995, p. 37). No distinction was made in this study between partners and roommates, and not all women in same-sex households would be lesbian (e.g., they could have been siblings). Nevertheless, these figures are provocative, for they suggest how easy it is for lesbians to "pass" and how likely it is that lesbians comprise a substantial proportion of nontraditional households.

Except for occasional reports that split older women into those who are still married and those who are widowed, in the gerontological literature generally, women are largely undifferentiated. While there is growing recognition of separation and divorce as powerful social forces increasingly affecting women, there is still little sustained examination of their impact on the lives of older women, especially on those who never remarry. Those who never married at all—a sizeable proportion of all women, often estimated to be 10%—remain virtually invisible. A pervasive assumption is that all women conform to heteronormative beliefs and behaviors, although a substantial proportion of both of the separated/divorced and never-married groups of older women is likely to be lesbian. Until population-based, representative samples of women are surveyed about their marital histories and sexual identities, and until data are analyzed sensitively and reported accurately by subgroup, the proportion of lesbians in any population will remain unknown.

From age 50 on, only around half of older lesbians reported having partners to whom they have been emotionally attached, on average, for over a decade (Grossman, D'Augelli, & O'Connell, 2001; Kehoe, 1988). Suggestions are that lesbians become friends before they become lovers, and that they maintain close friendships with former lovers (Adelman, 2000; Kehoe, 1988), and in this they differ greatly from gay men. Partners may be differentiated from other relationships or established on social, emotional, domestic, or sexual bases (Berger, 1982, pp. 130–131), but basically, there simply is not yet good information on lesbian partners. How long have the partners known each other? How did they meet? What is their friendship circle like? How have they organized their domestic life? What major social engagements or values do they share? How does partner status vary by religious, economic, political, racial/ethnic, regional or geographic location, health, or demographic (especially, but not exclusively, age) factors?

Not only are the patterns of temporary or permanent partnership at varying ages or life stages unknown for most "not currently married" women, but there is little clear conceptualization of what the term *partner* might actually encompass. The literature tends uncritically to assume that for a lesbian having a partner means the same thing as having a spouse—that is, being in an exclusive sexual relationship with a person, forming a single domestic unit, living in the same house, and sharing in the legal, financial, caring, and other benefits or burdens of that association. There is a growing body of work (Bell & Weinberg, 1978; Berger, 1982; Hooker, 1967; Kimmel & Martin, 2001), however, that raises questions about the cultural values hidden within this assumption.

Gay men—and possibly lesbians, too, although there is at this juncture less supporting evidence for them—seem to negotiate, organize, and maintain partnerships in ways quite distinct from those of marriage relationships (or, at least, from the sociocultural ideals assumed to underlie marriage relationships, for relatively little work has investigated the phenomenology of heteronormative spousal relationships as they are actually lived and experienced by the parties involved). Even the presence of an ideal of monogamy or lifelong commitments, ideals that older lesbians tend to uphold (Kimmel & Martin, 2001), does not mean that important differences between *spouse* and *partner* cannot exist. *Spouse* and *partner* are different because the social reference groups link their ideals and values to behavior in different ways and thereby ascribe different cultural meanings to these terms. Such differences could include, but are not limited to, having fewer restrictions around other temporary sexual unions, maintaining separate households even when resident in the same city, and not mingling resources, be these financial or otherwise. These differences would allow people to remain closeted to family, workmates, and the general community but able to disclose to friends and others if they so wish. It also represents a genuinely different cultural construction of the emotional and social meanings of partnering and of expectations of domesticity and support.

Children

It is often assumed that lesbians are childless. This assumption is woefully inadequate, an erroneous depiction of the complexity and trajectory across the lifespan of many lesbians' lives.

Compared with other women, only some lesbians have distinctive reproductive histories. Estimates vary somewhat, but around 40% of all lesbians have been married at some point in their lives, and approximately 25% to 33% report having children (Deevey, 1990; Kehoe, 1988). Lesbian child-bearing might have occurred within the normative time frame, presumably leaving them at the same level of risk for later developing reproductive cancers as heteronormative women, or they might have been late-age child-bearers, putting them at increased for certain cancers in old age, just as for heteronormative women in this category (Solarz, 1999). In contemporary times, too, the number of lesbian women having children is being bolstered through the use of newer reproductive technologies or "artificial insemination," techniques that circumvent the need for marriage or at least heterosexual intercourse in the customary fashion (Lewin, 1985; Mamo, 2002). The more conventional processes of adoption of children also occur. Resort to adoption is sometimes unavailable to lesbian women who wish to parent, especially in states that see a lesbian's membership in a sexual minority group as incompatible with good parenting.

Most surveys or studies investigate women's reproductive histories structurally and quantitatively, asking a woman about her age at first birth or the number of children born, and so forth. Few studies have assessed women's reproductive histories from the perspective of behaviors and relationships across the adult life course. For example, surveys have not asked about the reasons for, timing of, or meaning of shifts in partner status, the shift from male to female sexual partners being a particularly salient one for many lesbians. Nor have studies inquired about the decision to have children and the impact of this on partnership status, day-to-day life, occupational history, economic circumstances, and so forth.

Many sociocultural issues confronting lesbians match those facing other women in similar circumstances but are masked by an assumption that lesbians must always be different. Divorce, whether from legal marriages or same-sex partnerships, and subsequent "single" motherhood and parenting raise many similar issues for all women irrespective of their sexual identity, such as, for instance, child custody, alimony and property settlements, and mothering practices (Lewin, 1981; Lorde, 1995).

There is a great need to understand in much more detail the phenomenology of child-bearing in lesbians' lives, the when and the how of their reproductive choices and activities, and the influence of sexual minority status on associated behaviors, such as parenting. Nor can the role of child-bearing on risk or protective factors for certain diseases in late life be untangled (Solarz, 1999, pp. 55–63), or the availability of social support in late life be understood, without detailed attention to the role of children. Much more rigorous investigation of child-bearing on biomedical and social aspects of life needs to be done to establish convincing linkages between sexual identity and sexual orientation and health and social outcomes for older lesbian women.

"Coming Out"

Age at "coming out," that is, the realization of or mobilization of an intense and persistent emotional attachment to other women and not sexual activity per se, will have a major impact on women's aging throughout the life course. Some women develop this orientation to other women in adolescence or early adulthood; many women, however, do not do so until later in life, often not until after a period of conventional marriage and/or child-bearing. Deevey's (1990) account of 78 lesbians, for example, revealed that 11% of women came out in their 50s while two came out after age 60. Kehoe (1988) mentions a respondent who came out in her early 70s. Davis (1929), a pioneer investigator of women's sexual lives, also noted disjunctures between the timing of marriage and lesbian sexual activity/orientation for a significant subset of the 2,200 women she studied.

Older lesbians, in particular, are often said to have not disclosed—or perhaps not discovered—their sexual identity in early adulthood, using marriage and the production of children to remain closeted. Occasionally (e.g., Daniluk, 1998, p. 262; Genevay, 1982), suggestions are made that development of a lesbian relationship in late life would be a valuable resource for widows or other unattached women, a means to stave off isolation and loneliness. It is simply unknown how many widowed or formerly married women ever seriously contemplate, let alone establish or reject, lesbian connections in old age. To date, then, the full import of being at different stages in the life cycle or different developmental phases when "coming out" has not been examined, not for its immediate impact nor for its long-term consequences, especially but not exclusively in the domain of social support.

Cultural Ideals: Youth and Body Image

In gay male culture, being young and having a sleek, muscled, well-built body is a clearly acknowledged value and desired attribute

(Berger, 1982; Lee, 1990; Kimmel & Martin, 2001). In contrast, lesbians are said to not glorify either the early adult years or the corporeal ideals commonly ascribed for females, perhaps because these are central aspects of heteronormative life that supposedly govern to some degree sexual attraction and mate selection in male-female relationships. Claims are made that lesbians are not as drawn to establishing relationships based on chronological age or physique alone, to be more accepting of the gray hair, wrinkles, sagging body parts, or functional deficiencies that commonly occur in middle and old age (Daniluk, 1998, pp. 259, 323). The extent to which these claims are true is unknown, and may even differ in importance from cohort to cohort (Quam & Whiteford, 1992). Kehoe's (1988, p. 59) informants, for example, do not completely support this contention, nor do Adelman's (1987) older lesbians who describe growing up and/or coming out in the 1920s to 1950s.

True or not, these claims appear to have widespread acceptance and belief in the lesbian community. Collectively, they comprise an important foundational myth that allows lesbians as a group to distinguish themselves symbolically from other sexual minorities, especially gay men, and from the heteronormative world. At the same time, this myth reiterates and emphasizes the inner, emotional core that constitutes attachment to other women, while it eschews or even disavows that an outer, physical nature plays a role in social connections.

Older lesbians still live in a society where body image can be jeopardizing to emotional/psychological well-being. Youth, vigor, and nubile bodies are generally prized, and social, legal, civic, economic, and welfare responses are built around influential images of youth and desirable corporeal stature. Thus do old women who are rich and thin and white get to be treated differently (better) than those who are poor or big or nonwhite, lesbian or not (Cruikshank, 1990, p. 85).

Jeopardy—Double and Multiple

Older lesbians are vulnerable for disparities in health status and social resources not just because they are an invisible minority but also because they embody more than one jeopardy. The idea of "double jeopardy"—e.g., being old and also being a woman—has long been mooted in the gerontological literature and was developed to explain inequalities by racial/ethnic minority status in health and social out-comes (Ferraro, 1987; Ferraro & Farmer, 1996). Double jeopardy hinges around the idea that particular subgroups in society occupy more than one devalued social status at a time. Some writers extended the concept to "multiple jeopardy," referring to the simultaneous dis-play of several devalued statuses and thus exposure to systematic discrimination on many fronts at once. Hence, being old, female, African-American, and poor is to have many vulnerabilities, to be at multiple jeopardy for deleterious outcomes. A major problem with the concept of multiple jeopardy is that it is not composed of independent factors that can be neatly or simply added together. Rather, the same sociocultural processes create all the vulnerabilities; each jeopardy is inextricably linked to all the others because they result from a complex interplay of the same social forces. In other words, there is actually a single constellation of risk with multiple partial manifestations, created through the differential deployment of the same social forces and historical contingencies.

Ageism, Sexism, and Heterosexism

Embedded within the valorization of youth are "twin prejudices" (Daniluk, 1998, p. 317)—ageism and sexism—that affect older women in general. These are two insidious forms of stigmatization and discrim-ination, based on erroneous ideas about advanced chronological age and female gender, respectively. They affect access to health care and services and cause poorer outcomes, whether measured by morbidity or mortality (Daniluk, 1998; Kehoe, 1988; Quam, 1997, p. 2).

Discrimination can and does take many forms—from disapproval, social shunning, and gossip, through ejection from natal families, verbal abuse, and denial of rights or access to services, to blackmail and physical abuse. Eighty percent of Deevey's (1990) respondents aged 50–82 reported experiencing some form of discrimination at some time in their life. Family disapproval (31%) and verbal abuse (37%) were most common, along with fear of discovery (54%). Discrimination in access to jobs or housing also occurs and is particularly painful, even more than the actual violence that affects about one-third of gay men or lesbians (Grossman, D'Augelli, & O'Connell, 2001).

The specific impact of "ageism" on lesbians is unknown, although speculation exists that ageism (and presumably sexism, too) is less shocking or disturbing to midlife or older lesbians than to heteronormative women because lesbians experience when young the behavioral and psychological consequences of stigmatization (Adelman, 2000, p. 6). Even if less unexpected, the deleterious consequences of these forms of discrimination might be no less for lesbians than for their heteronormative peers. It is possible that the combination of ageism and sexism with discrimination stemming from a difference in sexual orientation might result in even greater inequalities, in even poorer outcomes for older lesbians than for older heteronormative women. The exact impact of this trio of factors, however, awaits rigorous investigation.

Of note is the possible role of what might be called "given" versus "chosen" stigma. One cannot alter given characteristics, so one cannot stop one's aging or (except for people under special compulsions and circumstances) change one's sex, but one can choose to not disclose one's sexual orientation to outsiders (although keeping this secret also has its "price" and consequences). How the visibility and degree of control over disclosure of stigmatized characteristics interact with other sources of discrimination and the outcomes thereof are not yet well known.

HEALTH AND DISABILITY

In general, women live longer than men, but with a greater number of medical disorders, more physical/emotional conditions, and greater functional deficits (DHHS, 2002; Guralnik et al., 1995; Kane, 1991; Merrill & Verbrugge, 1999; Verbrugge, 1989). Major disorders, in order of prevalence, are respiratory diseases, musculoskeletal conditions, mental disorders, and circulatory problems. As women age, from midlife (40–64 years) through being young-old (65–74 years), old-old (75–85 years) to oldest-old (85+ years), the prevalence rates of various disease categories change. The older women get, the more likely they are to have chronic rather than acute conditions (i.e., diabetes, degenerative joint diseases, asthma, and so forth, rather than appendicitis) and to have multiple chronic illnesses. It is common for people aged 75+ to have three or more health conditions simultaneously, each of which requires day-to-day management, most of which cause functional deficits.

Compared to men, women have a distinct pattern of developing certain kinds of disorders that have a huge impact on lifetime work and economic opportunities as well as on social connections (Annandale & Hunt, 2000; Verbrugge, 1989; Verbrugge, Gruber-Baldini, & Fozard, 1996). Women have more incapacitating chronic diseases and debilitating autoimmune disorders, such as rheumatoid arthritis and systemic lupus erythymatosus, that daily can cause pain and fatigue and so decrease occupational performance and social interaction. Moreover, these kinds of disorders tend to strike women at earlier ages than for men. There are ethnic and socioeconomic class differences in the prevalence of these types of disorder, too, although class issues are rarely discussed as such, usually being confounded with ethnicity and income.

In general, then, as women advance in age from 65 on, their health and well-being decline. As health declines so do social aspects of life. Increasing age increases the likelihood that eventually old women will need oversight and caregiving by others on a regular basis.

Lesbian Health

Compared to heteronormative women, lesbians display some differences in physical and mental health (Solarz, 1999). These are not so much a vastly different constellation of disorders but rather a greater prevalence, earlier onset, or more severe manifestation of the conditions affecting women in general. The higher biopsychological stress levels of lesbians from discrimination, stigma, and homophobia might trigger these conditions, but so too might unhealthy patterns of response. Lesbians are often claimed to have increased rates of substance use (cigarettes, alcohol, and illicit drugs), overeating, domestic violence, depression, and suicide, for example (Adelman, 2000), compared to their age peers. Presently, it seems that sexual orientation per se or any specific sexual practice or behavior is not related to health outcomes. Many methodological, definitional, funding, structural, and ideological issues undermine the adequacy of much previous biomedical study of lesbian health (Solarz, 1999; Terry, 1999). In general, there has been insufficient rigorous research on lesbian health of the kind necessary to make firm assertions about the existence of health disparities or the specific effects of risk or protective factors (Solarz, 1999).

Despite the rightful prominence given to the very aggressive cancers of young and middle adulthood, the greatest prevalence of all types of cancer is in old age. Older lesbians are at least as vulnerable as other older women to developing cancer in late life, possibly, although uncertainly so, even more vulnerable because of their distinct reproductive histories and higher rates of smoking and alcohol use (Solarz, 1999). There is increasingly well documented evidence suggesting that, compared to their age peers, lesbians might have different cancer experiences (e.g., Dibble et al., 2002). Investigation of exactly who experiences such conditions might reveal that being a childless lesbian rather than a biological mother is the major factor. Being a biological mother may be protective regardless whether a woman identifies as a lesbian.

Concern with cancer in old age is reasonable but needs to be put in context: cardiovascular disease kills more than 500,000 women annually (Maruccio et al., 2000), whereas breast cancer kills a distressingly large number but nonetheless far fewer women, around 44,000 per year (Solarz, 1999, p. 48). Indeed, by age 75, more women than men have cardiovascular disease, yet it is commonly thought to be a health condition affecting primarily men. Heart disease is a leading cause of morbidity and mortality for women in the "old-old" and "oldest-old" categories. Risk and protective factors for cardiovascular disease are not distributed equally between lesbians and heteronormative women. Risk factors uncomfortably mirror harmful behaviors that have been associated with lesbians: namely, depression, obesity, smoking, higher intake of alcohol, and stress. Cardiovascular disease is a major cause of functional disability in old age and, hence, of a need for assistance.

A major condition that affects people as they advance in age is memory loss or dementia. Around one-half of all people aged 85 or older have some degree of cognitive dysfunction. May Sarton's (1977) depiction of the loss of a lover to dementia is poignantly presented in her novel *The House by the Sea*. The impact of this gradual, irreversible erosion of memory and personhood takes a heavy toll on partners and caregivers, and will be especially onerous for lesbians who have remained closeted and so unable to share widely their grief and distress at this loss of companionship (Quam, 1997).

It is sad but unfortunately not surprising to note that older women and their health receive no direct mention in Solarz's (1999) several-hundred-page comprehensive review and assessment of the state of knowledge of lesbian health. In laying out a research agenda for future work, the only acknowledgement of aging comes as a single line in

Box 2.2 (p. 85), stating that attention should be devoted to "specific physical and mental health concerns of lesbians as they age, from childhood to old age." Simply not acknowledged in any way are the particular physical and mental conditions, functional limitations, and disabilities of late life, or their influence on the vast nursing home and pharmaceutical industries, the medical, nursing, and related professions, regulatory agencies, or public policy and governmental finances, including federal and state Medicare and Medicaid programs. Once again, older lesbians are an invisible minority.

Sexuality

Huge cultural roadblocks and assumptions abound about the impropriety of sexual activity or desire in old age (Daniluk, 1998, pp. 263–270). This general tendency to de-sex and de-sexualize the elderly as well as to depict them as a bundle of health problems waiting to happen, if not already being manifest, results in a view of old people as androgenous, dependent, and ineffectual. This reticence about sex occurs with respect to all older people, not just sexual minorities, and has been a long-standing issue besetting studies of sexuality. Even when considering midlife populations, discussion of female sexuality rarely extends beyond the physiological impact of menopause. A complicating factor for heteronormative women compared with lesbians is widowhood, which not only increases with increasing age but considerably reduces the number of potential partners and chance for sex.

Studies of gay men (e.g., Berger, 1982) and lesbians (Adelman, 1990; Kehoe, 1988) present some data showing that most older respondents remain sexually interested and active if an appropriate opportunity arises. Recall that "older" in some of these studies usually means aged 40 or above, with few respondents over age 65; data for those aged 70 or more are extremely skimpy. Essentially unknown for either the heteronormative population or sexual minorities is the extent to which sexual activity or sexual desire occurs in old age or how it is imagined, manifested, and managed, let alone its correlates or outcomes.

Health care providers and other social service agents, not to mention society in general, perpetuate the unwarranted assumption that older people lack not only sexual interest or desire but also the capacity for sexual activity. Old people are just not supposed to desire or engage in sex. When sexual activity is imagined, older men are represented—

usually through a stereotype of "dirty old men" or "randy old goats" (Daniluk, 1998, p. 346)—whereas older women are most frequently absent even in derogatory stereotype. The erroneous assumptions in these images are vastly exacerbated if an older person also happens to be a so-called sexual deviant, as this calls into play other stereotypes about his or her supposed nature—the sexual predator image of older gay men, for example, luring innocent young men from normality to sin. It is unknown but possible that rather than being de-sexed, the often assumed hypersexuality of the young and male sexual minority person becomes a stereotype ascribed to older lesbians, thereby exacerbating the prejudice of those already uncomfortable with any degree of sexuality in an older person.

Accessing Health Care

Key differences exist between lesbians and other women with respect to health beliefs, behaviors, and access to health care, some of which may affect lesbian morbidity or mortality. These effects probably come about largely through delay in seeking care as well as through creating such an atmosphere of miscommunication and mistrust that even when sought, professional advice is rejected or disbelieved (van Dam, Koh, & Dibble, 2001). These differences between lesbian and heteronormative women are primarily social in origin and consequence, and they impinge in subtle and not so subtle ways on the older woman and the adequacy of her care.

Many lesbians, both young and old, dislike disclosing their sexual orientation to health care providers because they both fear—and experience—subsequent embarrassment, punishment, rejection, discrimination, and poor-quality care (Eliason, 1996; Kimmel & Martin, 2001, pp. 7, 90–94; Ponticelli, 1998; Scarce, 1999; Solarz, 1999). Older lesbians who generally are already reluctant to disclose their sexual orientation are especially wary and fearful of health care and other service providers with their power to disrupt everyday life (Kehoe, 1986).

There are big differences by cohort in the degree of comfort women feel about acknowledging their sexuality and its impact on or importance to their life and health, and especially in their willingness to disclose their sexual identity to others, including health professionals. The cohort of women who came of age after the Boston Women's Health Collective published *Our Bodies, Our Selves* in the mid-1970s or, for lesbians, the cohort after Lyon/Martin, have a very different attitude than do women in older cohorts. Future cohorts of old lesbians will have yet other responses as they evaluate and respond to the social climate and events of their time.

TYPES OF LONG-TERM CARE

The entire life course provides resources, opportunities, and constraints that can be drawn upon in old age. Diverse trajectories through the lifetime of opportunities and constraints result in varying accumulations of social capital and expertise, so that in old age there is enormous heterogeneity along almost every social dimension. Diverse pathways helps explain both individual- and group-level exposure to, manifestation of, and impact of disease on older people's lives, as well as variations in social support and changes in that over time, an especially salient topic with respect to the mobilization of care for health-related decreases in functioning in old age.

Some of the greatest concerns of people regarding old age are those of loneliness or neglect—legitimate concerns, for 25% of older lesbians and gay men report experiencing loneliness and around 10% have thoughts of suicide at some point in their life (Grossman, D'Augelli, & O'Connell, 2001). A poignant picture of gay men's fears has been painted by Berger (1982, p. 148), a picture that is likely true for older lesbians, too: a fear that in old age no one will be there to care for them; that no one will mourn their deaths; that they will have no sense of immortality or opportunity to pass on wisdom accumulated in the course of their life; and that they will die alone.

Various social and cultural responses to these fears have been created by older lesbians and gay men, including mechanisms for receiving social support and caregiving in old age. But the central question remains: When they need care, who cares for older lesbians on a long-term basis?

There are two tiers of care, each with implications for adequacy of care available to lesbians in old age. The first tier is formal, institutional care; the second, much more extensive, tier is informal community-based care.

Formal Care

Formal long-term care is provided in an institutional framework, either as residential care or as long-term community-based services staffed by professionals. Perhaps the best recognized instance is the medical or nursing care provided 24 hours a day in nursing homes or skilled nursing facilities. At any one time, however, only 5% of all elderly are sufficiently impaired as to need care in this setting. Around 80% of long-stay (3 or more months) nursing home residents are women, most likely aged 75 years or more, and usually with two or more deficits in ability to perform ADLs[2] (or with one ADL impairment and moderate to severe cognitive decline). Since the average annual cost of nursing home care has reached about $50,000, this is not an option available to every lesbian unless she is sufficiently wealthy, or poor enough to qualify for public assistance.

For those being discharged from hospital after acute admissions or with chronic conditions needing periodic surveillance, there are community-based long-term care facilities offering skilled help on a temporary basis, such as hospice, adult day health centers, or home health care. A variety of health professionals (e.g., visiting nurses, speech and physical therapists, medical social workers) provide in-home care, paid for by Medicare, Medicaid, or private insurance. Other formal community-based helping services are also provided for those with a need for ongoing but a low-skill care, such as nutrition sites or Meals-on-Wheels, and board-and-care facilities.

The willingness—or, rather, lack thereof—with which older lesbians disclose their sexual identity to care providers has been the subject of a very small amount of research. Quam (1997, pp. 97–99, 105–107) and Deevey (1990), for example, document the fears of older lesbian women in nursing home settings about disclosure, and the pitfalls and problems that result thereby. The prejudices and misinformation health care staff have about sexual minorities, and the fear and distrust lesbians and their companions (and, for that matter, gay men, too, as Friend [1990, p. 1143] points out) evince towards health care providers, create hostile and unsupportive environments. More investigation needs urgently to be done, especially since sexual minority groups are experiencing exactly the same demographic shifts as the rest of the population. As greater numbers of elderly lesbians and gay men enter

---

[2]ADL stands for the basic, necessary Activities of Daily Living. These are usually taken to be transferring (e.g., from bed to chair), mobility, eating, bathing, dressing and grooming, and toileting. Impairment in a person's ability to perform one or more of these tasks is an important signal that he or she is becoming frail and in need of care. The greater the number of ADL tasks for which a person requires assistance, and the greater the degree of help needed, the greater the person's level of impairment.

nursing homes in the future, so will increase the need for knowledge, sensitivity, and training of staff and administrators about their distinct circumstances. Special nursing homes or units within long-term care facilities catering specifically to sexual minority populations could evolve, paralleling the move to create special housing and assisted-living situations, such as the Rainbow Adult Community Housing initiative in San Francisco (de Vries, personal communication) and "Crone's Nest," a housing complex for women run by a lesbian commune in Florida (Chalfie, 1995, p. D-5).

Informal Care

Older people living at home generally need informal (low technical skill) care and assistance with one or more IADL[3] tasks on a regular basis. Generally, help is needed first to maintain activities outside the home, such as shopping or transport. Then, as the older individual become more frail and homebound, additional help is given to preserve the older person's ability to remain living independently as long as possible.

The vast bulk, more than 75%, of care provided to the frail elderly is informal care—i.e., based in the community but undertaken by nonpaid, nonprofessional caregivers with minimal training or supervision. These caregivers are predominantly but not exclusively family members. Here lies a number of pertinent but at present vastly under-researched issues with respect to older lesbians.

Caregiving is a thoroughly gendered activity, that is to say, a predominantly female pursuit (Abel, 1991; Cancian & Oliker, 2000; Meyer, 2000; Olesen, 1997). The vast majority of informal care is undertaken by wives and daughters or daughters-in-law. These two categories of women provide some 80–85% of all community-based informal care to elders. An irony is that despite their poorer health and functional status, in old age many wives are caring for their often older, often less functionally impaired but nonetheless sicker

---

[3]IADL stands for Instrumental Activity of Daily Living, and it encompasses tasks that make continued community living possible. IADL tasks include activities such as transport to appointments, shopping, preparing a meal, cooking, cleaning, managing finances and medications, and using the telephone. Impairment in the ability to independently perform one or more of these tasks increases with age. Half of the population aged 85+ needs some but not necessarily complete assistance with at least one IADL task on a daily basis.

husbands. Between 10% and 15% of people aged 65+ receive care from more distant kin (e.g., collateral relatives such as nieces, grandchildren) or from nonkin such as neighbors, friends, tenants, or others (Barker, 2002).

Like other older women, lesbians will likely need care at some point in their old age, probably after age 75, because of declining health and increasing functional limitations. The question: Who is available, able, or willing to give informal care to older lesbians?

Among lesbians who have a partner, it is most likely the partner who will provide care, at least up until institutionalization if it should be necessary. It is likely that there will be two similar-aged, physically ailing, functionally failing, financially strapped women caring for each other into extreme old age. Under what circumstances can a lesbian couple sustain caregiving on their own? Moving case studies attest to difficulties encountered in long-term care settings (Deevey, 1990; Dorrell, 1990; Quam, 1997), difficulties stemming from care provider prejudice and stereotyping. Discrimination due to homophobia will most likely be exacerbated by prejudices and discrimination due to ageism and sexism.

CAREGIVING AND SOCIAL SUPPORT

When and why do others get drawn into the informal caregiving endeavor? Who is likely to assist an older lesbian couple or an unpartnered lesbian who needs day-to-day care in order to remain at home as long as possible? A range of possible caregivers and matters around social support that urgently need research attention are discussed here.

Natal Family

The family into which one is born (i.e., one's natal family or family of orientation) is not only expected to provide care when one is ailing but actually does so when the needy member is elderly. Infants and children can expect to receive care from parents, grandparents, siblings, and collateral kin such as aunts and uncles. In young adulthood, the availability of parents and their generation of kin as caregivers eventually ceases, being superseded by the family of procreation. Even so, the importance of natal kin does not totally subside. Siblings and cousins remain key resources, even though they are often resources of last resort, turned to only after marriage partners and children. In older adulthood, partners remain key resources, but eventually children and grandchildren rise to prominence in the caregiving constellation (Brubaker, 1990; Gubrium, 1991). The moral obligation of lineal kin to provide care for one another is a taken-for-granted cultural value underpinning much interaction within natal families and is reflected in both social theory distinguishing family from other social groups and throughout social policy (Croog, Lipson, & Levine, 1972; Karner, 1998; Qureshi & Walker, 1989). Adult children are expected to provide care for their elderly parents, whether this be actually undertaking caregiving themselves or organizing for its provision by others.

It is reasonable, then, to expect that for lesbians who have children these offspring will most probably be the human resources that are called on to provide informal care, especially if these children are daughters. After all, lesbians and their children are just as subject to the shaping and expectations of outside social forces, constraints, and opportunities as people in the larger society. Despite this, unanswered questions abound because of specific issues associated with being a lesbian.

Other relatives in the natal family network might be unwilling to provide care to distant kin who are lesbian. Nieces and nephews are important caregivers for a proportion of the elderly (Sussman, 1985), many times for the so-called familyless elderly. But the connection of nieces, nephews, grandchildren, or cousins to a lesbian family member might be quite different than to a heteronormative relative. Again, in general, the current literature lacks an extended discussion of the trajectory over the life course or the "natural history" of extended kin networks and the ways they are conceptualized and mobilized in old age.

Family of Procreation

Recall that around one-third of lesbians parent children. Lesbian families are just one of the many nontraditional forms of family on the contemporary American landscape. Newer family forms abound, or at least are more socially recognizable as different from the ideologically "proper family" (Coontz, 1999; Tufte & Myerhoff, 1979). These arise from a variety of factors: increased longevity; rising divorce rates;

greater numbers of middle- and upper-class women postponing marriage and child-bearing until in their 30s; increases in the proportion of
women working full-time; increases in surrogate parenting via nannies;
decreases in the size of completed families; change in the number and
composition of multigeneration households; and increases in remarriage and blending of families, which result in half-siblings and step-
parenting. Added to this is the creation of families through adoption,
or use of in-vitro and other technological developments that aid conception outside normal heterosexual union (Lewin, 1985; Mamo,
2002). While lesbian families share many of the issues common to
step- or blended families, they nonetheless need to negotiate, normal-
ize, and legitimize their distinct family form, and they need to keep
doing so throughout the life of their children, be it when the children
start school, become partnered as adults, or have offspring of their
own. These issues of negotiation, normalization, and legitimization
become salient in new ways when lesbian parents reach old age, however, especially when they begin to need care (see also Kimmel &
Martin, 2001, p. 90).

Will lesbians receive care from their children, as generally happens
for heteronormative women? Will the values, attitudes, and behaviors
inherent in the notion of filial piety be upheld for lesbian mothers?
The answer seems to be tentative "in general, yes." Tentative because
to date there exists very little research examining "filial piety" or moral
obligation to care for older members of deviant populations. Variation
in the exercise of caregiving duties and obligations can be expected
because of the personality and individual circumstances of the protago-
nists, the history and tenor of their relationship, as well as by the
now familiar list: ethnicity, social class, economic status, religious
affiliation, political association, occupation, regional or geographic
location, or immigrant status.

Availability of care by children will depend not just on the lesbian
mother's age and degree of need but also on the age or developmental
stage of the child, whether, for instance, the child is a young adult
still establishing her own identity, career, or family, or middle-aged
and so firmly immersed in adult life, or an older woman herself facing
the changes that old age brings. The age at which a lesbian mother
"came out" in relation to her age at child-bearing will also have an
impact. Women raising children from birth in a lesbian household
versus women becoming lesbian when their children are older, even
teenagers, will have quite different experiences. Kehoe (1988) reports

that, with a few exceptions, women who come out late in life successfully maintain contact with their children or grandchildren.

Sons are already characterized in literature, perhaps unjustly, as generally standing outside the provision of "hands-on" care, such as assistance with bathing, dressing, and grooming, while being willing to perform other care activities, such as management of finances, transportation, heavy lifting, and so forth (Stephens & Christianson, 1986). This distancing of sons from personal care is especially but not exclusively present with respect to opposite-sex parents, probably because of general societal taboos or incest rules prohibiting certain kinds of intimacy. Barker and Mitteness (1990, p. 117) noted this taboo with respect to the activities of a son caring for his frail elderly mother, while Abel and Nelson (2001, p. 28) discuss the phenomenon with respect to their care for their ailing father. It is unclear the extent to which this gendered dichotomy of care provision will be exacerbated when the parent requiring assistance is a lesbian. Kehoe (1988, p. 30) reports that brothers and sons of lesbians feel most threatened by their relative's sexual orientation, a phenomenon that could strengthen societal taboos on intimacy and further reduce their availability for certain types of informal care in old age.

But, what happens to the step-parent in a blended lesbian family? How will notions of filial piety or kinship obligation and duties be played out in these circumstances? Will care be parceled out according to biological connection? Will the children of a lesbian couple provide care but only to, or disproportionately to, the biological mother? Will the coparent or adoptive mother be relegated to a subsidiary role, eliminated from decision making around her partner's well-being? Urgent investigation into these issues is needed.

Estrangement

The effects of the estrangements that many lesbians experience from their natal family at earlier times not only cuts them off from maintaining meaningful ties with socially significant people, but might constrain caregiving possibilities in later life. Many lesbians describe strained relationships or expulsion from families after they "come out" (Adelman, 1990, pp. 29–31; Kehoe, 1988, p. 36; Kimmel & Martin, 2001, p. 4). Some report eventual reconciliation with family after varying periods of time. Stories abound, too, of families remaining absent until after death, at which point they reenter the scene, often excluding partners or friends from making funeral arrangements or estate decisions.

Along with sexual identity, other devalued states or activities—for example, drug use, prostitution, violence, or other criminal behaviors—can also lead to the expulsion of women from their natal families. Lesbians having a dual deviant status are likely to face harsher consequences than that due to sexual identity or sexual orientation alone. There are a few indications (Isaacs, 1971) that even after years of absence or estrangement, children often will respond and provide care to parents with criminal, drug-using, or such like pasts. But the children frequently do so with strict limits on contact between the frail elder and their own family of procreation, or on the scope and nature of care provided.

Estrangement from natal kin could work another way. It could also prevent lesbians from being mobilized as a source of care for aging parents or siblings, an activity that many would not only be willing but desire to undertake. Or, of course, the need for the aged parents to receive care could motivate natal kin groups to ameliorate or begin to heal breaches of relationship with lesbian family members. The extent to which lesbians provide care to older family members is unknown, but anecdotes suggest that a substantial proportion of mid-life and young-old lesbians have solid and supportive connections with aged parents.

The trajectory over the life course, or the "natural history" of filial obligations or estrangement from and restoration into family of orientation, is largely unexplored territory for adults of any age, not just lesbians. At this juncture, however, very little is known about the sources, timing, duration, or negotiation of estrangements or reincorporations of lesbians into their family of orientation. Are estrangements total or partial? Temporary or permanent? Under what circumstances do they occur and get repealed? What are the processes by which breaches occur and get ameliorated? Which estrangements are never resolved and why? Who is estranged—just the parents of a lesbian, all or only some siblings, and if so, which ones? How do estrangements and their resolution vary by ethnicity, social class, economic status, religious affiliation, political association, occupation, or regional or geographic location? These key questions concern the social life and circumstances of lesbians in general and influence importantly their access to care in late life.

Friends and Community

No matter how well connected lesbians are to kin, it is hard for lesbians to convey to them the full impact of the silences and invisibilities, the guarding of public behaviors, the stereotyping, the discrimination and rejection that is constantly experienced. Even the most supportive kin can and do on occasion inadvertently exacerbate the hostility of the social world in which lesbians live because they do not experience, and so understand, the often subtle but real ways in which insult, hurt, and prejudice operate. Lesbians seek solace, find refuge, and survive in this intimidating environment in several ways, but the most important ways involve the formation, mobilization, and sustenance of friendship links.

Suggestions abound (Adelman, 1987, 1990, 2000; Kehoe, 1988) that lesbians have distinct patterns of behavior concerning the building and maintenance of ties with friends or lovers and that they follow particular paths when incorporating these people into social circles or families. Once again, there is a paucity of research data on lesbian friendships. Little work has investigated systematically the role of friends or the meaning of friendship for lesbians, especially in relation to or distinction from sexual partner. And the impact of age, gender, ethnicity, social class, economic status, religious affiliation, political association, occupation, regional or geographic location, or immigrant status of friendship formation, maintenance, and meaning has not been well researched.

While it is unknown whether lesbian friendship groups will cluster into distinct psychosocial groups on the basis of partner status, degree of sexual activity, life satisfaction and self-esteem, and so forth, as Bell and Weinberg (1978) found for gay men, there is some variation across networks. Most women seem to have more than one style of friendship group present in their lives. All such groups help lesbians cope with an unfriendly wider world. Some older lesbians, for example, remain closeted, interacting freely with only a small circle of trusted friends with whom they share activities and sentiments. In other words, they form tight groups or "cliques," as Hooker (1967) called them when discussing the social world of gay men. Nondisclosure can be a successful adaptive strategy, especially for older lesbians or those whose jobs require them to "pass" in the heteronormative world.

Many lesbians survive because of connections with the wider homosexual community, through the use of targeted social services (such as "gay" senior centers) or participation in voluntary organizations (such as the Metropolitan Community Church, or arts and music organizations, sports teams, or the like). This affords the development of what Hooker referred to as "loose networks" composed of multiple acquaintances and friends, spread across a range of networks with different interests. Such networks confer esteem and validate members' lives, often in a nonintimate fashion in a strictly limited context. Not all lesbians are, or indeed should be, well integrated to the "gay community" (Adelman, 2000), but many find connection to an empowering community an important source of validation. While a move out of the closet reduced some tensions in the lives of some cohorts of lesbians, it created yet other tensions for other cohorts. Included among these new tensions are pressures to embrace or conform to the political agendas of some activists (such as the "outing" of closeted gays or lesbians) and the consequences of coming out to family and at work.

Families of Choice

A particular variant of Hooker's (1967) "sociometrically central groups" constitutes the most important means that lesbians use to reduce the psychic and social costs of living in an unwelcoming social milieu. This comprises a third type of friendship network, best described as the formation of a nontraditional or alternative type of family: a "family of choice." Families of choice, comprising various constellations of peers, friends, lovers, and former lovers, help compensate for weak or lost ties to natal families or families of procreation (Adelman, 2000; Cruikshank, 1990, pp. 82–83), which is why Bell and Weinberg (1978) describe them as "surrogate family." But families of choice do much more than simply compensate for losses (Stacey, 1999; Weston, 1991). Indeed, Friend (1990) argues that while families of choice might serve as "replacement" family for those who have lost ties to other types of family, they function as "reinforcements" for those who have good, active relationships with other types of family.

The idea of "reinforcement" emphasizes that families of choice are culturally produced, similar to but nonetheless different from other families. Lesbian families of choice are formed and function in a stigmatized environment, in response to strong social pressures of prejudice and discrimination, in order to meet their members' psychosocial needs for validation and legitimization. Families of choice demonstrate emotional sentiments, social values, and domestic obligations similar to those in kin-based families but value and arrange these in alternate ways because different issues and concerns rise to prominence. The point here is that lesbians and gay men have creatively manipulated the taken-for-granted cultural meanings of kinship to provide themselves with social support resources equivalent to those in the outside world. The joys, burdens, duties, obligations, pleasures, exasperations, and expectations looked for and found in heteronormative families exist also in families of choice. Though equally real and important, the meanings of kinship, friendship, and social connectedness are different in these two cultural systems.

When older lesbians do not have partners or kin able or willing to provide informal care, friends take over—especially those who have coalesced into a family of choice (e.g., Dorrell, 1990). That this happens is not really remarkable, for resort to and reliance on nonkin caregivers—neighbors, friends, tenants, workmates, landlords, and similar people—is an avenue to care commonly used by many older people who otherwise lack the necessary economic or kin resources (Barker, 2002). What is probably different for lesbians is the rapidity or ease with which such nonkin caregivers become a family constellation. Dorrell (1990) provides a case example of the formation of family of choice by seven unrelated women drawn into caring for an 84-year-old lesbian. Much more extensive investigation of this phenomenon is needed. While there is an important literature replete with suggestions on the ways in which families of choice have been mobilized to provide care for young adults, especially younger gay men with HIV/AIDS (Aneshensel et al., 1995; Billings et al., 2000; Folkman, Chesney, & Christopher-Richards, 1994; Folkman et al., 1997), there has been little exploration of when and how families of choice manage or provide care for older people who are becoming frail.

Planning for Care

A small proportion of gay men and lesbians, partnered or not, deliberately organize for care in old age through a particular commitment combined with the features of family of choice. As the intent, sentiment, and activity match those in a specific business relationship, Barker (forthcoming) has given this constellation of care the same name—*tontine*. A tontine is a pact among a group of people to uphold, promote, or safeguard a desired good or outcome in which the last survivor has exclusive rights of access, use, or ownership. This type of informal care's most distinguishable characteristics are that it is planned, albeit sometimes rather casually until actually needing to be mobilized, and that it is a serious commitment which members intend to fulfill. (Chalfie [1995, p. D-5] also notes the uncommon existence of planned care groups.)

Caregiving tontines, then, are groups of individuals who agree that throughout their life they will care for one another as long as necessary. The twist on the usual meaning is that here there is no highly desired (economic) prize or outcome, just one last, sad individual who has outlived all the others to whom he or she has given care. In Barker's study (2002; forthcoming), caregiving tontines among gay men and lesbians comprised small groups (five to six individuals) who met initially either through their employer (e.g., the military) or at their residence (e.g., a single-room-occupancy [SRO] hotel in the inner city), often decades before reaching old age. A lifetime of enforced silence, hassle, discrimination, persecution, and rejection by family, service agencies, and the wider society has made these older lesbians and gay men prefer tontines composed of peers to other forms of care, or be unwilling to request or accept help from outside the sexual minority population.

CONCLUSION

The sociocultural, institutional, legal, and emotional contexts within which lesbians live and grow old make a highly unusual environment with specific characteristics and demands that shape and constrain their lives. A pervasive climate of prejudice, discrimination, and stigmatization exists, based on sociocultural norms and ideals that devalue their sexual identity and emotional and social attachments. Alienation from the heteronormative world results in and leads to a life filled with secrets, wariness, hypervigilance, psychosocial stress, and depression that for some ends in suicide. Abuse and violence are all too common accompaniments. An institutional environment with policies or procedures that deny or limit access to services, such health care or counseling, further exacerbates this. The legal environment is unsympathetic and hostile for lesbians compared to their age peers, too, there being different conditions for taxation, inheritance of property, or receipt of survivor benefits from pensions and insurances, and refusal of adoption or custody of children or rights to visit children or grandchildren. The emotional environment can be chilling. Nondisclosure of sexual identity, an effective and successful survival strategy at younger ages, becomes a source of pain and loneliness in late life, especially during bereavement. Painful, too, is exclusion or denial of status as next-of-kin, with a right to help make treatment decisions, especially end-of-life decisions, for a terminally ill partner, to visit if she is hospitalized, or to make funeral or burial arrangements (Berger, 1982, pp. 194–201; Chalfie, 1995, pp. 45–84; Quam, 1997).

Lesbians have adapted to this world and these environmental demands in innovative ways, mobilizing, negotiating, and resisting standard cultural values and social norms in ways that enable them not merely to survive but also to thrive. For example, the word *partner* and its associated assumptions of fidelity, coresidence, and domesticity have been culturally reconstructed to meet the unique environmental demands of lesbian lives. Reworked, too, are the central ideas of *kin*, *family*, and *friend* and the meanings and means of achieving social connectedness and their corollary so important in late life—*care*. These apparently familiar but actually re-created cultural values mitigate the effects of psychic and environmental demands, compensate for losses, and reinforce and validate life choices. These meanings, symbols, behaviors, and sentiments help create a social order that sustains and nurtures lesbians in the face of debilities and losses so common in late life.

In this chapter, social aspects of the life of older lesbians have been discussed only in the broadest of descriptive terms. Before greater social justice can be achieved for any oppressed sexual minority population, rigorous, detailed, accurate, and extensive empirical data must be gathered and used to present contextualized and complete descriptions of their life and circumstances. Only after this has been achieved will adequate analysis or explanatory theory be able to be developed and tested.

Only the most immediate and obvious topics and issues have been raised in this research agenda, which is aimed at making an overlooked population visible. No doubt, as this suggested program of investigation is scrutinized and pondered, other interesting and compelling questions will arise and, hopefully, generate discussion and exploration. Here, then, is an opportunity not just to answer questions and immediate issues plaguing aging lesbians but also to advance the entire field of social gerontology, to provide answers, spur new questions, and raise new knowledge important to all older women.

REFERENCES

Abel, E. K. (1991). *Who cares for the elderly? Public policy and the experiences of adult daughters*. Philadelphia: Temple University Press.

Abel, E. K., & Nelson, M. K. (2001, May 21). Intimate care for hire. *American Prospect, 12*(9), 26–29.

Adams, D. L. (Ed.). (1995). *Health issues for women of color: A cultural diversity perspective*. Thousand Oaks, CA: Sage Publications.

Adelman, M. (Ed.). (1987). *Long time passing: Lives of older lesbians*. Boston: Alyson Publications.

Adelman, M. (1990). Stigma, gay lifestyles, and adjustment to aging: A study of later-life gay men and lesbians. In J. A. Lee (Ed.), *Gay midlife and maturity* (pp. 7–32). Binghamton, NY: Haworth Press.

Adelman, M. R. (Ed.). (2000). *Midlife lesbian relationships: Friends, lovers, children and parents*. Binghamton, NY: Harrington Park Press.

Aneshensel, C. S., Pearlin, L. I., Mullan, J. T., Zarit, S. H., & Whitlatch, C. J. (1995). *Profiles in caregiving: The unexpected career*. San Diego: Academic Press

Annandale, E., & Hunt, K. (Eds.). (2000). *Gender inequalities in health*. Philadelphia: Open University Press.

Barker, J. C. (2002). Neighbors, friends and other non-kin caregivers to community-living dependent elderly. *Journal of Gerontology: Social Sciences, 57B*, S158–S167.

Barker, J. C. (forthcoming). Constellations of care among non-kin caregivers.

Barker, J. C., & Mitteness, L. S. (1990). Invisible caregivers in the spotlight: Non-kin caregivers of frail older adults. In J. F. Gubrium & A. Sankar (Eds.), *The home care experience: Ethnography and policy* (pp. 101–127). Newbury Park, CA: Sage.

Bayne-Smith, M. (Ed.). (1996). *Race, gender and health*. Thousand Oaks, CA: Sage.

Bell, A., & Weinberg, M. (1978). *Homosexualities: A study in diversity among men and women*. New York: Simon & Schuster.

Bengston, V. L., Rice, C. J., & Johnston, M. L. (1999). Are theories of aging important? Models and explanations in gerontology at the turn of the century. In V. L. Bengston & K. W. Schaie (Eds.), *Handbook of theories of aging*. New York: Springer.

Bengston, V. L., & Schaie, K. W. (Eds.). (1999). *Handbook of theories of aging*. New York: Springer.

Berger, R. M. (1982). *Gay and gray: The older homosexual man*. Chicago: University of Illinois Press.

Billings, D. W., Folkman, S., Acree, M., & Moskowitz, J. T. (2000). Coping and physical health during caregiving: The roles of positive and negative affect. *Journal of Personality & Social Psychology, 79*, 35–42.

Brubaker, T. H. (Ed.). (1990). *Family relationships in later life.* (2nd ed.). Newbury Park, CA: Sage.

Cancian, F. M., & Oliker, S. J. (2000). *Caring and gender.* Walnut Creek, CA: Rowan & Littlefield.

Chalfie, D. (1995). *The real golden girls: The prevalence and policy treatment of midlife and older people living in nontraditional households.* Washington, DC: Office of Special Activities, American Association of Retired Persons.

Coontz, S. (Ed.). (1999). *American families: A multicultural reader.* New York: Routledge.

Croog, S. H., Lipson, A., & Levine, S. (1972). Help patterns in severe illness: The roles of kin network, non-family resources, and institutions. *Journal of Marriage and the Family, 34* 32–41.

Cruikshank, M. (1990). Lavendar and gray: A brief survey of lesbian and gay aging studies. In J. A. Lee (Ed.), *Gay midlife and maturity* (pp. 77–88). Binghamton, NY: Haworth Press.

Daniluk, J. C. (1998). *Women's sexuality across the life span: Challenging myths, creating meanings.* New York: Guilford Press.

Davis, K. B. (1929). *Factors in the sex lives of twenty-two hundred women.* New York: Harper & Brothers.

Deevey, S. (1990). Older lesbian women: An invisible minority. *Journal of Gerontological Nursing, 16*(5), 35–39.

DHHS. (2002). *Health, United States, 2001: Special Excerpt: Trend tables on 65 and older population.* Washington, DC: Department of Health and Human Services, Centers for Disease Control and Prevention, and National Center for Health Statistics.

Dibble, S. L., Roberts, S. A., Robertson, P. A., & Paul, S. M. (2002). Risk factors for ovarian cancer: Lesbian and heterosexual women. *Oncology Nursing Forum, 29*(1), E1–7.

Dorrell, B. (1990). Being there: A support network of lesbian women. In J. A. Lee (Ed.), *Gay midlife and maturity* (pp. 89–98). Binghamton, NY: Haworth Press.

Eliason, M. J. (1996). *Who cares? Institutional barriers to health care for lesbian, gay, and bisexual persons.* New York: NLN Press. (National League for Nursing Publication No. 14-6762.)

Ferraro, K. F. (1987). Double jeopardy to health for Black older adults? *Journal of Gerontology, 42,* 528–533.

Ferraro, K. F., & Farmer, M. M. (1996). Double jeopardy to health hypothesis for African Americans. *Journal of Health and Social Behavior, 37,* 27–43.

Folkman, S., Chesney, M. A., & Christopher-Richards, A. (1994). Stress and coping in caregiving partners of men with AIDS. *Psychiatric Clinics of North America, 17,* 35–53.

Folkman, S., Moskowitz, J. T., Ozer, E. M., & Park, C. L. (1997). Positive meaningful events and coping in the context of HIV/AIDS. In B. H. Gottlieb (Ed.), *Coping with chronic stress* (pp. 293–314). New York: Plenum Press.

Friend, R. A. (1990). Older lesbian and gay people: A theory of successful aging. In J. A. Lee (Ed.), *Gay midlife and maturity* (pp. 99–118). Binghamton, NY: Haworth Press.

Genevay, B. (1982). In praise of older women. In M. Kirkpatrick (Ed.), *Women's sexual experience: Explorations of the dark continent* (pp. 87–101). New York: Plenum Press.

Grossman, A. H., D'Augelli, A., & O'Connell, T. S. (2001). Being lesbian, gay, bisexual, and 60 or older in North America. In D. C. Kimmel & D. L. Martin (Eds.), *Midlife and aging in gay America* (pp. 23–40). Binghamton, NY: Harrington Park Press.

Gubrium, J. F. (1991). *The mosaic of care: Frail elderly and their families in the real world.* New York: Springer.

Gubrium, J. F., & Holstein, J. (1999). Constructionist perspectives on aging. In V. L. Bengston & K. W. Schaie (Eds.), *Handbook of theories of aging* (pp. 287–305). New York: Springer.

Guralnik, J. M., Fried, L. P., Simonsick, E. M., Kasper, J., & Lafferty, M. E. (Eds.). (1995). *The women's health and aging study: Health and social characteristics of older women with disability.* Bethesda, MD: National Institute on Aging. (NIH Publication No. 95-4009.)

Hendricks, J., & Achenbaum, A. (1999). Historical development of theories of aging. In V. L. Bengston & K. W. Schaie (Eds.), *Handbook of theories of aging* (pp. 21–39). New York: Springer.

Henry, J. (2000). *Singing Myself a Lullaby* (Video). New York, ADF Video.

Hooker, E. (1967). The homosexual community. In J. H. Gagnon & W. Simon (Eds.), *Sexual deviance.* New York: Harper & Row.

Isaacs, B. (1971). Geriatric patients: Do their families care? *British Medical Journal,* 4(782), 282–286.

Kane, P. (1991). *Women's health: From womb to tomb.* New York: St. Martin's Press.

Karner, T. X. (1998). Professional caring: Homecare workers as fictive kin. *Journal of Aging Studies, 12,* 69–82.

Kehoe, M. (1986). Lesbians over 65: A triply invisible minority. *Journal of Homosexuality, 12,* 139–152.

Kehoe, M. (1988). *Lesbians over 60 speak for themselves.* Binghamton, NY: Haworth Press.

Kertzer, D. I., & Keith, J. (Eds.). (1984). *Age and anthropological theory.* Ithaca, NY: Cornell University Press.

Kimmel, D C., & Martin, D. L. (Eds.). (2001). *Midlife and aging in gay America.* Binghamton, NY: Harrington Park Press.

Lee, J. A. (Ed.). (1990). *Gay midlife and maturity.* Binghamton, NY: Haworth Press.

Lewin, E. (1981). Lesbianism and motherhood: Implications for child study. *Human Organization, 40,* 6–14.

Lewin, E. (1985). By design: Reproductive strategies and the meaning of motherhood. In H. Thomas (Ed.), *Sexual politics of reproduction* (pp. 123–138). Brookfield, VT: Gower.

Lorde, A. (1995). Man child: A Black lesbian feminist's response. In M. L. Anderson & P. H. Collins (Eds.), *Race, class, and gender: An anthology* (2nd ed., pp. 275–281). Belmont, CA: Wadsworth.

Mamo, L. (2002). *Sexuality, reproduction and biomedical negotiations: An analysis of achieving pregnancy in the absence of heterosexuality.* Ph.D. dissertation, Department of Social and Behavioral Sciences, University of California San Francisco.

Martin, D., & Lyon, P. (1970). The older lesbian. In B. Berzon (Ed.), *Positively gay*. Los Angeles: Media Mix.

Marshall, V. W. (1999). Analyzing social theories of aging. In V. L. Bengston & K. W. Schaie (Eds.), *Handbook of theories of aging* (pp. 434–458). New York: Springer.

Maruccio, E., Loving, N., Bennett, S. K., & Hayes, S. N. (2000). A survey of attitudes and experiences of women with heart disease. *Women's Health Issues, 13*, 23–31.

Merrill, S. S., & Verbrugge, L. M. (1999). Health and disease in midlife. In S. L. Willis & J. D. Reid (Eds.), *Life in the middle: Psychological and social development in middle age*. San Diego: Academic Press.

Meyer, M. H. (Ed.). (2000). *Care work: Gender, labor and the welfare state*. New York: Routledge.

Morgan, D. L. (Guest Ed.). (1998). The baby boom at midlife and beyond. *Generations, 22*(1). Spring issue.

Olesen, V. L. (1997). Who cares? Women as informal and formal caregivers. In S. B. Ruzek, V. L. Oleson, & A. Clarke (Eds.), *Women's health: Complexities and differences* (pp. 397–424). Columbus: Ohio State University Press.

Ponticelli, C. M. (Ed.). (1998). *Gateways to improving lesbian health and health care*. New York: Haworth.

Quam, J. K. (Ed.). (1997). *Social services for senior gay men and lesbians*. Binghamton, NY: Harrington Park Press.

Quam, J. K., & Whitford, G. S. (1992). Adaptations in age-related expectations of older gay and lesbian adults. *The Gerontologist, 32*, 367–374.

Qureshi, H., & Walker, A. (1989). *The caring relationship: Elderly people and their families*. Philadelphia: Temple University Press.

Sang, B., Warshow, J., & Smith, A. J. (1991). *Lesbians at midlife: The creative transition*. Los Angeles: Spinsters Ink.

Sarton, M. (1977). *The house by the sea*. New York: Norton.

Scarce, M. (1999). *Smearing the queer: Medical bias in the health care of gay men*. New York: Haworth.

Settersten, R. A. (1999). *Lives in time and place: The problems and promises of developmental science*. Amityville, NY: Baywood Publishing Co.

Settersten, R. A. (Ed.). (2003). *Invitation to the life course: Toward new understandings of later life*. Amityville, NY: Baywood Publishing Co..

Solarz, A. L. (Ed.). (1999). *Lesbian health: Current assessment and directions for the future*. Washington, DC: National Academy Press.

Stacey, J. (1999). Gay and lesbian families are here; All our families are queer; Let's get used to it! In S. Coontz (Ed.), *American families: A multicultural reader* (pp. 372–405). New York: Routledge.

Stephens, S. A., & Christianson, J. B. (1986). *Informal care of the elderly*. Lexington, MA: Lexington Books.

Stone, D. (2000). Caring by the book. In M. H. Meyer (Ed.), *Care work: Gender, labor and the welfare state* (pp. 89–111). New York: Routledge.

Stone, R., Cafferata, G. L., & Sangl, J. (1987). Caregivers of the frail elderly: A national profile. *The Gerontologist, 27*, 616–626.

Sussman, M. B. (1985). The family life of old people. In R. H. Binstock & E. Shanas (Eds.), *Handbook of aging and the social sciences* (2nd ed., pp. 414–449). New York: van Nostrand Reinhold.

Terry, J. (1999). *An American obsession: Science, medicine and homosexuality in modern society.* Chicago: University of Chicago Press.

Tufte, V., & Myerhoff, B. (Eds.). (1979). *Changing images of the family.* New Haven, CT: Yale University Press.

Turner, B. F., & Troll, L. (Eds.). (1994). *Women growing older: Psychological perspectives.* Thousand Oaks, CA: Sage.

van Dam, M. A. A., Koh, A. S., & Dibble, S. L. (2001). Lesbian disclosure to health care providers and delay of care. *Journal of the Gay and Lesbian Medical Association, 5,* 11–19.

Verbrugge, L. M. (1989). The twain meet: Empirical explanations of sex differences in health and mortality. *Journal of Health and Social Behavior, 30,* 282–304.

Verbrugge, L. M., Gruber-Baldini, A. L., & Fozard, J. L. (1996). Age differences and age changes in activities: Baltimore Longitudinal Study of Aging. *Journal of Gerontology: Social Sciences, 51,* S30–S41.

Weston, K. (1991). *Families we choose: Lesbians, gays, kinship.* New York: Columbia University Press.

CHAPTER 3

From a Far Place: Social and Cultural Considerations About HIV Among Midlife and Older Gay Men

E. Michael Gorman and Keith Nelson

INTRODUCTION

Gay men in their midlife and senior years (those born approximately before 1955) represent a population that has been disproportionately affected by HIV/AIDS. As others have documented (see for example, Linsk, 1994, 2000; Ship, Wolff, & Selik, 1991), this cohort contributed most of the earliest cases of AIDS. Currently more than one in nine alive AIDS cases are older than 50, and more than one in eight are older than 45; most of these individuals are gay or bisexual men. Moreover, in addition to having been impacted by HIV itself, it is this cohort, along with their lesbian, bisexual, and transgender allies, their friends, and their families, that has borne the primary tasks of advocacy, caregiving, grieving, and other social, economic, and political consequences of this epidemic. This generation also came of age during an era when gay, lesbian, and bisexual lifestyles had been hidden and often scorned by the larger society. These factors continue to influence how AIDS is addressed among older people overall. This essay reflects on both current HIV/AIDS challenges facing gay and bisexual men in their middle and senior years as well as hopefully providing some measure of insight as to their strengths and resilience in light of their life experiences.

As the population of the United States as a whole is "graying," the issues facing those who are open about their sexual orientation and those who are HIV infected merit serious and thoughtful consideration. As of December 2001, 90,513 people over the age of 50 (CDC, 2001) had been reported with AIDS, about 11% of the total number of people with this diagnosis. If one includes those over 45, then more than 20% of all cumulative AIDS cases in adults and adolescents, or more than 170,000 persons, are now grappling with that host of concerns that we subsume under the rubric of "aging with HIV/AIDS." This does not include the growing numbers of HIV-positive people who are not yet diagnosed with AIDS. This demographic portends an increase in the number of older people with HIV/AIDS (PWHA) needing health and social services and carries implications for planning for these services as well as for caregiving and other kinds of emotional and social support. These figures also provide some sense of the burden not just on society but especially on the lesbian, gay, bisexual, and transgender (LGBT) communities, often both to their families of choice and of biological origin, and on those cities and places where most of these individuals live.

In this paper we review social and epidemiological data with respect to HIV as it impacts middle-aged and older gay men and then shift focus to a microlevel with an emphasis on the discourse (or discourses) attending to HIV in this aging and middle-aged cohort of gay and bisexual men and their partners, survivors, and families. In developing the major discussion points of the paper, we have drawn on our own research and community and clinical experiences as well as of other writers whom we have cited. Gorman has been involved in social scientific research on gay men since before 1980 and in HIV-related research since 1982. Nelson has had extensive clinical and community experience in dealing with substance abuse and HIV issues over the course of the last decade in a variety of agency and community-based settings. Some of the discourses have been drawn from participant observations, field notes, and individual and group interviews over the last half-decade of NIH-supported research in western Washington State and the San Francisco Bay Area (NIDA R01 DA). While the ostensible focus of that particular research enterprise was not aging per se, observations, interviews, and field notes provided insight into many issues facing middle-aging and older gay men in respect of HIV. In addition, we have also utilized the anthropological convention of paraphrasing and/ or developing composite discursive statements that reflect sentinel cultural values and scripts relevant to the topic gleaned from ongoing fieldwork. We have generally chosen to utilize such paraphrases sparingly, but nonetheless believe them to be useful in conveying a sense of subjectivity and giving voice to the experiences of those middle-aging and senior gay men we are concerned with here.

HIV/AIDS: THE CONTEXT OF THE THIRD DECADE FOR LGBT COMMUNITIES

Since the emergence of AIDS over two decades ago (CDC, 1981), the devastating effects of the pandemic continue to mount. In the United States, where AIDS has been strongly associated with male homosexual activity, social and political currents have strongly affected how the disease has been approached. It may be that this particular dimension of the issue has only just begun to be framed in specific terms, and, of course, any such discourse may well vary from region to geographic region, depending on the sociodemography of caseload and political and social ideology. But the reality is that in many parts of the United States, at least, when one speaks of "HIV in older adults" one often means mostly gay men, however that is finessed. The results of the interface of the two domains "aging" and "AIDS" as they come together in the specific cohort of gay baby boomers will be very important to observe and will certainly represent a considerable part of the complex set of challenges facing AIDS practitioners in the years to come.

This having been said, it is also important to note that even as the political stigmatization of AIDS as a "gay disease" shaped the contours of the nascent gay liberation movement, so the contours of those same cultural battles continue to shape the psychic landscape of this cohort as it ages and deals with its unique relationship to the AIDS epidemic. Paradoxically, as AIDS decimated the gay community, it became a rallying point for the legitimation of gay rights because the HIV virus became a symbol of the irrational nature of homophobia and sharpened the historical realization that gays and lesbians could not depend on the presumed beneficence of government as far as their lives were concerned. At the same time there occurred the growing recognition that gays and lesbians existed throughout all segments of American society and had done so throughout history. Still, the overt discrimination included extremely prejudicial notions of AIDS being a scourge on "sinners" who engaged in "abominations" (homosexual acts) and put homosexuals in the unique position of having to fight for the legitimation of a major public health problem *as well as their own civil rights* against charges of moral depravity.

THE CURRENT STATE OF HIV/AIDS

The World Health Organization has estimated that in the year 2000 approximately 40 million individuals were living with HIV/AIDS worldwide, including approximately 37 million adults (WHO, 2000). In the United States more than 800,000 cumulative AIDS cases had been reported, of which some 420,000 were in gay or bisexual men, or MSM (men who have sex with other men): that is, about 53% of all adult cases and 64% of all male adult AIDS cases, respectively (CDC, 2002). There had been 33,000 cases of AIDS in adolescents or young adults age 13–24, and of these, about 54% were gay or bisexual males. Of particular note, the order of magnitude of AIDS mortality and morbidity among gay and bisexual men constitutes a huge and disproportionate burden on the LGBT community in particular. By the year 2002, there had been approximately 460,000 U.S. adult deaths from AIDS or AIDS-related causes, with the number of adult male deaths being on the order of 400,000. Of these deaths, some 267,000 of these were MSMs, a very large number when one considers the relatively small likely size of the gay/bisexual male population (some estimates range from 2–4% of the adult male population).

By comparison, the United States experienced 57,000 combat deaths in Vietnam, 37,000 in the Korean conflict, and 404,000 combat-related deaths in World War II, but these combat deaths were spread over an entire generation and more, as well as across all geographical areas of the country, not primarily in a concentrated subgroup. In other words, in the case of AIDS, deaths have been concentrated in certain states, in certain major urban centers, and among a relatively small subsample of the adult male population. It may well be argued that the longer-term social and psychological impact of these losses will not be comprehended fully for decades, but the shorter and more near-term consequences have already manifested themselves in terms of mortality and in a tremendous toll of the psychological, political, and financial resources of the LGBT community as well upon the families of PWA (Linsk & Poindexter, 2000; Poindexter & Linsk, 1999).

Finally, in addition, these mortality figures do not take into account HIV/AIDS-related morbidity, and thus one must include at least another 150,000 plus individuals living with AIDS, plus *an undetermined number with HIV alone, which have not in many circumstances historically been reportable.* In other words, the ongoing and probable future burden of HIV among MSM who are aging is considerable and must be taken into account when viewing the problem from an environmental perspective.

HIV AND GENERAL DEMOGRAPHIC CONSIDERATIONS

The elderly (age 65 and above) are the fastest-growing segment of the population and use proportionately more medical care than any other age group other than infants (Anderson, Barrett, & Bogue, 1997). In addition, those in their "middle years" or older represent a very large population soon to be making further demands on the nation's health care resources. It is this cohort of gay men whom AIDS has literally decimated.

Because of these large numbers, there is a genuine risk that older and to an extent middle-aged people with HIV/AIDS pose potentially difficult and significant challenges to health care and social service systems in providing health and economic security, unless appropriate research and planning efforts are undertaken soon. In addition, individuals who are HIV positive *and* who are seniors or in later middle age face the threat of being further marginalized (Linsk, 1994), especially given the difficulties facing the health care system as a whole as the population ages (Clinton, 1999; National Bipartisan Commission on the Future of Medicare, 1999). Even in the self-described LGBT communities, there has been candid discussion of "AIDS fatigue" and concerns raised that too many scarce resources were diverted to HIV/AIDs in the 1980s and that it is now important to balance the competing needs of the various LGBT constituencies, e.g., women and men, transgenders, bisexual persons, those with different health issues such as breast cancer and mental health issues, and those of different cohorts, such as generation Xers, post–baby boomers, and boomers themselves. By "AIDS fatigue" one understands the particular and peculiar experience of both ennui and psychological burnout that not infrequently accompanies work in the AIDS epidemic, which has been historically so all-consuming given the particular social, political, and ideological barriers to care that have existed. When one adds to this consideration a policy of nonrecognition, delegitimization, and overt hostility toward GLBT cultural and social needs articulated by conservative American politicians, one conjures a scenario of painful choices and of potentially grave proportions, which still faces society. While the initial challenges of the first decade of AIDS may have been met to some degree over time, there still remain significant *emerging* challenges with respect to the needs of the aging baby boomers.

While the policy implications of such scenarios are not clear, a likely possibility is that there may well be fewer resources available to care for aging HIV-positive individuals, most of whom are gay men, as well as fewer resources for prevention in this still sexually active population. In fact, of course, sexual activity continues throughout the lifespan, and HIV risk is far from nonexistent among the elderly, regardless of gender or sexual orientation (Adams & Cox, 1995; Rosenberg, 1995), although topics such as sexual activity and/or concomitant "recreational" drug use or alcohol abuse may be avoided by health care providers (Blow, 1998; Linsk, 1994). A point to be noted is that as the AIDS epidemic has broadened to a variety of groups, it appears even more likely that many older adults may have not received HIV/AIDS prevention education appropriately targeted to them in a timely manner (Linsk, 1994). Stigma related to AIDS can thus be inadvertently reinforced by the health care system, preventing effective interventions (Kooperman, 1994).

Aside from HIV itself, LGBT individuals over 45, whether or not they are seropositive, face the typical demands of their heterosexual contemporaries in caregiving for aging parents, often creating dilemmas about how to prioritize constrained resources, especially where individuals themselves are living with disabilities, including HIV, that often add to their additional economic burdens.

Along these same lines, psychological issues facing middle-aging and older gay or bisexual men (MSM) compound difficulties faced by the elderly in general. Issues regarding gay identity, adaptation, and integration into the gay community are pivotal to an individual's feelings about himself as an aging gay person, and AIDS has certainly had a major impact on the developmental processes involved in the life course of this cohort (Cohler, Hostetler, & Boxer, 1998).

CURRENCY OF LGBT AGING CONSIDERATIONS

There has been growing attention to issues of "aging" with respect to LGBT populations, witnessed by a growing number of programs, outreach efforts, and workshops on LGBT seniors, as well as increasing attention to those in their middle years (see, for example, Boxer, 1997; Herdt, Beeler, & Rawls, 1997; Isensee, 1999; Kooden & Flowers, 2000). We argue that the effects of the AIDS epidemic are central to understanding the needs of this population, since the initial phases of the AIDS epidemic so severely affected this cohort. It would be reasonable to say that virtually every gay person of this age cohort alive today has been touched by the AIDS epidemic in one form or another, either by needing to cope with having an HIV diagnosis, or to cope with loved ones and friends suffering from the disease, or to caretake those same loved ones. These experiences have been compounded by having to engage in the political struggles to legitimize HIV/AIDS as a disease and a public health concern rather than as a moral issue while simultaneously participating in the evolution of the gay struggle for equality and recognition as a legitimate minority.

In fact, the likelihood is that AIDS, in both its biology and its social history, compounds psychological issues facing middle-aging, older gay or bisexual individuals, adding to the typical difficulties faced by the elderly in general. Furthermore, most gay men (and lesbians) share issues in common with others who are aging, such as concerns about the availability of adequate health care, fears of loneliness, fears of becoming invisible, and fears about loss of income and autonomy. However, gay men, along with lesbians and transgendered persons, also have unique concerns about discrimination, which make their experiences likely to be different from those of their heterosexual agemates. They may in fact experience discrimination in housing and health care. They may experience fears of rejection in disclosing their sexual orientation and coming out to their family or others if they have hidden their gay lives (Quam & Whitford, 1992). For most LGBT persons, in fact, entering middle and late life, older adult developmental issues interact with issues regarding gay or lesbian or transgender identity, including unresolved internalized homophobia and adaptation to both the aging process and to societal responses to being an aging homosexual both within and outside of the gay community. Although not well described, it makes sense that the AIDS epidemic with its concomitant social meanings has had considerable impact upon the psyche of not only gay men but also of other members of the other LGBT communities who experience similar anxieties about their roles in society in terms of their own identities and life experiences. *It would astonishing if an event of such psychological, cultural, social, political, and economic magnitude as AIDS did NOT impact the psyches of these individuals.* How and in what ways remain to be seen, yet it is certain from what we have gleaned already that these individuals have not only been challenged, but they have also survived, and many have come to experience great inner strength and resilience as part of this process. This inquiry may shed light on the intrapsychic processes of aging and the ways in which deep-seated psychological, social, and cultural conflicts can be better understood in individuals dealing with stigma and oppression.

SOCIAL AND POLITICAL CONSEQUENCES OF AIDS

Socially nuanced themes such as gay identity, adaptation, and integration into the gay community have been significantly influenced by AIDS for gays as well as for lesbians and transgenders. The disease brought together those persons affected in a fight for their lives and may well have been the impetus for the creation of a plethora of community-based organizations and self-help groups, which have in turn promoted the solidarity of the community. In addition, the coming together of impacted LGBT populations provided a catalyst to forge alliances with other groups, and this continuum provided critical mass to the AIDS movement, resulting in a number of important social and political gains (Gutierrez, 1989).

Among these were greater visibility of LGBT individuals and greater support for AIDS-specific causes, including greater federal spending on HIV/AIDS research, treatment, and prevention. In addition, this social movement was able to push for other kinds of legislation that provided some increasing measure of protection for LGBT individuals, often at the state level.

A variety of health care organizations and related professional associations, both public and private, also have specifically included sexual orientation as a target of policy to ensure that LGBT rights are protected and that culturally competent care is given to LGBT populations (Lohman, Kennedy, Levin, Wong, & Chng, 2000).

The growth of organizations recognizing and addressing LGBT needs has been encouraging. However, the need for an activist approach for

LGBT human rights and advocacy for LGBT-specific care continues in the face of growing political challenges. The first decade of AIDS involved acute challenges and the need for radical action; the second and third decades involve the more prosaic tasks involved in coalition building, working for systemic changes, and engaging in increased competition for resources.

CHALLENGES AND DIFFICULTIES FACING OLDER HIV-POSITIVE GAY MEN

A number of issues confront HIV-positive gay men in particular in their middle and later lives. Among these include a heightened sense of mortality ("How long do I really have to live now that I am not dying?"), an expectation on the part of some of a shortened life expectancy ("This stuff [i.e., antiviral medication] takes its toll on the body and I figure I won't see real retirement"), and disability often accompanied by depression as a result of many years of fighting the virus and many years on antiretroviral therapy. In addition, there are a variety of social and psychological issues, including having a kind of "pariah" status (both old and with AIDS) and a disillusionment as the acute challenges of the first decade of AIDS transformed into the more bureaucratic and one might say more tedious organizational tasks of the second decade.

There is no question about the lifesaving properties of "the cocktail," since AIDS-specific mortality has plummeted. Yet these lifesaving antiviral medications have taken a physical and psychological toll since their introduction in the mid-1990s. Often, the secondary side effects of these medications wreak havoc with the body's organs, resulting in increasing incidence of serious medical complications, including neuropathy, nausea, cholesterolemia, and risk for heart attacks, liver function problems resulting in some cases in liver failure, and lipidystrophy, often resulting in a peculiarly disfiguring redistribution of body fat to the stomach and back and loss of fatty tissue in the facial area.

This last-mentioned syndrome is referred to by many simply as "The Look" and is unfortunately readily identifiable. Already feeling marked by their lifestyle, and often scarred by fighting for a plethora of AIDS and related civil rights causes over the last two decades, many older gay men say they experience additional stigma at this time because of the effects of AIDS medications themselves. Open any AIDS information bulletin or any gay newspaper and one finds ample discussion of this issue, which further serves to underscore the particular liminality of current gay midlife aging concerns. Many older gay men report feeling "invisible" when they walk about in their own neighborhoods and frequent popular haunts, which they attribute to the commonplace "graying" of their agemates in general. This is further exacerbated in HIV-positive persons by the peculiar physical manifestations of HIV treatments. "I feel like a leper at times" is a not uncommon refrain. Some report less than kind reactions by younger and/or HIV-gay men and even by some health care providers, therapists, and AIDS workers. "I feel like they're telling me, 'Look, you've had your quota of services and now it's time for somebody else's turn,' or 'The community went out of its way to support AIDS issues in the 80s and we just can't afford to fight that fight in the same way now. There are just too many competing demands on scarce community resources, so just try and make do, won't you?' " Some men report even more pointed barbs reflecting perhaps either deep-seated resentment against gay men generally or lack of understanding of the issues facing these individuals, which make many feel all the more guilty or ostracized or both.

The politics and the national rhetoric around AIDS also are cited by some men as contributing to their sense of anomie and isolation. "I mean, what do they want us to do, just go away?" posed one man. Another man said, "This is going to sound really weird and self-indulgent, but I remember hearing about Eskimo old people who just walked off into the tundra when food got scarce so as to be less of a burden to their villages. Sometimes I wonder if some people think we shouldn't do the same thing. Just kind of fade away." Perhaps this represents an extreme case of self-recrimination, but some have suggested that certain national AIDS information campaigns may inadvertently contribute to a sense of marginalization of middle-aging and older gay men. This might be as a result of emphasizing the most current trends in HIV sero-conversions without taking into account either regional or local variations in the HIV epidemic. For instance, in the western United States, 75% of the new AIDS cases are still among men who have sex with other men and many of the individuals over 45 with HIV are gay men who have survived.

In addition, many HIV-positive gay men experience an acute sense of grief because of multiple losses, as they have experienced deaths of life partners, close friends, and support systems with whom they had anticipated going through life. "You know, it's very hard every time I think about this," one man in his mid-50s explained, "but I am the only survivor of all of the guys I came out with. It's very painful. And really there are no words for it. It is real hard trying to convey that experience to younger gay men or others, including people in my own family."

A great many older HIV-negative men report survivor guilt. "Why me? Why am I one of the few to live?" While this experience is shared by many who survive any catastrophic event or disaster, in this case the experience of AIDS survivorship is acutely bound up with a sense of identity, of having been somehow "marked" as vulnerable because one belongs to a certain class or group of individuals, of having been "singled out" in some sense. One man related, "I find I really have to struggle against the notion that we [the gay community] somehow deserved this because of our lifestyle or that the fickle finger of fate somehow had it in for us." Often such sentiments are accompanied by the self-deprecation already described in their thoughts about having made "too many demands on the health care system already."

There is also a sense of frustration voiced by some older gay men that at times younger gay men do not appreciate the experiences and lessons learned from the survival of their older gay brothers. One man said, "I don't mean they should be grateful or anything, but if they could just imagine what it was like. Like many young guys seem to think that there was a decade of party and then AIDS. It isn't that simple, obviously, and I get the sense of little appreciation for the real political and social hurdles or the relatively low level of consciousness and organizational savvy that existed at the time. It took years of struggle and hard work by both men and women and lots of blood, sweat and tears. It didn't just happen."

In light of these concerns, not surprisingly depression is a frequent complaint of men in this age group, and reports of suicide attempts and suicide itself are higher than in the general population. Recent reports in the literature attest to the much higher frequency of suicide, especially among urban gay men, among who AIDS has taken its greatest toll (see, for example Mills et al., 2001). In many respects, such a finding is not surprising, and it may well be the result of the compounding of several risk factors: chronic illness over many years, co-occurrence of substance abuse and mental health issues, loss of significant life partners and agemates, disenchantment growing from the perceived youth centeredness and preoccupation with whatever is currently sexy and hot in mainstream urban gay culture, and a sense of marginality and social isolation. "Where *do* I fit?" Or even, "Why bother to try?"

Along similar lines, many health experts also see substance abuse being an increasingly important part of middle-aging and aging LGBT concerns. Substance abuse, and especially alcohol abuse, has been frequently described as a particular concern for the LGBT communities (Stall & Purcell, 2000). This is not a new issue, and while there remains a measure of debate as to the precise extent of alcoholism in the gay-lesbian-transgendered world (see, for example, Stall & Wiley, 1988; Ostrow, 2000; Gorman et al., 1997; Cabaj & Gorman, 2000), what remains clear is that there is a subset of LGBT individuals who abuse alcohol and illicit substances with deleterious health consequences. Among gay men who are HIV-positive, these authors and others have found self-medication with a variety of drugs, such as methamphetamine, MDMA (ecstasy), GHB, ketamine, and marijuana to be a prevalent coping mechanism for dealing with both the physical and the psychological pain that often accompanies HIV (see Gorman & Carroll, 2000; Gorman, 2002).

However, by the same token, it is important to state that many HIV-positive gay men also found meaning in their diagnosis. One man said, "I hate to say this but being diagnosed with AIDS and accepting that I had a drug problem actually saved my life in an emotional and spiritual way. I was forced to stop running on empty and get real. I have been clean and sober now for ten years and am studying Buddhism. It's unfortunate that it took AIDS for me to get in touch with myself, and come to terms with my internalized homophobia." This turning to a deeper reality, a sense of spiritual awakening, is not uncommon and seems to be a keystone to living with AIDS with dignity and self-acceptance. Along these lines, "gay or gay/lesbian spirituality" has now received considerable attention from a variety of denominational, traditional, and nontraditional perspectives. There now exist gay/lesbian groups and websites for every major religious tradition (Christian, Jewish, Buddhist, Moslem, Sikh, Hindu) as well as for pagan, new age, and atheist points of view. Hundreds of websites exist worldwide, and dozens of books and articles have been written from both perspectives of believers as well as from the perspectives of sociology and anthropology of religion. (Along the lines of the latter, see, for example, Gorman, 1980, 1991.) Still, spirituality in relation to aging per se has not yet received significant attention by gay and lesbian writers, perhaps because the LGBT community has been preoccupied with its own coming-of-age concerns as well as by those brought on by the AIDS epidemic itself. That situation may be starting to change as LGBT individuals face their own middle-aging and aging issues. In addition to the general concerns with meaning and eschatological considerations, however, substance abuse concerns became a catalyst for the community in the wake of the AIDS epidemic in the 1980s, and over the course of the last 15 years dozens of 12-step programs (e.g., Alcoholics Anonymous, Narcotics Anonymous, Gay-Lesbian Alanon, Crystal Meth Anonymous) have been established that speak to clear and evident social need in this regard, at least in North America.

CHALLENGES TO HIV-NEGATIVE GAY MEN AND THE LARGER LGBT COMMUNITY

The challenges posed by HIV are by no means limited to those infected by HIV. The reality is that a majority of men in the middle adult and aging years are *not* HIV positive, yet they are still impacted by the AIDS epidemic in significant ways (as are lesbians and heterosexual friends, family, and colleagues of those who are infected). How and in what ways are HIV-negative individuals impacted? And, what about the larger LGBT community and their biological families, friends, and colleagues?

There are several challenges. In the first place, the magnitude of HIV-related mortality inflicts the same sense of stigmatized multiple loss on the entire LGBT community and the families of those who have died. HIV-negative men and women, gay, lesbian, and straight, have often borne much of the brunt of AIDS caregiving and advocacy and have had to pick up and go on with their lives after the deaths of loved ones to HIV. For gay HIV-negative health care professionals, the burden of HIV has created a tremendous personal challenge. Some also feel that too many resources have been diverted to one segment of the LGBT community. Yet in many respects it could be argued that the HIV etched the LGBT community with grief in an unprecedented way as it took a similar toll of the families of those who died. AIDS exhaustion and the multiple loss syndrome could be said to have impacted these individuals in much the same way. The psychological impact has been varied: sublimation of feelings in activism, depersonalization such as might be realized through alcohol or drug abuse, and isolation.

Along these lines, some have speculated (see Ostrow, 1996; Gorman & Carroll, 2000; Gorman et al., in press) that one possible consequence of the magnitude of such multiple losses may be the current epidemic of the recreational club drug methamphetamine and polysubstance abuse, which may in turn be facilitating increased transmission of HIV in men who have sex with other men. In other words, some may be experimenting with or using such illicit substances, often in combination with alcohol, to "deal" with their grief. One man in his early 50s related:

> For myself, I feel like it [ecstasy] saved my life in a way. I was in a terrible hole of depression. I had lost my lover and every single one of my best friends—the guys I thought I would grow old with. I felt overwhelmed by guilt and terribly lonely. I had become despondent. Then one day at the Laundromat I struck up a conversation with this young punk gay guy who invited me to go with him to a rave that evening. I did and got introduced to "E," which seemed to free me of my self-absorption and allowed me to forget my depression at least somewhat. I met a whole new circle of mostly younger gay guys whom I never would have met otherwise and began to feel like I had a life once again. They became my new circle of friends and over the next weeks and months I got involved heavily in the local dance and rave scenes. I continued using ecstasy, which has started creating problems for me that it didn't do at first. But there is a sense that "E" got me out of my black hole.

Many men and women report that knowing and caring for HIV-infected and/or AIDS-diagnosed individuals have opened doors for them in terms of coming to terms with their own capacity for personal growth. These people have provided leadership in HIV care, policy development, and prevention, wanting to spare future generations the pain that they have known. One man explained. "In learning to deal with AIDS I learned about myself and to get over myself for the first time in my life. Based on my experience caring for my lover and a close friend, I feel I became a better person. I decided to leave the job I had had and went to nursing school and now I have a whole new career and a job that means so much more to me despite its stresses and demands."

Turning to yet another domain, the effects of homophobia upon the development of aging gays has not been well studied, but concerns about rejection by family and discrimination in health care, employment, housing, and long-term care due to sexual orientation compound the fears already experienced by many older people in general related to these issues (Quam & Whitford, 1992). However, Quam and Whitford observed that because of facing the struggles of "coming out" and facing societal disapproval, many of their respondents felt a deep sense of strength and satisfaction with their lives, and their creation of community with other gays and lesbians imbued them with the sense of altruistic fulfillment Erikson (1964) described as necessary to the "integrity" of a life well lived in relationship with others. However, the association with other aging gay men and women was underscored as essential to the feeling of connection and authenticity in a world that is still quite biased against gays.

HIV AND AGING FROM A DEVELOPMENTAL PERSPECTIVE

In addition to the specific health challenges posed by AIDS, another dimension of the impact of HIV on older LGBT individuals might be thought of in terms of one's life stages or passages. While this essay can only touch upon the issues impacting gay development in later life, it is important to acknowledge the reciprocal nature of social events and the life passages of gays.

The changes occurring during an individual's life have been described in terms of fairly discrete stages (Erikson, 1963, 1964) and in terms of life course. Erikson (1964) conceptualized the individual's life stages as being socially integrated, with midlife a time of generativity and late life as a time of perceiving oneself in terms of either integrity or despair, related to how one has lived one's life. *Generativity*, originally conceptualized by Erikson (1964) in his model of human developmental psychology, has been widely used to describe the contributions one makes to the generation that follows, and is especially salient during middle and later life. Others have provided more detailed models of the psychosocial attributes of generativity (McAdams & de St. Aubin, 1992; McAdams, Hart, & Maruna, 1998) and alternative developmental models targeting nondominant groups (e.g., Borysenko's [1996] model of the feminine life cycle) that have expanded the concept of generativity to reflect the different life courses inherent in the spectrum of human diversity.

Erikson (1964) viewed "integrity" as the ability of an older person to "envisage human problems in their entirety" (p. 134) in order to pass on such vision to the next generation, thus imbuing one's life with meaning. Erikson recognized that generativity and integrity emerged within "the total cultural milieu" (p. 142) and cautioned against confusing generativity with social conformity, an observation amplified in Cohler, Hostetler, and Boxer's (1998) examination of generativity in gay men in midlife. Cohler, Hostetler, and Boxer observed that heterosexual development is not affected by the prejudice and stigma inherent in gay development; the dynamics of having to learn to cope with social discrimination and personal identity conflict often result in a gay man or lesbian developing "off-time" with the AIDS pandemic, resulting in "a telescoping of developmental concerns" (p. 278). If, in an existential sense, the meaning of one's life is shaped by one's responses to the social influences defining the broad parameters of one's life, for those whose very identity could be viewed as having been in social flux, such as gays and other minorities, this process involves unique challenges. Personal development in such circumstances likely does not mirror the dominant paradigm. In many respects, the collision of events of gay liberation and the AIDS epidemic combined to create a unique opportunity for the explanation of this developmental phenomenon.

Johnson and Colucci (1999) posited four themes necessary to understanding lesbian and gay issues related to family and aging: relationship with family, the invisibility of important events in the gay person's life in the scheme of the dominant culture, intergenerational responsibility, and legacy. Generativity needs may be met through mentorship to younger gays, contributions to and participation in the LGBT community, and as a legacy of courage for others who feel "different" in some way (Cohler, Galatzer-Levy, & Hostetler, 2000; Johnson & Colucci, 1999). The connection to a larger supportive milieu appears to be essential to engaging successfully in such generativity; for all too many older gay men, a life of alienation and isolation has resulted from the toll of discrimination. The necessity to make sense of one's life within a social structure often in opposition to one's core being may well intensify the issues of integrity versus despair for LGBT people.

For gay men as well as lesbians experiencing midlife and later life, it is quite likely that the traditional structures or contexts of generativity and integrity are not available, or are often found wanting in the sense that historically there was no extended "gay or lesbian community" to anchor or inform one's developmental process, and there were few real gay or lesbian role models who had attained old age in any commonly understood sense of that term. By this same token, it is also the case that many gay men and lesbians now considered to be seniors or middle-aging may not fit into their families of origin or other transgenerational societal institutions. Instead, they have had to define their own roles and reframe their relationships both with families of origin and with society generally, including if they happen to be biological parents. This process is of a cultural and personal order difficult to appreciate even by those undergoing it and those who are on the very vanguard of that process.

Some of this dynamic may express itself in the creation of "families of choice," i.e., the selection of a life partner of the same gender and the establishment of an extended (or not so extended) support system along those lines. Such families may well include having children, either by adoption or by birth. Many gay men and lesbians have chosen to become parents in these ways, and of course numerous others are parents by virtue of having been heterosexually partnered or married and subsequently transitioned into a gay or lesbian life. Whether or not such a family of choice involves children, it could be seen as a psychological, sociological, and cultural response to the nascent issues of generativity faced by LGBT persons in contemporary society. This cultural and sociological dynamic may in turn facilitate new ways of experiencing generativity and challenge both LGBT and heterosexual individuals and society with respect to integration and resilience. In other words, in respect of aging concerns, a particular creative tension may be occurring at this point in history for those LGBT individuals on the cusp of becoming "seniors" and those who have already achieved that status. For gay men and indeed all LGBT persons, HIV/AIDS has had and continues to exert a profound impact on this process, which has significant psychological, sociological, and cultural dimensions.

CONCLUSION

In sum, we believe that we as a society (here we refer to the United States experience in particular) appear to be at a crossroads in terms of articulating and understanding HIV and aging concerns as they impact society generally, the LGBT community, and especially gay men in their late middle and senior years, regardless of their HIV status. The impact of the HIV/AIDS epidemic on both global and U.S. society has been epochal and no less so on the gay community in terms of the loss of the lives of so many gay men in their prime of life, especially in the first decade of the pandemic, as well as in terms of the ongoing economic, psychological, medical, and caregiving needs of those who are living with HIV. Indeed, it could be said that so trenchant is the relationship between HIV and gay male identity and survival (and only to a slightly lesser degree with respect to the LGBT community generally), that one cannot comprehend the exigencies of "aging" in this community without reference to HIV.

The challenges facing older gay and bisexual men in the age of AIDS are numerous, and they include the provision of both appropriate prevention and treatment services in a health care system admittedly already strained by competing needs. Furthermore, such planning must necessarily incorporate a systems approach that can take into account the extended networks and families and communities in which these individuals live and the meaning and context in which they have lived their lives. Parallels and linkages to other populations, such as lesbians, heterosexual friends, and others likewise need to be explored further, and social planning and policy must be inclusive of the needs of the aging who are HIV positive and their caregivers. The authors believe that to neglect the particular needs of this far from negligible population would be a great misfortune and could result in significant societal costs. We believe that several areas would benefit from further exploration. Specifically, what can we learn from the unique experiences of such gay [and lesbian] elders that can help us understand the important psychological and social changes attendant to biological aging? What can we learn specifically from *this* cohort about its struggles and its victories, its challenges and its resilience? Finally, what can we learn about the inner strengths and intrapsychic as well as sociological and cultural dimensions of aging from this unique cohort of individuals and the tapestry of their lives ?

Finally, with respect to AIDS, it must be acknowledged that we are only beginning to understand the longer-term impacts of the epidemic in terms of the psychological and cultural landscape of the LGBT community. There is a genuine need to comprehend better not only the toll and the needs of those affected by HIV, but likewise the positive lessons, possibly applicable to other aging populations. In the third decade of the HIV/AIDS epidemic, its interface with the processes related to aging gay and lesbian populations offers potentially rich opportunities to discern how gay, lesbian, transgender, and bisexual cultural systems emerge almost phoenix-like from the ashes of that HIV/AIDS epidemic and to document how these systems evolve and survive.

REFERENCES

Adams, W. L., & Cox, N. S. (1995). Epidemiology of problem drinking among elderly people. *International Journal of the Addictions, 30*(13/14), 1693–1716.

Anderton, D. L., Barrett, R. E., & Bogue, D. J. (1997). *The population of the United States* (3rd ed.). New York: The Free Press.

Blow, F. C. (1998). Substance use among older adults. Rockville, MD: Center for Substance Abuse Treatment.

Borysenko, J. (1996). *A woman's book of life: The biology, psychology and spirituality of the feminine life cycle.* New York: Riverhead Books.

Boxer, A. M. (1997). Gay, lesbian, and bisexual aging into the twenty-first century: An overview and introduction. *Journal of Gay, Lesbian, and Bisexual Identity,* 2(4), 187–197.

Cabaj, R., & Gorman, M. (2000, Spring). Lesbian/gay/bisexual/transgendered individuals and substance abuse: A profile. In *A provider's guide to substance abuse treatment for lesbian, gay, bisexual and transgendered individuals, Vol. 1.* Rockville, MD: U.S. Department of Health and Human Services, Substance Abuse and Mental Health Services Administration.

Centers for Disease Control. (1981). Pneumocystis pneumonia—Los Angeles. *Morbidity and Mortality Weekly Report, 30,* 250–252.

Centers for Disease Control. (2001, June). *HIV/AIDS surveillance report.*

Centers for Disease Control. (2002). *HIV/AIDS surveillance report.*

Clinton, W. J. (1999). Medical issues in the State of the Union Address delivered by President Clinton before a joint session of Congress—January 19, 1999. Available online: *http://www.amaassn.org/ama/asic/article/0,1059,2053491,00.html.*

Cohler, B. J., Galatzer Levy, R. M., & Hostetler, A. J. (2000). Lesbian and gay lives across the adult years. In B. J. Cohler & R. M. Galatzer-Levy (Authors), *The course of gay and lesbian lives* (pp. 193–251). Chicago: University of Chicago Press.

Cohler, B. J., Hostetler, A. J., & Boxer, A. M. (1998). Generativity, social context, and lived experiences. Narratives of gay men in middle adulthood. In D. P. McAdams & E. de St. Aubin (Eds.), *Generativity and adult development. How and why we care for the next generation.* Washington, DC: American Psychological Association.

Erikson, E. H. (1963). *Childhood and society* (2nd ed.). New York: W. W. Norton.

Erikson, E. H. (1964). Human strength and the cycle of generations. In *Insight and Responsibility. Lectures on the ethical implications of psychoanalytic insight* (pp. 109–157). New York: W. W. Norton.

Gorman, E. M. (1980). *A new light on Zion.* Ph.D. dissertation, University of Chicago, Department of Anthropology.

Gorman, E. M. (1991). A special window: An anthropological perspective on spirituality in contemporary U.S. gay male culture. In M. L. Stemmler & J. M. Clark (Eds.), *Constructing gay theology, contemporary issues in religion* (pp. 44–61). American Academy of Religion Series, Vol. 2.

Gorman, E.M. (2002). Research with gay drug users: Current methodological issues. In W. Meezan & J. I. Martin (Eds.), *Research methods and issues with gay, lesbian, bisexual and transgender populations.* New York: Harrington Press.

Gorman, E. M., Barr, B., Hansen, A., Robertson, B., & Green, C. (1997). Speed, sex, gay men and HIV: Ecological and community perspectives. *Medical Anthropology Quarterly, 11*(4), 505–515.

Gorman, E. M., & Carroll, R. (2000). The interface of substance abuse and HIV: Considerations regarding methamphetamines and other "party drugs" for nursing practice and research. *Journal of Nursing and AIDS Care, 11*(2), 51–62.

Gorman, E. M., Nelson, K., Applegate, T., Scrol, A., & Amato, E. (in press). Club drugs and polysubstance use and HIV among gay/bisexual men: Lessons gleaned from a community project and implications for practice, outreach and education. *Journal of Gay and Lesbian Social Services.*

Gutierrez, F. J. (1989). *Gays and lesbians. An ethnic identity.* Paper presented at the annual meeting of American Psychological Association Convention, August 1989.

Herdt, G., Beeler, J., & Rawls, T. W. (1997). Life course diversity among older lesbians and gay men: A study in Chicago. *Journal of Gay, Lesbian and Bisexual Identity, 2*(3/4), 231–246.

Isensee, R. (1999). *Are you ready? The gay man's guide to thriving at midlife.* Los Angeles: Alyson Books.

Johnson, T. W., & Colucci, P. (1999). Lesbians, gay men, and the family life cycle. In B. Carter & M. McGoldrick (Eds.), *The expanded life cycle: Individual, family, and social perspectives* (3rd ed.). Boston: Allyn and Bacon.

Kooden, H., & Flowers, C. (2000). *Golden men: The power of gay midlife.* New York: Avon.

Kooperman, L. (1994). A survey of gay and bisexual men age 50 and older. (1994). *AIDS Patient Care, 8*(3), 114–117.

Linsk, N. L. (1994). HIV and the elderly. *Families in Society: The Journal of Contemporary Human Services, 5*(6), 362–372.

Linsk, N. L. (2000). HIV among older adults: Age-specific issues in prevention and treatment. *AIDS Reader, 10*(7), 430–444.

Linsk, N. L., & Poindexter, C. (2000). Older relatives as caregivers for HIV-infected persons: Reasons for caring. *Journal of Applied Gerontology, 19*(2), 181–202.

Lohman, R., Kennedy, N., Levin, S. M., Wong, F. Y., & Chng, C. L. (2000). Using alliances and networks to improve treatment for lesbian, gay, bisexual, and transgender clients. In *A provider's guide to substance abuse treatment for lesbian, gay, bisexual and transgendered individuals* (Vol. 1; pp. 147–158). Rockville, MD: U.S. Department of Health and Human Services, Substance Abuse and Mental Health Services Administration.

McAdams, D., & de St. Aubin, E. (1992). A theory of generativity and its assessment through self-report, behavioral acts and narrative themes in autobiography. *Journal of Personality and Social Psychology, 62,* 1003–1015.

McAdams, D., Hart, H., & Maruna, S. (1998). The anatomy of generativity. In D. McAdams & E. de St. Aubin (Eds.), *Generativity and adult experience: Psychosocial perspective on caring and contributing to the next generation* (pp. 7–43). Washington, DC: American Psychological Association Press.

Mills, T. C., Stall, R., Pollack, L., Paul, J. P., et al. (2001). Health-related characteristics of men who have sex with men: A comparison of those living in "gay ghettos" with those living elsewhere. *American Journal of Public Health, 91,* 980–983.

National Bipartisan Commission on the Future of Medicare. (1999). Draft working document. Author. Available: *http://rs9.loc.gov/medicare/breauxplan.html.*

Ostrow, D. G. (1996). Substance use, HIV, and gay men. *Focus. A Guide to AIDS Research and Counseling, 11*(7), 1–3.

Ostrow, D. G. (2000). The role of drugs in the sexual lives of MSM. *AIDS & Behavior, 4*(2), 205–219.

Poindexter, C. P., & Linsk, N. L. (1999). HIV-related stigma in a sample of HIV-affected older female African-American caregivers. *Social Work*, 4(1), 446–461.

Quam, J. K., & Whitford, G. S. (1992). Adaptation and age-related expectations of older gay and lesbian adults. *The Gerontologist*, 32(3), 367–374.

Rosenberg, H. (1995). The elderly and the use of illicit drugs: Sociological and epidemiological considerations. *The International Journal of the Addictions*, 30(13/14), 1925–1952.

Ship, J., Wolff, A., & Selik, R. (1991). Epidemiology of acquired immune deficiency syndrome in persons aged 50 years or older. *Journal of Acquired Immune Deficiency Syndrome*, 4, 84–88.

Stall, R., & Purcell, D. (2000). Intertwining epidemics: A review of research on substance abuse among MSMS. *AIDS and Behavior*, 4(2), 181–192.

Stall, R., & Wiley, J. (1988). A comparison of alcohol and drug use patterns of homosexual and heterosexual men: The San Francisco Men's Health Study. *Drug and Alcohol Dependence*, 22, 63–73.

World Health Organization. (2000, June). *Report on the global HIV/AIDS epidemic*. Geneva, Switzerland.

SECTION 2

Empirical Contributions

CHAPTER 4

Psychological Well-Being in Midlife and Older Gay Men

Robert Kertzner, Ilan Meyer, and Curtis Dolezal

Psychological well-being in middle-aged and older gay men connotes both a sociocultural context for positive mental health as well as the interactive effects of personality, psychiatric vulnerabilities, and the idiosyncracies of life experience. In addition, historical age cohort effects such as social attitudes toward older adults' sexuality, in general, and homosexuality, in particular, significantly shape psychological well-being in older gay men. Perhaps because of these complexities, there is little systematic research that examines determinants of well-being in this population. This chapter will review the literature describing psychological health in older gay men, examine data on gay men's well-being derived from a nationally representative sample, and consider how the life course experience of gay men might shape psychological well-being.

We will focus on the potential applicability of a multidimensional construct of psychological well-being (Ryff & Keyes, 1995) that may help "map" the landscape of well-being in gay adults and, in so doing, underscore the differential mental health significance of social processes that affect the identity of being gay and of becoming older. Ryff's model of well-being serves several purposes relevant to this chapter. First, by including the assessment of domains related to self-realization and personal fulfillment, it registers a highly salient process in the lives of gay men, that of coming out and assuming a stigmatized and developmentally resisted identity. Second, the model is sensitive to age-related change in dimensions of well-being and thus captures the relationship between subjective appraisals of well-being and location within the life course. As such, this model of well-being addresses the central question of how the maintenance of male homosexual identity and the assumption of related social roles confer psychological strengths or vulnerabilities at particular ages throughout the life course. Finally, Ryff's measure moves beyond limitations of other assessments that capture short-term affective well-being (i.e., happiness) to explore more enduring life challenges, such as sense of purpose in life and, implicitly, the philosophical notion of what constitutes the good life. To consider this dimension is to ask the question of how being gay influences the human predicament of maintaining meaning and morale throughout the second half of life. As Herdt (1997a) has written, "What moral action defines the role of the self following the act of coming out? In part, the question of a gay self concerns the nagging sense that the self in the stories of gay life has not yet found a moral voice . . . a moral sensibility and ethics that go beyond the act of coming out" (p. 168).

We turn first to several preconceptions that underlie this chapter. First, to fully appreciate the significance of social identities constructed around homosexuality, later chapters of individual life histories must be considered in order to provide a context for interpreting earlier chapters. Moreover, a focus on positive psychological health may best capture the longitudinal effects of assuming a homosexual identity in young adulthood from this chapter's perspective that homosexual identity is a minority identity characterized by discordant values and norms regarding sexuality, intimacy, and, perhaps, human existence and purpose (Meyer & Dean, 1998).

We also focus on gay men's experience in the belief that gender imparts significant differences to life course experience, regardless of sexual orientation. While the life course of lesbians and gay men is affected by similar social processes such as the stigmatization of sexual desire, male gender socialization is associated with a different sexual culture and different patterns of relational life that selectively shape psychological and subjective well-being across the life course.

LITERATURE ON PSYCHOLOGICAL HEALTH
IN GAY MEN

What, then, do we know about psychological health in gay men's lives from a life course perspective? Earlier studies describe a variety of positive mental health findings in older gay men. In his landmark study of gay aging, Berger (1982) noted that his respondents had traveled a "long and tortuous road" toward self-acceptance, but believed that their journey resulted in improved psychological adjustment characterized by less depression and fewer psychosomatic symptoms in older age. Similar findings were reported by Weinberg and Williams (1974), who described levels of life satisfaction and stability of self-concept in older gay men that were equal to those of heterosexual controls and higher than those of younger homosexual men. These findings of positive mental health were attributed to adaptations integral to the coming-out process: developing skills to master crises in social and family rejection, cultivating new sources of social support, and acquiring greater independence from conventional social mores in defining personal aspirations and identity (Kimmel, 1978).

This literature reflects the formative influence of the social stigma attached to aging, homosexuality, and the dual status of being old and gay as major determinants of psychological well-being in earlier generations of gay men entering middle age and old age. Contemporary generations of gay men, however, are likely to experience a greater range of formative social influences on homosexual identity formation, and, as such, stigma may be less uniformly operative. Furthermore, as more overt gay-related stigmatization and discrimination wane in certain quarters in Western societies, a different contextual factor influencing psychological health in older gay men's lives may be increasingly important: that of psychosocial valuation of life experience, or lack thereof. Here, invisibility rather than stigmatization per se is key, although the two processes are closely linked. As reviewed by Boxer (1997) and Cohler and Galatzer-Levy (2000), social age norms and the related ascription of social roles, expectations, and behaviors strongly shape an individual's sense of being "on schedule" with respect to life experiences and, from the perspective of social comparison theory, influence an individual's sense of well-being. Yet gay men, as they age, may increasingly feel that their lives are unreflected by either heteronormative culture or gay sexual culture, neither of which elaborates upon the age-related social roles and identities of older gay men. Lacking the role of progenitor, legally recognized spouse, or desirable sexual partner, to cite several salient examples, older gay men may feel increasingly marginalized by their social worlds.

This generalization, of course, is subject to several important caveats. First, historical change in social and legal tolerance of homosexuality has broadened the range of gay lives now possible to live and this trend pertains to older men as well. The AIDS crisis, the establishment of gay community institutions, greater recognition of domestic partnerships, and increasingly public profile of gay adult lives provide social identities for gay men that were nonexistent in past generations (Herdt, 1997b; Yang, 1999). Second, older gay men manage other identities beside that of being homosexual, some of which are likely to significantly shape life experience and mediate the effects of aging on psychological well-being; these include vocational, family, relationship, and health-related identities as well as the broader demographic factors of race, education, and income.

Still, several overriding social characteristics of gay lives remain relevant to a discussion of psychological well-being in middle-aged and older men. Gay men are more likely to be unpartnered over the life course compared to heterosexual men and are less likely to have children (Fowlkes, 1994); without built-in kinship networks that include members of younger generations, many aging gay men experience diminished family and social supports, particularly as parents die or friendship networks decrease in size (Kimmel, 1978; Lee, 1987). In addition, older gay men may find themselves disinclined to start new relationships or disadvantaged because of gay sexual culture's preference for youthfulness in prospective partners (Gagnon & Simon, 1973; Coleman, 1981). Some gay men approaching their forties experience an increasing sense of marginalization within gay sexual culture that results in a heightened distress about aging or an adaptive decrease in participation in gay social worlds (Gagnon & Simon, 1973; Weinberg & Williams, 1974); these observations, though dated, may still be partially applicable. Of note, Harry (1982) reported that among the young, middle-aged, and older gay men he studied, those in their forties were most anxious about aging, particularly if they were experiencing a crisis in attachment to work or in their relational life.

Two other aspects of the gay male life course significantly affect psychological well-being, although little research has studied their longitudinal dimension and meaning. First, age-related change in the objective and subjective realms of sexuality is not well studied in gay men. Systematic study of male sexuality in older adults has not inquired about sexual orientation (Schiavi, 1999). Little research, to this author's knowledge, has studied the relationship between age-related changes in sexual interest, arousal, and activity, on the one hand, and more general indices of well-being, on the other, in gay men's lives. Clinical reports suggest that for some gay men entering midlife, diminished sexual desire creates an uncertain sense of gay social identity and precipitates psychological distress (Isensee, 1999). In one of the few studies of sexuality in older gay men, Pope and Schultz (1991) found that sexual activity diminished with age but that satisfaction with sexual life remained unchanged for most men. This finding is similar to that reported for heterosexual men and may reflect decreasing expectations of sexual satisfaction or the emergence of other means of expressing intimacy within ongoing relationships (Schiavi, 1999). The latter interpretation, however, is rooted in the more frequent occurrence of long-term and primarily monogamous relationships in heterosexual men's lives; the proper interpretive lens for understanding gay men's sexuality is unclear, given higher rates of single lives and the greater frequency and tolerance of sex outside of established relationships. Further research is needed to study how gay men react to age-related change in sexuality and to explore the significance of partnership status as a factor shaping sexual satisfaction, interest, and behavior in gay men's adult lives (Hostetler & Cohler, 1997).

A second factor relevant to well-being across the life course of gay men is predisposition to mood and anxiety states (most gay men, of note, do not have these clinical diagnoses). Although our main emphasis in this chapter is to consider the effects of the sociocultural context on positive psychological health in older gay men's lives, the question of psychiatric diatheses is relevant because of increased rates of mood and anxiety disorders reported in gay men (Gilman et al., 2001; Sandfort, deGraff, Bijl, & Schnabel, 2001) and the likely interactive effects between social factors and individual risk factors in affecting mental health. Preexisting psychopathology sensitizes individuals to several factors that are themselves linked to psychological distress: stigma, changes in social role that are poorly mediated by culture, and life transitions deviating from an expectable timetable (Vaillant, 1993). Depression itself may make it more difficult for adults to enter into or sustain relationships (Cui & Vaillant, 1997), while being partnered, in turn, is associated with enhanced psychosocial adjustment to aging and greater life satisfaction (Weinberg & Williams, 1974; Berger, 1982; Quam & Whitford, 1992; Sandfort, deGraff, Bijl, & Schnabel, 2001).

Little systematic research has examined whether rates of psychiatric disorders are higher in older gay men than in younger gay men or how premorbid psychopathology affects adaptation to life stressors and developmental tasks in the life course of gay men. A recent community-based study of men and women that compared young with middle-aged adults found a significant sexual orientation-by-age interaction for alcohol misuse; homosexual and bisexual orientations and middle age were associated with greater alcohol misuse in men and women (Jorm et al., 2002). No sexual orientation-by-age interactions were reported for anxiety or depressive symptoms or for negative or positive affect.

THE ADULT LIFE COURSE PERSPECTIVE IN HETEROSEXUAL POPULATIONS

The life course of adult men as described in the general population provides an additional perspective on factors associated with well-being in gay men. As mentioned above, gay men maintain other identities and social roles beside those related to being homosexual; as participants in larger social worlds, gay men are influenced by the social age structures and age norms of heteronormative culture. Vocational identity, for example, strongly influences a sense of aging in men. Men often perceive the onset of middle age by cues such as the differential behavior accorded them in the work setting, make appraisals of life experience based on career-related events, and perceive a close relationship between life line and career line (Neugarten, 1968; Ryff, 1989). This may explain why heterosexually and bisexually/homosexually identified men describe similar estimates of the age at which midlife begins and ends: ages 43 and 58, respectively (unpublished data based on analysis of MIDUS data, Brim et al., 1995).

Middle age is also associated with other change in psychological life and social roles that is relevant to the present discussion. Looking at dimensions of psychological well-being by age, Ryff (1989) found that middle-aged compared to young adults in the United States' population had higher levels of personal autonomy and environmental mastery and, compared to old adults, a greater sense of personal growth and purpose in life. Neugarten (1968) characterized midlife as a time of peak complexity in social roles with an increasing emotional, social, and cultural distance from the young. Central to many descriptions of middle age is a heightened awareness of less time remaining in life; this incremental awareness of life's finitude spurs greater introspection, a need for solitude, and a reappraisal of what is possible and desirable to achieve in the time remaining in life (Cohler & Galatzer-Levy, 1990). Levinson (1978) described a normative questioning of purpose in life experienced by men in their early forties, often leading to a restructuring of individual lives and the discovery of new sources of life meaning.

The applicability or modification of these observations to gay men's lives is unclear (Cornett & Hudson, 1987). Perhaps midlife gay men's withdrawal from youth-oriented gay social worlds partially reflects a more generic distance from the young as described by Neugarten (1968). On the other hand, the notion of a midlife reappraisal of social identity may be less applicable to gay men, who already stand outside social norms defining full adult personhood based on procreation and heterosexual marriage (Herdt, personal communication). As mentioned above, gay men may also experience earlier social dislocations from their communities, if such communities are largely defined by youth-oriented venues of gay sexual culture (Weinberg & Williams, 1974). The ability to experience a sense of continuity in life narrative despite these social processes may be particularly important to midlife gay men's psychological well-being (Kertzner, 1999).

SECONDARY DATA ANALYSIS OF MIDUS STUDY

To test the applicability of descriptions of age-related change in psychosocial attributes and well-being in gay men's lives, we examined data from the National Survey of Midlife Development in the United States (MIDUS) study, a collaborative, interdisciplinary investigation of patterns, predictors, and consequences of midlife development in the areas of physical health, psychological well-being, and social responsibility (Brim et al., 1995). We were interested in exploring how sexual orientation together with age might selectively shape psychological well-being, life satisfaction, and satisfaction with current sex life in gay men.

Given the literature cited above describing a sense of crises mastery and self-sufficiency forged by the coming-out process, we hypothesized that compared with heterosexual peers, older gay men would have higher levels of personal autonomy and, compared with younger gay men, higher levels of personal autonomy, self-acceptance, and life satisfaction. We also hypothesized that, as noted in the general population (Diener, Lucas, & Oishi, 2002), being in a relationship, experiencing less depressive symptomatology, receiving more education, and reporting better health would be associated with higher scores on well-being and life satisfaction measures, including satisfaction with current sex life.

Sample

MIDUS respondents were drawn from a nationally representative random-digit-dial sample of noninstitutionalized, English-speaking adults aged 25–74 selected from working telephone banks in the coterminous United States. Those queried participated in an initial telephone interview and responded to a mail questionnaire. Data used in this analysis were taken from the Main Data Set, the main survey of 4,242 respondents. The following sample description and subsequent data analysis are based on unweighted data.

Respondents were asked whether they were "attracted to men, women, or both." Using this definition of sexual orientation, 1,730 male respondents were classified as heterosexual, 31 as homosexual, and 26 as bisexual, with 368 nonresponses or missing data points, out of a total of 2,155 men. Because of the small number of men defined as homosexual or bisexual ($n = 57$), both categories were collapsed into homosexual/bisexual. There were no differences between homosexual and bisexual men in education, income, age, health status, or number of depressive symptoms.

For data-analytic purposes, age was stratified into two groups: men under 40, and those 40 and older; this stratification is in accordance with the adult developmental literature that posits significant change in self-identity associated with men's early forties and with previous reports suggesting change in gay social identity at this age (Weinberg & Williams, 1974; Levinson, 1978).

Among the 57 homosexual/bisexual men, 14 were married and 13 were living with someone in a "steady-marriage like relationship." Most of the homosexual/bisexual men were childless, although 16 had biological children and 4 had nonbiological children. The racial composition of the homosexual/bisexual group was almost entirely white; of the 56 men responding to questions about race, 93% were white; 2%, black; and 4%, other; in contrast, 87% of the heterosexual men were white; 5%, black; and 3%, other. Of note, only 6 respondents among all men reported that they had experienced or been treated for AIDS or HIV in the past 12 months; 3 of these men were homosexual/bisexual, and 3 were heterosexual.

Measures

The main outcomes of interest in this data analysis were Ryff's multidimensional assessment of psychological well-being (Ryff, 1989) and single-item assessments of current life and sexual life satisfaction. The Ryff instrument assesses dimensions of personal autonomy, environmental mastery, positive relations with others, sense of purpose in life, sense of personal growth, and self-acceptance. This measure was designed to address the observation that structural social factors only account for part of the variance of mental health outcomes and that idiosyncratic life experiences and opportunities are reflected in self-appraisals of well-being (Ryff, 1989).

Satisfaction with current life was assessed by the single question "Using a scale from 0 to 10 where 0 means 'the worst possible life overall' and 10 means 'the best possible life overall,' how would you rate your life overall these days?" Similarly, satisfaction with current sex life was assessed by asking, "Using a scale from 0 to 10 where 0 means 'the worst possible situation' and 10 means 'the best possible situation,' how would you rate the sexual aspect of your life these days?"

Other assessments include demographic indices, a continuous measure of depressive symptomatology using the CIDI-SF (Wittchen, 1994), and single-item assessments of partnership status and overall physical health.

Statistical Analyses

Heterosexual and homosexual/bisexual men were compared on measures of education, income, self-reported health status, and depression using t-tests and on partnership status by chi square. To examine the effects of sexual orientation and age on subscales of psychological well-being and assessments of life satisfaction and satisfaction with sex life, multiple regression analyses were conducted in several steps. First, age and sexual orientation were entered to examine possible main effects (Model One); then, a sexual orientation-by-age interactive term was added as an independent variable in the regression analysis (Model Two). To adjust for the effects of education, income, self-reported health status, partnership status, and depression on main effects, these covariates were entered along with sexual orientation and age in the above analyses (Model Three). Finally, an analysis with these covariates was repeated, with the addition of a sexual orientation-by-age interactive variable (Final Model).

Results

Comparisons of Heterosexual Versus Homosexual/Bisexual Men (Table 4.1)

Among all men, no significant differences were found in levels of income, education, or health. Homosexual/bisexual men had higher levels of depressive symptomatology and were younger than heterosexual men, with a mean age of 42 years compared to 47 years. Heterosexual men were also more likely to be in relationships than homosexual/bisexual men and to have children under the age of 18 (data not shown).

Among men 40 years of age and older, no differences by sexual orientation were found in income, education, or age. Heterosexual men rated their overall health at slightly better levels, at a trend level of significance; homosexual/bisexual men had higher numbers of depressive symptoms than heterosexual men.

Regression Analyses of Sexual Orientation and Age on Well-Being (Table 4.2)

Homosexual/bisexual men compared to heterosexual men had lower scores on self-acceptance and sense of purpose in life (Model One). These differences were no longer significant when the sexual orientation-by-age interactive term was entered into the analyses (Model Two); however, older age together with homosexual/bisexual status predicted lower scores on these measures. This remained true when adjusting for depressive symptoms, income, educational levels, health

TABLE 4.1 Sample Characteristics

Differences in age, education, income, self-reported health status, depressive symptomatology (t-tests), and partnership status (chi square) by sexual orientation

	Adults < 40 years of age		Adults ≥ 40 years of age		All Adults	
	HT (572)	HM/BI (30)	HT (1143)	HM/BI (27)	HT (1728)	HM/BI (57)
Age	32.4±4.4	32.3±4.4	54.1±9.6	53.0±10.1	46.9±13.2	42.1±12.9**
Education	3.0±.9	3.0±.99	3.0±1.00	3.0±1.1	3.0±1.0	3.0±1.1
Income	25.1±14.0	24.9±15.4	23.7±18.6	24.6±23.9	24.2±17.1	24.8±19.7
Health	3.7±.9	3.7±1.0	3.5±1.0	3.1±1.1^	3.5±.9	3.4±1.1
Depression	.7±1.9	2.1±2.7*	.5±1.6	1.6±2.6*	.60±1.7	1.84±2.7**
In relationship	71%	47%**	80%	44%**	77%	46%**

* p ≤ .05 ** p ≤ .01, all comparisons within age grouping (^ p = .055).
HT, Heterosexual; HM/BI, Homosexual/Bisexual.
Educational coding: (1) some grade school to some high school, (2) GED or graduated high school, (3) some college (no bachelor's degree), (4) graduated college or other professional degree.
Income: respondent's personal income over past year: category 23: $20,000–24,999; 24: $25,000–29,999; 25: $30,000–34,999; 26: $35,000–39,999.
Health: (1) poor, (2) fair, (3) good, (4) very good, (5) excellent.
Depressive symptomatology: summative score of depressive symptoms, with scores ranging from 0 to 7 in male respondents. Mean for all men is .65; median .00.
Relationship: % of respondents living with someone in a marriage-like relationship.

status, and relationship status. As expected, more education, being in a relationship, better self-reported health, and fewer symptoms of depression were each associated with higher levels of self-acceptance and sense of purpose in life.

Regression Analyses of Sexual Orientation and Age on Life and Sex Life Satisfaction (Table 4.3)

Homosexual/bisexual status was associated with lower scores on measures of present life and sex life satisfaction, although no significant

TABLE 4.2   Regression Analysis: Effects of Age, Sexual Orientation, and Interaction of Age and Sexual Orientation on Self-Acceptance and Sense of Purpose in Life

	Model 1	Model 2	Model 3	Final model
	Beta	Beta	Beta	Beta
Self-acceptance				
Age	−.003	.007	−.007	.002
Sexual orientation	−.084**	−.035	−.040(.078)	.004
Age × orientation		−.071*		−.063*
Education			.068**	.068**
Partnership			.125**	.124**
Depression			−.187**	−.188**
Income			.001	.002
Health			.176**	.174**
Adj R^2	.006**	.008**	.111**	.113**
F	11.54**	9.46**	32.82**	29.37**
Sense of purpose				
Age	−.088**	−.078**	−.083**	−.074**
Sexual orientation	−.078**	−.026	−.050*	−.003
Age × orientation		−.075*		−.068*
Education			.189**	.190**
Partnership			.124**	.123**
Depression			−.083**	−.084**
Income			.022	.023
Health			.151**	.149**
Adj R^2	.012**	.014**	.112**	.114**
F	6.23**	5.71**	32.52**	29.92**

*$p \leq .05$, **$p \leq .01$.

effect was found for the interaction of age and sexual orientation. Sexual orientation no longer predicted life satisfaction when regression analyses were adjusted for the above covariates. Partnership status, better health, and less depression were each associated with higher levels of life satisfaction.

The effect of sexual orientation on satisfaction with current sex life was significant at a trend level (p = .076) in the direction of lower ratings for homosexual/bisexual men after adjusting for the above covariates. Partnership status, better health, less depression, less education, and greater income were each associated with higher levels of satisfaction with current sex life.

TABLE 4.3   Regression Analysis: Effects of Age, Sexual Orientation, and Interaction of Age and Sexual Orientation on Life and Sex Life Satisfaction

	Model 1	Model 2	Model 3	Final Model
	Beta	Beta	Beta	Beta
Life satisfaction, current				
Age	.109**	.113**	.101**	.103**
Sexual orientation	−.095**	−.076**	−.042(.062)	−.031
Age × orientation		−.028		−.015
Education			−.021	−.021
Partnership			.195**	.195**
Depression			−.186**	−.186**
Income			.015	.015
Health			.223**	.223**
Adj R^2	.021	.021	.165	.164
F	19.99**	13.58**	49.89**	43.67**
Sex life satisfaction, current				
Age	−.128**	−.128**	−.135**	−.137**
Sexual orientation	−.085**	−.085**	−.040(.076)	−.051
Age × orientation		.000		.016
Education			−.067**	−.067**
Partnership			.239**	.239**
Depression			−.074**	−.074**
Income			.075**	.075**
Health			.183**	.183**
Adj R^2	.021	.021	.134	.134
F	19.51**	12.97**	39.44**	34.53**

$^*p \leq .05$, $^{**}p \leq .01$.

Discussion

The above data analysis explores the significance of sexual orientation and age in relation to positive psychological health in gay men's lives. Although we had expected to find higher scores on personal autonomy in older gay men compared to heterosexual peers and higher personal autonomy and self-acceptance in older gay compared to younger gay men, we did not find these differences. We did find, however, that homosexual/bisexual status was associated with lower scores on self-acceptance and sense of purpose of life. Of particular interest to this chapter, these differences were no longer significant when the interaction of age and sexual orientation was included in regression analyses; we found that older age together with homosexual/bisexual status accounted for lower scores on these measures. This interactive effect remained significant after adjusting for differences between heterosexual and homosexual/bisexual men in depression, health status, and relationship status, suggesting that the finding was not solely attributable to observed differences by sexual orientation in these covariate measures. Nonetheless, it should be noted that age, sexual orientation, and the interactive effect of both, while significant, still only explained relatively little of the variance in self-acceptance and sense of purpose in life.

Homosexual and bisexual men rated their satisfaction with current life and, in particular, sex life, less positively than heterosexual men, with no significant interactive effect of sexual orientation and age. As above, age and sexual orientation accounted for little of the variance in these outcome measures, with the addition of the partnership status, depression, and self-reported health variables modestly improving the amount of variance explained. It is interesting to note, however, that the differences in satisfaction indices by sexual orientation were no longer significant when adjusting for the above covariates, which themselves were associated with life and sex satisfaction. Perhaps unlike measures of sense of purpose in life and self-acceptance, which may be sensitive to social valuation of the life course experience of older gay men, satisfaction indices may be more affected by proximal circumstances such as the availability of a partner and how well or unwell individuals feel on a daily basis.

Before more fully exploring these data and returning to this chapter's main interest, several important caveats about data interpretation warrant consideration. First, the criteria of sexual attraction in defining sexual orientation as used in this study is not synonymous with social identity as gay or bisexual. In a probability sample of the U.S population, Laumann et al. (1994) found that most men who reported desire for same-sex partners did not self-identify as gay or bisexual. Findings associated with sexual orientation in the present study, therefore, are of uncertain generalizability to men who self-identify as gay or bisexual; the process and consequences of self-identification may have significant effects on psychological well-being and satisfaction measures. As a further consideration, the creation of a single homosexual/bisexual predictor variable for data-analytic purposes may obscure important differences between these two sexual orientations. Recent work by Jorm et al. (2002), for instance, found that bisexual adults had poorer mental health than homosexual adults or heterosexual adults.

With a larger subsample of homosexual/bisexual men, more differences by sexual orientation status may have been detected on measures of well-being and satisfaction. Although this data analysis attempted to enhance power by using regression analyses and utilizing data from all male respondents, the relatively small number of homosexual and bisexual men in this cohort limit inferences that can be made about negative findings, including the lack of difference in personal autonomy by sexual orientation as hypothesized by this chapter. Furthermore, the very small number of minority homosexual/bisexual men precludes an analysis of well-being by race, an important factor shaping the experience of being gay and growing older (Adams & Kimmel, 1997).

Although the main measure of psychological well-being used in this study has good psychometric properties as established in studies with general population samples, it is possible that the measures comprise "yardsticks of self-evaluation that are unattainable, unattractive, or irrelevant for individuals at different locations in the social structure" (Ryff, 1989, p. 1079). The social location of gay men may be different enough to weaken the reliability of Ryff's measure of psychological well-being. Of note, in a study of 3,200 gay and bisexual men that used this measure, researchers were unable to replicate a six-dimensional model of well-being in factor analysis (personal communication, Jay Paul). The phenomenology of psychological well-being in gay men's lives may differ in ways that are not tapped in the Ryff measure, reflecting the salience of developing a stigmatized identity, the different configurations of emotional and sexual intimacy characterizing gay men's interpersonal worlds, or the psychological impact of the HIV epidemic.

With these caveats in mind, there may be important differences in the quantitative and qualitative dimensions of sense of purpose in life and self-acceptance in older gay men's lives. One possible explanation of these findings is that age cohort effects may have shaped the self-ratings of currently older homosexual/bisexual respondents; some of these men came of age before Stonewall and may have been exposed to early and sustained experiences of stigmatization related to their homosexuality. As mentioned above, younger gay and bisexual men are likely to have experienced stigma differently and, perhaps, less pervasively. Stigmatization and discrimination preclude full realization of individual potential and may affect a sense of fulfillment and purpose in life (Erikson, 1946; Baumeister, 1991). Being married and experiencing same-sex desire, as typifies a sizeable minority of older homosexual/bisexual men in this study, may represent one attempt to manage stigmatized desire in this cohort of older men; in contrast, the vast majority (26 out of 30) of younger men who describe same-sex desire are unmarried. Although this may reflect an age-related prevalence of marriage, it may also reflect historical differences in the social acceptability of nonmarital lifestyles.

The interactive effect of sexual orientation and age on sense of purpose in life and self-acceptance could also reflect the lack of psychosocial valuation of older gay men's life experience by heteronormative and gay sexual culture. This absence undermines sexuality as an organizing theme in life narrative and thereby interferes with a salutary sense of personal integration and continuity in the second half of life (Cohler & Galatzer-Levy, 1996). Older gay men may see little reflection of their lives in social norms and institutions, feel that their contributions are less valued, or have fewer opportunities for such contribution. In contrast, male heterosexual identity is generally assumed, reflected, and valued throughout the adult life course regardless of the strength of sexual desire and, to some extent, age. Thus, heterosexual adulthood benefits from cultural scenarios of adult sexuality that are organized around family life and, to some extent, conventional gender roles that are expressed in many relationships (Gagnon & Simon, 1973). Thus, even if sex loses its luster as heterosexual men age, the institution of heterosexuality provides ongoing sources of social identity and meaning for men. In current work (unpublished manuscript), the authors are exploring how social valuation of life experience affects psychological well-being in older homosexual and bisexual men. Older adults' appraisals of their social contributions and integration may have particular salience in influencing their sense of purpose in life and self-acceptance (Keyes, 1998); how these social processes apply to homosexual and bisexual men warrants further study.

CONCLUSION

Psychological well-being in older gay men reflects a convergence of sociocultural processes, historical context, and idiosyncracies of individual life experience and attributes. Beyond broad demographic factors, on the one hand, and mental health strengths and vulnerabilities, on the other, the social organization of gay lives has significance for the experience of well-being in the second half of life. Further research is needed to replicate these findings of differential psychological well-being and to corroborate such findings with qualitative interviews that capture the conditions under which particular ideals of well-being are obstructed or realized (Ryff, 1989). This, in turn, will inform public policy and health interventions to optimize the psychological health of older gay men and increase our understanding of how sexual orientation influences the experience of purpose and meaning in life.

REFERENCES

Adams, C. L., & Kimmel, D. C. (1997). Exploring the lives of older African-Americans. In B. Greene (Ed.), *Ethnic and cultural diversity among lesbians and gay men* (pp. 132–151). Thousand Oaks, CA: Sage.

Baumeister, R. F. (1991). *Meanings of life*. New York: Guilford Press.

Berger, R. M. (1982). *Gay and gray: The older homosexual man*. Urbana-Champaign, IL: University of Illinois Press.

Boxer, A. M. (1997). Gay, lesbian, and bisexual aging into the twenty-first century: An overview and introduction. *Journal of Gay, Lesbian, and Bisexual Identity*, 2(4), 187–197.

Brim, O. G., Baltes, P. B., Bumpass, L. L., Cleary, P. D., Featherman, D. L., Hazzard, W. R., Kessler, R. C., Lachman, M. E., Markus, H. R., Marmot, M. G., Rossi, A. S., Ryff, C. D., & Shweder, R. A. (1995). National Survey of Midlife Development in the United States (MIDUS) [Computer file]. ICPSR version. Ann Arbor, MI: DataStat, Inc./Boston, MA: Harvard Medical School, Dept. of Health Care Policy [producers], 1996. Ann Arbor, MI: Interuniversity Consortium for Political and Social Research [distributor], 2000.

Cohler, B. J., & Galatzer-Levy, R. M. (1990). Self, meaning, and morale across the second half of life. In R. A. Nemiroff & C. A. Colarusso (Eds.), *New dimensions in adult development* (pp. 214–260). New York: Basic Books.

Cohler, B. J., & Galatzer-Levy, R. M. (1996). Self psychology and homosexuality: Sexual orientation and the maintenance of personal integrity. In R. P. Cabaj & T. S. Stein (Eds.), *Textbook of homosexuality and mental health* (pp. 207–223). Washington, DC: American Psychiatric Press.

Coleman, E. (1981). Developmental stage of the coming out process. *Journal of Homosexuality*, 7(2/3), 31–43.

Cornett, C. W., & Hudson, R. A. (1987). Middle adulthood and the theories of Erikson, Gould, and Valliant: Where does the gay man fit in? *Journal of Gerontological Social Work*, 10(3/4), 61–73.

Cui, X. J., & Vaillant, G. E. (1997). Does depression generate negative life events? *Journal of Nervous and Mental Disease, 185*(3), 145–150.

Diener, E., Lucas, R. E., & Oishi, S. (2002). Subjective well-being: The science of happiness and life satisfaction. In C. R. Synder & S. J. Lopez (Eds.), *Handbook of positive psychology* (pp. 63–73). Oxford, Great Britain: Oxford University Press.

Erikson, E. H. (1946). Ego development and historical change. *Psychoanalytic Study of the Child, 2,* 359–396.

Fowlkes, M. (1994). Single worlds and homosexual lifestyles: Patterns of sexuality and intimacy. In A. S. Rossi (Ed.), *Sexuality across the life course* (pp. 151–186). Chicago: University of Chicago Press.

Gagnon, J. H., & Simon, W. (1973). *Sexual conduct: The social sources of human sexuality.* Chicago: Aldine Publishing Company.

Gilman, S. E., Cochran, S. D., Mays, V. M., Hughes, M., & Ostrow, D. (2001). Risk of psychiatric disorders among individuals reporting same-sex sexual partners in the National Comorbidity Study. *American Journal of Public Health, 91*(6), 933–939.

Harry, J. (1982). Being out: A general model. *Journal of Homosexuality, 1,* 25–40.

Herdt, G. (1997a). *Same sex, different cultures: Exploring gay and lesbian lives.* Boulder, CO: Westview Press.

Herdt, G. (1997b). Intergenerational relations and AIDS in the formation of gay culture in the United States. In M. P. Levine, P. M. Nardi, & J. H. Gagnon (Eds.), *In changing times: Gay men and lesbians encounter HIV/AIDS* (pp. 245–281). Chicago: University of Chicago Press.

Hostetler, A. J., & Cohler, B. J. (1997). Partnership, singlehood, and the lesbian and gay life course: A research agenda. *Journal of Gay, Lesbian, and Bisexual Identity, 2*(3/4), 199–229.

Isensee, R. (1999). *Are you ready? The gay man's guide to thriving at midlife.* Los Angeles: Alyson Books.

Jorm, A. F., Korten, A. E., Rodgers, B., Jacomb, P. A., & Christensen, H. (2002). Sexual orientation and mental health: Results from a community survey of young and middle-aged adults. *British Journal of Psychiatry, 180,* 423–427.

Kertzner, R. M. (1999). Self-appraisal of life experience and psychological adjustment in midlife gay men. *Journal of Psychology and Human Sexuality, 11,* 43–64.

Keyes, C. L. (1998). Social well-being. *Social Psychology Quarterly, 61,* 121–140.

Kimmel, D. C. (1978). Adult development and aging: A gay perspective. *Journal of Social Issues, 34*(3), 113–130.

Laumann, E. O., Gagnon, J. H., Michael, R. T., & Michaels, S. (1994). *The social organization of sexuality.* Chicago: University of Chicago Press.

Lee, J. A. (1987). What can homosexual aging studies contribute to theories of aging? *Journal of Homosexuality, 13,* 43–69.

Levinson, D. J. (1978). *The seasons of a man's life.* New York: Alfred A. Knopf.

Meyer, I. H., & Dean, L. (1998). Internalized homophobia, intimacy, and sexual behavior among gay and bisexual men. In G. Herek (Ed.), *Stigma and sexual orientation* (pp. 160–186). Thousand Oaks, CA: Sage.

Neugarten, B. L. (1968). The awareness of middle age. In B. L. Neugarten (Ed.), *Middle age and aging* (pp. 93–98). Chicago: University of Chicago Press.

Pope, M., & Schultz, R. (1991). Sexual attitudes and behavior in midlife and aging homosexuals males. In J. A. Lee (Ed.), *Gay midlife and maturity* (pp. 169–177). Binghamton, NY: Harrington Park Press.

Quam, J. K., & Whitford, G. S. (1992). Adaptation and age-related expectations of older gay and lesbian adults. *The Gerontologist, 32*(3), 367–374.

Ryff, C. D. (1989). Happiness is everything, or is it? Explorations on the meaning of psychological well-being. *Journal of Personality and Social Psychology, 57*(6), 1069–1081.

Ryff, C. D., & Keyes, C. L. M. (1995). The structure of psychological well-being revisited. *Journal of Personality and Social Psychology, 69*(4), 719–727.

Sandfort, T. M., de Graaf, R., Bijl, R. V., & Schnabel, P. (2001). Same-sex behavior and psychiatric disorders. *Archives of General Psychiatry, 58*, 85–91.

Schiavi, R. C. (1999). *Aging and male sexuality.* Cambridge, UK: Cambridge University Press.

Vaillant, G. E. (1993). *The wisdom of the ego.* Cambridge, MA: Harvard University Press.

Weinberg, M. S., & Williams, C. J. (1974). *Male homosexuals: Their problems and adaptations.* New York: Oxford University Press.

Wittchen, H. U. (1994). Reliability and validity studies of the WHO-composite international diagnostic interview (CIDI): A critical review. *Journal of Psychiatric Research, 28*, 57–84.

Yang, A. (1999). *From wrongs to rights: Public opinion on gay and lesbian Americans moves toward equality.* The Policy Institute of the National Gay and Lesbian Task Force.

CHAPTER 5

Disclosure and Depression Among Older Gay and Homosexual Men: Findings from the Urban Men's Health Study

Todd W. Rawls

During the 1970s and early 1980s, researchers turned away from seeking the causes of homosexuality to understanding the precursors of successful psychological adaptation to a widely stigmatized identity and minority group membership. During this time, several social scientists offered remarkably similar, theoretical stage models of the process of homosexual identity formation, some of which were ultimately subjected to empirical investigations (Cass, 1979; Coleman, 1982; Dank, 1971; De Monteflores & Schultz, 1978; Hencken & O'Dowd, 1977; Lee, 1977; McDonald, 1982; Plummer, 1975; Troiden, 1979). As is well known, prior stage models of homosexual identity formation suggest a normative, linear, and sequential progression of life events (Herdt & Boxer, 1996).

According to McDonald (1982), these events alter "from initial awareness of same sex feelings through homosexual behavior to eventual self-labeling, self-disclosure, and the final stabilization of a positive gay identity" (p. 48). Furthermore, many stage theorists hypothesize that individuals are motivated to "progress" from one stage to another because they experience some form of psychic tension resulting from cognitive dissonance or interpersonal incongruency; individuals are motivated to "achieve" a public gay or lesbian identity that is congruent or consistent with their behaviors, their self-identities, their public presentations of self, and/or others' impressions of themselves. This is, perhaps, best represented in theoretical attempts based on Cass's (1979) Homosexual Identity Formation (HIF) model, according to which "the process of striving for congruency between perceptions about one's behavior, one's self-identity, and others' beliefs about oneself provides the momentum that propels a person from one stage of HIF to another" (Brady & Busse, 1994, p. 4). Moreover, many stage theorists suggest that individuals can experience some form of "arrested development" by failing to progress beyond any particular stage, and that failing to progress through the hypothesized stages will have negative consequences for individuals' overall psychological well-being or mental health.

Empirical investigations suggest that the "coming-out" process, if completed, usually takes most subjects ten or eleven years to complete, and that most subjects complete the process by their mid-20s (see McDonald, 1982). However, nearly all of these studies were concerned with understanding the recalled "coming-out" experiences of younger gays and lesbians during the 1970s and 1980s, and they disregarded older subjects.

Because these studies were primarily concerned with understanding people's movement into, and involvement with, new urban gay subcultures that became established communities during the 1970s, most researchers recruited convenience samples of predominantly young, self-identified gay and/or lesbian subjects from gay bars, women's bars, homophile organizations, bathhouses, and so forth. However, McDonald's (1982) sample did include some older, male respondents, and he reported significant cohort differences with respect to the timing of developmental "milestones" in the coming-out process—finding significant differences between his 20-year-old subjects ($n = 106$) and those in their 30s ($n = 54$) and 40s ($n = 19$). McDonald found that, on average, older subjects came out later in life and exhibited much greater variability in the ages with which they achieved various milestones in the coming-out process (pp. 53, 56).

Also during the 1970s and 1980s, a number of important studies illuminated processes by which homosexuals can achieve high levels of psychological adaptation and develop healthy identities in the face of social oppression and stigmatization. These studies identified factors that are important for the mental health and well-being of gay men and lesbians, such as accepting one's homosexuality, being committed to homosexuality, developing a positive homosexual identity, building supportive social relationships, having satisfying sexual relations, being a member of homosexual groups, and being involved in gay or lesbian social contexts (Bell & Weinberg, 1978; Farrell & Morrione, 1974; Hammersmith & Weinberg, 1973; Jacobs & Tedford, 1980; Schmitt & Kurdek, 1987; Weinberg & Williams, 1974).

Similarly, research on older, self-identified gay men and lesbians suggests that many of these same factors are important and that most older gays and lesbians are generally happy, well-adjusted, sexually active, and socially engaged (Adelman, 1991; Almvig, 1982; Beeler, Rawls, Herdt, & Cohler, 1999; Bennett & Thompson, 1991; Berger, 1980, 1982, 1984, 1992, 1996; Berger & Kelly, 1996; Davis & Kennedy, 1990; Deevey, 1990; Ehrenberg, 1996; Francher & Henkin, 1973; Friend, 1980, 1987, 1989; Gray & Dressel, 1985; Herdt, Beeler, & Rawls, 1997; Kehoe, 1986a, 1986b, 1989; Kelly, 1977, 1980; Kimmel, 1979, 1992; Laner, 1978, 1979; Lee, 1987a, 1987b; Levy, 1979; Lipman, 1986; Minnigerode, 1976; Minnigerode & Adelman, 1978; Quam & Whitford, 1992; Raphael & Robinson, 1984; Ryan & Bradford, 1993; Vacha, 1985; Weeks, 1983; Weinberg, 1970; Weinberg & Williams, 1974). Indeed, one may say that a canonical position has emerged in the research literature that homosexuals, of all ages, who are more "out," open, and actively involved in gay community contexts will enjoy higher levels of mental well-being than those who are more "closeted" and less involved.

However, this canonical position should not seem surprising, because the research supporting it has nearly always relied upon nonrepresentative, convenience samples of younger, self-selected respondents who were recruited through gay or lesbian institutions, community organizations, advertisements, personal networks, and so forth. Consequently, most respondents in these studies report high levels of satisfaction with, or acceptance of, their previously formed gay or lesbian self-identities. They also tend to be open about their sexual self-identities, have extensive gay and lesbian friendship networks, and are relatively active within gay or lesbian social contexts or communities—all of which are cultural ideals within the contexts in which these studies were conducted. Also, these highly selective samples are mostly white, highly educated, and affluent, and they typically underrepresent older persons. For example, respondents over 65 years of age are almost entirely absent from this research.

NORMALIZING THE OLDER HOMOSEXUAL

Research during the last 25 years has attempted to refute negative stereotypes or cultural myths that have so often characterized older gay men and lesbians as being socially isolated, depressed, sexually frustrated, unhappy, prone to alcoholism or substance abuse, and so forth (Berger, 1992, 1996; Friend, 1980, 1989; Kehoe, 1986a, 1989; Kimmel, 1978, 1979; Vacha, 1985; Weinberg & Williams, 1974). Indeed, Wahler and Gabbay (1997) recently reviewed 58 empirical studies on gay male aging and concluded that the negative stereotypes about older gay men that have been so prevalent in American society are not warranted. Instead, they note that happiness and successful adaptation to aging are commonly reported by older gay men, perhaps due to coping skills and competencies that are unique to aging homosexuals.

However, many of the studies focusing on older gay men (and sometimes lesbians) were specifically conducted with the aim of dispelling prevalent stereotypes, as summarized in Berger's landmark book *Gay and Gray*:

> The older homosexual . . . is alienated from friends and family alike, and he lives alone, not by choice but by necessity. At thirty he is old. Since he is no longer sexually attractive to other homosexuals, he is forced to prey on children and to pursue anonymous sexual contacts in public places such as restrooms and parks. He is desperately unhappy. (Berger, 1996, p. 25)

In addition to showing that most of the gay men in his convenience sample (over 40 years of age) enjoyed high levels of psychological adjustment, Berger (1996) went further and argued that mental well-being among gay men may actually increase with age—a line of reasoning that has led some researchers to conceptualize gay aging using the mastery of stigma and/or crisis competence hypotheses (Berger, 1982, 1996; Berger & Kelly, 1986; Francher & Henkin, 1973; Kelly, 1977; Kimmel, 1979; Vacha, 1985; Weeks, 1983).

Several researchers studying gay and lesbian aging argue that older gay men and lesbians may be better suited to cope with age-related changes as a result of having weathered the trials and tribulations of being homosexual in a homophobic society or of having "come out" and formed self-affirming gay or lesbian identities within oppressive social contexts. They argue that older homosexuals have additional coping strategies or skills that allow them to enter old age at an advantage.

However, as the sociologist Lee (1991) notes, it may be misleading to characterize older gays and lesbians as "extraordinary agers," because such a perspective might lead researchers to overlook the yet unknown, but less desirable, realities of aging among persons who have remained hidden to social research. The counterintuitive can be found in Lee's (1987b) own research: Older gay men who remained closeted were happier than those with higher rates of disclosure. Lee also argued that gay men with higher rates of disclosure had a higher lifetime prevalence of stressful events and were more likely to experience lower levels of psychological well-being in old age. Similarly, Adelman (1991) found that low disclosure was related to high life satisfaction and lower levels of self-criticism among her relatively small sample of homosexual men and women over the age of 60 in San Francisco.

METHOD

This study is based on secondary analysis of a subsample of older homosexuals from the Urban Men's Health Study (UMHS), which was conducted between November 1996 and February 1998. The Urban Men's Health Study was primarily supported by National Institute of Mental Health grant MH54320. Supplementary support for the UMHS was provided by the National Institute on Aging and the Centers for Disease Control and Prevention Division(s) of HIV/AIDS (Catania et al., 2001). The following analysis was partially supported by the Social Science Research Council Sexuality Research Fellowship Program.

Working under contract for researchers at the University of California Center for AIDS Prevention Studies (CAPS), the Survey Methods Group of San Francisco used computer-assisted telephone interviewing (CATI) technology and random digit dialing (RDD) techniques to survey a probabilistic sample of men who have sex with men (MSM) in San Francisco, Los Angeles, Chicago, and New York City. Using over 195,000 telephone numbers to screen over 60,000 households, they completed interviews with 2,881 men who either identified themselves as gay or who reported any same-sex contact since age 14.

The overall goal of the sampling plan was to minimize RDD costs while maximizing the representativeness of the sample from selected ZIP codes in each city with higher percentages of MSM respondents. Thus, the UMHS does not provide a "true" probability sample of MSMs in each of the four cities. Rather, the UMHS provides a probability sample of MSMs within selected ZIP codes in each city. However, prior studies conducted in San Francisco using RDD techniques only sampled the two densest ZIP codes, whereas the UMHS sampled thirteen ZIP codes. Consequently, the UMHS provides much better representation of MSMs living outside of ZIP codes with "gay ghetto" neighborhoods. By sampling much larger sociogeographic areas, well beyond the "gay ghettos" in San Francisco, Los Angeles, Chicago, and New York, the UMHS undoubtedly provides increased representation of gay men of color, men with lower incomes, men without partners, men who are marginally involved in gay communities, and men with lower educational levels (as has been confirmed in San Francisco). Furthermore, the demographic profile of the UMHS sample suggests that it is far more representative than previous convenience samples of self-selected gay men recruited through community contexts (see Catania et al., 2001). Consequently, the UMHS represents a quantum leap in the sampling of MSMs and overcomes the substantial limitations associated with more common techniques for sampling rare populations.

Measures in the final UMHS interview protocol were extensively field-tested using procedures developed by Cannell and colleagues (1989) that combine qualitative and quantitative methods to determine if items are problematic for respondents or interviewers. After the items were tested and revised, they were again briefly field-tested for timing and editing purposes.

Because most of the variables in the following analysis are either on a nominal level of measurement (categorical) or resulted in highly skewed distributions (and therefore violate the assumptions of more powerful statistical tests), I have opted to use a more conservative approach and restrict much of the following to chi-square analyses of contingency tables. While more powerful approaches are available, chi-square analysis also reduces the probability of reporting statistically significant relationships that are so small that they are actually trivial. However, given the limited sample size, the number of control variables that can be considered at any one time is also limited, due to the problem of "diminishing n's," in which expected cell frequencies fall below five.

RESULTS

The UMHS surveyed 372 self-identified homosexual men between the ages of 50 and 85. However, half of the respondents in this subsample were between the ages of 50 and 55 at the time of their interviews, and the median age was used to divide the sample into two groups of roughly equal size. For the purposes of some age comparisons, the sample was also divided into three groups: men in their 50s, 60s, and men aged 70 years and above. Because only three respondents reported ages of 80 years and above, they were included in the last group. Table 5.1 displays the frequency distribution for respondents' ages grouped by decades.

When examining Table 5.1, one might infer that the prevalence of male homosexuality varies greatly by age in America's four largest cities. However, this is probably not the case. Based on data from the General Social Survey (GSS) and the National Health and Social Life Survey (NHSLS) reported by Laumann, Gagnon, Michael, and Michaels (1994), if the UMHS had been successful at sampling men who have had sex with another male since adolescence, as it had intended, then the distribution of respondents' ages by decade would have looked much different, being more evenly distributed across age categories. In other words, one would have expected many more respondents in their 60s, 70s, and 80s. In my opinion, the telephone "screener" (or script) used to select respondents for the UMHS was

TABLE 5.1   Frequency Distribution of Respondents' Ages Grouped by Decades

Respondents' ages	Frequency	Percent
50 to 59 years	242	65.0
60 to 69 years	91	24.5
70 years and above	39	10.5
Total	372	100.0

more successful at sampling men who think of themselves as gay, rather than men who have sex with other men.

Nearly all of the studies utilizing convenience samples of self-identified gay men report that gay men have higher educational attainment and enjoy higher annual incomes than comparable members of the general population do. Several researchers have argued that this nearly universal finding in the research literature may be an artifact of convenience sampling, but the following analysis tends to refute this view.

Table 5.2 compares the educational attainment of older men in the UMHS with that of white men 50 years of age and above residing in the urban and suburban areas of the 12 largest cities in the United States who completed the 1993, 1994, and 1996 General Social Surveys (see Davis & Smith, 1992; Davis, Smith, & Marsden, 1999). Here we see that, when controlling for age, race, and place of residence, higher percentages of the men in the UMHS have obtained advanced degrees compared to men from the general population.

Similarly, most research utilizing convenience samples of gay-identified men recruited from urban gay settings reports higher annual incomes compared to members of the general population. Table 5.3 compares 1996 gross household incomes reported by the older, white men residing with another adult male from the UMHS with roughly comparable data from the 1998 and 2000 GSS, specifically 1997 and 1999 total family income reported by married white men aged 50 to 89 years of age from the urban and suburban areas of the 12 largest cities in the United States.

Table 5.3 shows that the total household incomes of older, white men residing in households with another adult male from the UMHS

TABLE 5.2 Percentage of White Urban Men Aged 50 Years and Above From the UMHS and the GSS Reporting Various Educational Degrees

	GSS (1993, 1994, 1996)	UMHS (1996)
Less than high school	12.6	1.5
High school/some college	43.1	26.6
Bachelor's degree	30.5	40.6
Graduate degree	13.9	31.4

TABLE 5.3   Percentage of White Urban Men 50 Years of Age and Above From the UMHS and the GSS Reporting Various Incomes

	GSS: 1997, 1999 total family income	UMHS: 1996 gross household income
$9,999 or less	0.0	3.3
$10,000 to $19,999	3.3	5.4
$20,000 to $39,999	18.3	13.0
$40,000 to $59,999	15.0	16.3
$60,000 and above	63.3	62.0

are nearly equal to the total family incomes of married white men 50 years of age and older residing in the urban and suburban areas of the top 12 largest cities from the GSS. However, if one does not control for race, it does indeed appear that urban gay men make more money annually than men in the general urban population. Perhaps this is because the racial composition of gay communities, as well as of the men in the UMHS, more closely resembles the racial composition of the United States as a whole, rather than the racial composition of men living in our largest cities, where Caucasians may even be a minority (e.g., Chicago).

Ninety-two percent of the older men in the UMHS report that they are white, whereas 88.1% of the men aged 50 years and above from the entire 1996 GSS are white. However, if one restricts the 1996 GSS to older men residing in the urban areas of the 12 largest cities, only 67% are white. The higher percentages of white homosexual males in urban areas are partly due to the fact that large numbers of gay men have migrated to our largest cities, rather than remaining in their places of birth (Michaels, S., 1997; Pollack, L., 2000, personal communications).

The Center for Epidemiologic Studies Depression Scale

The UMHS included the Center for Epidemiologic Studies Depression Scale (CES-D; Radloff, 1977), which is a well-known scale that has been used to measure depressive symptomology in the general population. See Appendix for a list of items comprising the Center for Epidemiologic Studies Depression Scale (CES-D) used in the UMHS. In this study, the 20 items of the CES-D were first recoded to 0 for "less than 1 day," 1 for "1–2 days," 2 for "3–4 days," and 3 for "5–7 days." Appropriate items were reverse-coded and then summed, providing a possible range of scores of 0 to 60. Scores were not calculated for Rs who did not answer at least 16 of the items.

Clinicians often use a score of 16 or above on the CES-D to identify clients for additional in-depth, diagnostic interviews, and many researchers use this score to classify respondents as "depressed." While virtually all of the members of the general population who provide scores of 16 or above may be considered "distressed," or even subclinically depressed, recent research suggests that not all may be subsequently diagnosed as suffering from clinical depression or a severe depressive episode (Fava et al., 1982; Herman et al., 1994; Lyness et al., 1997; Turk & Okifuji, 1994). When used as a research tool to classify respondents with clinical depression, CES-D scores provide the greatest specificity and sensitivity in the range of 21 to 23. For the purposes of this study, respondents with a CES-D score of 16 or greater will be considered "distressed/depressed."

A total of 367 respondents completed the CES-D, and all of them answered a sufficient number of items to calculate an overall score. The distribution of CES-D scores is highly skewed, with a range of 0 to 50 and a median value of 7. Twenty-one percent of the respondents provided scores of 16 or above, indicating the presence of depressive symptoms or distress, and 12% provided scores of 22 or above on the CES-D, indicating a high likelihood of clinical depression. Because the majority of older gay men in the UMHS provide CES-D scores in the "normal" range, these findings should not be misconstrued as supporting a pathologizing view of homosexuality. However, it also appears that a larger minority of older gay males than previously assumed may be suffering from depression, perhaps as a result of enduring the trials and tribulations of being gay in a homophobic society (cf. Cochran & Mays, 2000; Gilman et al., 2001; Sandfort et al., 2001).

Disclosure of Sexual Orientation

Respondents were asked five Likert-scale items in the UMHS assessing the current extent to which they have disclosed their sexual orientation to friends, family members, coworkers, employers, and neighbors.

This series of items began with the statement "Men vary in the degree to which they report being 'out of the closet' or open about being gay or bisexual to others. I would like you to tell me how 'out' you are about your sexual orientation to the following groups of people, relative to other gay men." Each of the items was worded the same, except for the group referent, and provided five response categories: "About how many of your (friends) are you 'out' to about your sexual orientation at present? Would you say you are out to all of your (friends), almost all, about half, less than half, or none of them?" The distribution of scores for the five items is provided in Table 5.4.

Table 5.4 shows that 86.5% of the men 50 years of age and above in the UMHS are "out" to all or almost all of their friends, and just over half of the respondents are "out" to all of their family members. Conversely, Table 5.4 also shows that 18.8% are not "out" to any of their family members, and 26.6% are "out" to none of their employers. Conversely, 22.2% of the respondents in Weinberg and Williams's (1974) study of predominantly younger homosexual men reported that about half or more of their work associates knew or suspected that they were homosexual. On the other hand, Berger (1982, 1996) found that 42.5% of his respondents reported that about half or more of their work associates knew or suspected that they were homosexual (pp. 189–190). In comparison, 74.2% of the older respondents in the UMHS indicate that they are "out" to about half or more of their co-workers.

Berger (1982, 1996) compared his results of the degree to which respondents' homosexuality was known or suspected by others with

TABLE 5.4   Percentage of Respondents Reporting Varying Levels of Sexual Orientation Disclosure to Friends, Family Members, Co-workers, Employers, and Neighbors

	All	Almost all	About half	Less than half	None
Friends	65.1	21.4	7.0	5.4	1.1
Family members	51.8	13.6	5.5	10.2	18.8
Coworkers	53. 6	11.3	9.3	12.3	13.6
Employers	55.9	7.0	3.9	6.6	26.6
Neighbors	44.9	15.1	8.3	16.6	15.1

similar items from Weinberg and Williams's (1974) study. Berger concluded that older homosexuals are "less worried about exposure of their homosexuality" and "more likely to be known as homosexual" than younger men (p. 189). However, by the time Berger had conducted his study, seven years of cultural change had transpired since that of Weinberg and Williams. Thus, I strongly suspect that the differences in the three studies reported above are at least partly due to increases in perceived social tolerance and acceptance of homosexuality in American society since 1975.

For the present analysis, a scale of average level of sexual orientation disclosure was constructed by summing the values from each of the items and dividing by 5. Missing values were replaced by the mean value of the completed items, except that respondents had to answer at least three of the five items for a score to be computed. A total of 364 respondents answered a sufficient number of items for an average score to be computed. The Cronbach's Alpha for the values comprising the scale of average level of disclosure is .84.

Once again, the distribution of scores indicating average level of disclosure is highly skewed, such that 24.7% of the respondents produced an average score of 1, indicating that they are currently "out" about their sexual orientations to all of their friends, family members, coworkers, employers, and neighbors. The range of these scores is 1 to 5, and the median value is 1.80. Because of the non-normal nature of the resulting distribution, the median value of the average disclosure scores was used to classify respondents into two groups: those reporting high versus low levels of average disclosure. Average overall disclosure scores are moderately related to age in the UMHS, such that 58.6% of the respondents aged 50 to 59 years report higher levels of disclosure, compared to 40.4% of the respondents in their 60s, and only 27.8% of the respondents aged 70 years and above ($\chi^2 = 17.22$, $p \leq 0.0001$; see below). In other words, the percentage of men who have disclosed their sexual orientation to many friends, family members, employers, coworkers, and neighbors declines with age. Thus, the older men in the UMHS are not "more likely to be known as homosexual," as suggested by Berger (1982, 1996, p. 189).

Levels of Disclosure and Additional Variables

Other than respondent's age, reported above, one might presume that several additional variables would be related to average levels of disclosure. However, in the UMHS, neither race, education, nor income are significantly related to average levels of disclosure of sexual orientation. Thus, data from the UMHS do not support the argument that older gay men with higher incomes or higher levels of educational attainment are more likely to disclose their homosexuality, as some researchers have suggested.

Overall, 21.0% of the older men in the UMHS think of themselves as homosexual, rather than as gay, queer, or something else. However, age and sexual self-identity are strongly related, such that 16.5% of the men in their 50s think of themselves as homosexual, 19.8% of the men in their 60s self-identify as homosexual, and 51.3% of the men 70 years of age and older think of themselves as homosexual, rather than as gay ($\chi^2 = 24.58$, $p \leq 0.0001$).

One must remember that the meanings of modern gay and lesbian identities were first fashioned through discursive social interactions within private social spaces, such as Mattachine Society meetings and gatherings of the members of the Daughters of Bilitis during the late 1950s and the early 1960s. After the Stonewall incident in 1969, a nationally recognized gay and lesbian rights movement gained momentum, and the meanings associated with being gay or lesbian (as opposed to being "homosexual") became intertwined with the political and social objectives of the gay rights movement. Then, during the 1970s, new gay and lesbian identities became widely recognized features of the cultural landscape in the United States. The distinction between the identity constructs "homosexual" and "gay/lesbian," first reviewed by Herdt and Boxer (1993), may be a hallmark of this sociohistorical change in culture formation and individual development.

One might hypothesize that older men who think of themselves as being gay would be more open about their sexual orientation than those who think of themselves as homosexual, because one of the tenets of the gay rights movement has been to proudly disclose one's sexual orientation or identity. However, sexual self-identity (homosexual versus gay) is completely unrelated to average levels of disclosure in this sample, even when controlling for age. Thus, although disclosure levels decline with age, the older men in the UMHS who think of themselves as gay report similar levels of disclosure to friends, family, work associates, and neighbors as men who self-identify as homosexual.

Another way of thinking about this is that, generally speaking, the oldest respondents in the UMHS show lower levels of disclosure than respondents in their 50s or 60s, regardless of their sexual self-identities. Respondents over 70 years of age entered adulthood before the end of World War II, and it should not seem surprising that larger numbers of them would adopt an enduring strategy of more selectively disclosing their sexual orientations, compared to younger respondents. Perhaps, one should also not be too surprised to learn that roughly half of the men aged 70 years and above have chosen to think of themselves as gay, given that the label *homosexual* has often been thought of as connoting pathology. But, are men who think of themselves as homosexual more likely to experience poorer mental well-being, compared to those who think of themselves as gay? The answer is a resounding "no." In this sample, sexual self-identity has no bearing on CES-D scores. Thus, older men who think of themselves as homosexual are no more likely to suffer from depression than men who think of themselves as gay.

Respondents in the UMHS were asked, "At what age did you first tell someone that you were gay or bisexual?" Seventeen men (4.6%) in the UMHS had never told someone else that they were gay or bisexual, and their responses were treated as missing values. Excluding other missing values (i.e., "don't know/remember"), this item produced a range of ages from 9 to 61 years ($n = 335$). Half of the men in the UMHS did not tell someone else that they were gay/bisexual until after the age of 21 years, and approximately 25% of the sample did not disclose their sexual orientation until after the age of 26 years. One might presume that homosexuals who first told someone else about their sexual orientation at an earlier age might have had more time to disclose their sexual orientation or to adjust to their sexual self-identity than men who did not "come out" until relatively late in life.

The age at which respondents first told someone else that they were gay/bisexual is weakly related to average overall disclosure scores ($\chi^2 = 6.07$, $p \leq 0.05$), such that 58.9% of the respondents who first told someone else that they were gay/bisexual at the age of 21 or younger reported higher average levels of disclosure, compared to 45.4% of those who first told someone else after the age of 21. However, age of first disclosure is unrelated to CES-D scores, indicating that older gay men who "came out" relatively late in life have comparable levels of depressive symptomology with those who "came out" at earlier ages. Thus, it appears that older men who first disclosed their sexual orientation relatively "late" in life have similar levels of mental well-being as those who first "came out" at earlier ages. Given that 75% of the older respondents in the UMHS first began the process of "coming out" prior to the age of 26 years, it would appear that they have had sufficient time to adapt, psychologically, to being known as gay or homosexual.

Age, Disclosure, and Depression

Many prior studies concerned with the psychological adaptation of homosexual males in the United States find that lower levels of disclosure are associated with higher rates of depression (see, especially, Weinberg & Williams, 1974; Berger, 1982, 1996), and we know that in the UMHS, older men report lower levels of disclosure (see above). So, are older gay and homosexual men with lower levels of disclosure at risk for elevated levels of depression? While not statistically significant, the percentage of men in the UMHS with scores in the distressed/depressed range of the CES-D actually declines with age. Furthermore, the relationship between levels of disclosure and CES-D scores in the UMHS is specified by age. That is, the relationship between levels of disclosure and depression is only significant for men between the ages of 50 and 59 years, such that 31.6% of the men in their 50s with low levels of disclosure scored in the distressed/depressed range on the CES-D, compared to 16.5% of the men with high levels of disclosure ($\chi^2 = 7.44$, $p \leq 0.01$). However, homosexual men 60 years of age and older with lower levels of disclosure are no more likely to experience distress/depression than men reporting higher levels of disclosure.

Mental Well-Being and Additional Variables

Strong relationships between well-being and income, education, and race are common and enduring findings in the gerontological literature. Among the older men in the UMHS, there is a moderate, linear relationship between income and depression ($\chi^2 = 11.50$, $p \leq 0.05$). Figure 5.1 shows that 38.2% of those with 1996 gross household incomes under $10,000 provide CES-D scores that are within the distressed/depressed range, compared to only 13.6% of those with household incomes greater than $60,000 ($\chi^2 = 11.50$, $p \leq 0.05$). However, both education and race are unrelated to CES-D scores in this sample.

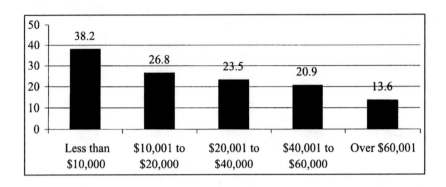

FIGURE 5.1   Percent distressed/depressed by gross household income.

The UMHS contains several additional variables that could be presumed to have a bearing on mental well-being, such as employment and partnership status, HIV status, and recent sexual problems. Regarding employment status, 17.8% of the older men in the UMHS who are working full or part-time have CES-D scores in the "distressed/depressed" range, and 18.8% of those who are retired provided scores in the "distressed/depressed" range. However, 47.1% of the respondents who are not working or retired have CES-D scores in the "distressed/depressed" range. These primarily include respondents who are disabled, laid off from a job, or looking for work. Thus, employment status and depression is strongly related ($\chi^2 = 15.79$, $p \leq 0.0001$).

Unfortunately, the UMHS could have included better items assessing partnership status, but two items may serve as proxies. Seventy-five percent of the older men in UMHS reported that they had at least one sex partner in the 12 months preceding their interview. Of these, 41.6% said that they were currently in love with or felt a special commitment to someone, and this proportion did not significantly differ by age. Of the 274 men who had a sex partner in the previous year, 15.2% of those who also said they were in love or felt a special commitment to someone had CES-D scores in the "distress/depressed" range, compared to 29.6% of those who were not in love ($\chi^2 = 8.13$, $p \leq 0.01$). Thus, being in love or feeling a special commitment to someone is significantly related to CES-D scores.

Among the older men in the UMHS, 14.3% either reported or believed that they were HIV positive, which almost perfectly corresponds with the results of home HIV test kits respondents returned to the principal investigators. Not surprisingly, HIV status is related to depression, albeit weakly, such that 32.7% of the respondents who reported or believed they were HIV positive had CES-D scores in the "distressed/depressed" range, compared to 18.6% of the HIV-negative respondents ($\chi^2 = 5.36$, $p \geq 0.05$).

Regrettably, the UMHS also did not include measures of general physical health, as poor health is commonly thought to increase the likelihood of depression. Furthermore, the UMHS did not include a measure of sexual satisfaction, which is also known to influence mental well-being among gay males (Bell & Weinberg, 1978; Berger, 1982, 1996; Weinberg & Williams, 1974). However, the UMHS did include an item concerning sexual problems in the past year, which reads as follows:

> These next questions ask about any sexual problems or difficulties that you might have. Many people have had some type of sexual difficulty at some point in their life, for example, sometimes men have difficulty getting an erection or sometimes women have difficulty having an orgasm. In the past 12 months, has there been something either physical or emotional that has made it difficult for you to have a satisfying sexual relationship?

In response to this item, 38.5% of the older men in the UMHS said that they had experienced sexual difficulties in the past year, and 64.5% of these men indicated that the problem affecting their sexual satisfaction was caused by a medical health problem or medications, whereas 38.6% of these men cited psychological difficulties affecting themselves or their partner. Incidentally, these percentages did not significantly differ by age. However, not surprisingly, the presence of some sexual difficulty in the past year is significantly related to CES-D scores, such that 28.6% of the men who had difficulty having a satisfying sexual relationship provided CES-D scores indicating "distress/depression," compared to 16.1% of those without recent sexual difficulties ($\chi^2 = 8.15$, $p \leq 0.01$).

DISCUSSION

During the height of the Cold War and the antihomosexual "witch-hunts" of the McCarthy era, most Americans believed that homosexuality was a mental illness, a crime, and a threat to mainstream American society. During the early to mid-1960s, police raids on homosexual bars intensified in America's largest cities, including Chicago, San Francisco, and New York. It was not until after the great social movements for women's liberation and civil rights of the tumultuous 1960s that the gay rights movement and publicly visible gay communities emerged as urban phenomena in the United States. Then, during the early 1970s, gay men and lesbians began to successfully argue that, rather than being mentally ill, they were simply members of yet another minority group that had been oppressed by a "sick" society. In 1957, Evelyn Hooker's pioneering work planted a seed, and a growing body of academic research began providing evidence that homosexuals were as psychologically well adjusted as their heterosexual counterparts. Finally, most academics and clinicians concluded that homosexuality was not a mental illness nor a cause of psychopathology, and in 1973, members of the American Psychiatric Association voted to remove homosexuality from their list of disorders in the *Diagnostic and Statistical Manual* (Bayer, 1987).

Today, the vast majority of academics, clinicians, and social reformers no longer believe that homosexuality is proof of underlying pathology. Rather, they contend that psychological, interpersonal, or behavioral problems experienced by some gay men and lesbians are probably the result of environmental risk factors or negative cultural attitudes toward homosexuality, such as social intolerance directed toward gays and lesbians. Thus, when gay men or lesbians seek counseling today, treatment modalities often involve attempts to heal psychological scars resulting from stigma and social oppression, or attempts at improving patients' skills in coping with heterosexism, homophobic discrimination, or sexual prejudice (cf. Herek & Berril, 1990; Herek et al., 1998).

While a great deal of research has demonstrated that most older gay men are happy and well adjusted, it must be remembered that many of these studies were conducted with the aim of dispelling negative views about older homosexuals. Furthermore, these studies relied almost exclusively upon convenience samples of self-identified gay men recruited directly from gay and lesbian cultural contexts. Therefore, the rather rosy picture many of these studies paint concerning the positive mental health of older gay men may be somewhat misleading. Clearly, substantial proportions of older gay and homosexual men are suffering from depression, and additional research is warranted to identify the best ways to help these men. While the methodology employed in the UMHS represents a substantial improvement over prior studies, our understanding of the lives and mental well-being of older homosexuals is still deficient.

Prior stage models of the coming-out process, as well as subsequent research on the psychological adaptation of gay males, suggests that homosexuals of all ages who are more "closeted," or less "out," will experience lower levels of mental well-being than those who are more open about their sexual orientations. However, despite the high face validity of this assertion, this study finds that this only holds true for homosexual men under the age of 60 years. Conversely, homosexual men 60 years of age and older with lower levels of disclosure are not more likely to experience distress/depression, compared to those reporting higher levels of disclosure. Furthermore, the oldest men in this study were far more likely to think of themselves as homosexual, rather than as gay, yet sexual self-identity was completely unrelated to levels of disclosure or CES-D scores. This suggests that, perhaps, clinicians should think twice before counseling older homosexual men to adopt and widely disclose a gay self-identity, when a more holistic treatment modality that considers other factors may be more appropriate. While this study is far from comprehensive, it does suggest the importance of such factors as employment and partnership status, general health, and sexual satisfaction for the mental well-being of older homosexual men.

In this study, the men over 60 years of age were born prior to 1937, and many will remember the Great Depression. Those currently over 70 years of age may have served in the military during World War II. These men came of age during a time in American history when homosexuality was heavily stigmatized, and concealment of their sexual orientation was the only viable adaptive strategy available to them. Perhaps homosexual men over 60 years of age have grown accustomed to their levels of disclosure, or they may have avoided many stressful life events associated with "coming out," as Lee (1987a) suggests. However, in-depth interviews with older gay men suggest that, during the 1930s, 1940s, and 1950s, sexuality was not a polite topic of discussion, and many kept their sexual feelings to themselves. On the other hand, the youngest respondents in this sample of the UMHS were born in 1947 and reached 20 years of age in 1967, a time of great social change in America when traditional gender roles and sexual norms were in flux. During the 1960s, America experienced the "sexual revolution," and young people admonished one another to "be true to yourself," as well as to others. Given the changes in American sexual culture during the 1960s and the advent of "gay pride" after 1970, it seems understandable that men currently in their 50s with lower levels of disclosure might experience more cognitive dissonance, interpersonal incongruency, and poorer levels of mental well-being, as many stage theorists have suggested. Thus, even though the oldest respondents in the UMHS are less likely to have widely disclosed their sexual orientation to others, being more "closeted" is not associated with higher rates of depressive symptomology. Perhaps, given the cultural climate when these men reached adolescence and early adulthood, when concealment of homosexuality was the norm, it should not seem too surprising that lower levels of disclosure are unrelated to psychological distress or depression for gay and homosexual men over the age of 60.

APPENDIX 1: ITEMS COMPRISING THE CENTER FOR EPIDEMIOLOGIC STUDIES DEPRESSION SCALE (CES-D)

The CES-D is a self-report scale designed to measure depressive symptomology in the general population. The items were recoded to 0 for "less than 1 day," 1 for "1–2 days," 2 for "3–4 days," and 3 for "5–7 days" (except for items B, K, and O, which were reverse-coded) and then summed. At least 16 of the 20 items had to have nonmissing responses for a scale score to be calculated.

Now we'd like to know how you've been feeling over the last week. Thinking about the past 7 days, how often . . .

A. Was your sleep restless? Would you say . . .
B. Were you happy? Would you say . . .
C. Did you talk less than usual? Would you say . . .
D. Were you bothered by things that usually don't bother you?
E. Was your appetite poor?
F. Did you feel that you could not shake off the blues even with help from your family or friends?
G. Did you feel that you were not as good as other people?
H. Did you have trouble keeping your mind on what you were doing?

I.   Did you feel depressed?
J.   Did you feel that everything you did was an effort?
K.   Did you feel hopeful about the future?
L.   Did you feel fearful?
M.   Did you feel lonely?
N.   Did you feel that people were unfriendly?
O.   Did you enjoy your life?
P.   Did you have crying spells?
Q.   Did you feel sad?
R.   Did you feel that people disliked you?
S.   Did you feel you could not "get going"?
T.   Did you think your life had been a failure?

REFERENCES

Adelman, M. (1991). Stigma, gay lifestyles, and adjustment to aging: A study of later-life gay men and lesbians. *Journal of Homosexuality, 20*(3/4), 7–32.

Almvig, C. (1982). *The invisible minority: Aging and lesbianism.* New York: Utica College of Syracuse University.

Bayer, R. (1987). *Homosexuality and American psychiatry: The politics of diagnosis.* Princeton, NJ: Princeton University Press.

Beeler, J., et al. (1999). Needs of older lesbians and gay men in Chicago. *Journal of Gay and Lesbian Social Services, 9*(1), 31–49.

Bell, A. P., & Weinberg, M. S. (1978). *Homosexualities: A study of diversity among men and women.* New York: Simon and Schuster.

Bennett, K. C., & Thompson, N. L. (1991). Accelerated aging and male homosexuality: Australian evidence in a continuing debate. In J. A. Lee (Ed.), *Gay midlife and maturity* (pp. 65–75). New York: Haworth Press.

Berger, R. M. (1980). Psychological adaptation of the older homosexual male. *Journal of Homosexuality, 5,* 161–175.

Berger, R. M. (1982). The unseen minority: Older gays and lesbians. *Social Work, 27,* 236–242.

Berger, R. M. (1984). Realities of gay and lesbian aging. *Social Work, 29,* 57–62.

Berger, R. M. (1992). Research on older gay men: What we know, what we need to know. In N. J. Woodman (Ed.), *Lesbian and gay lifestyles: A guide for counseling and education* (pp. 217–234). New York: Irvington.

Berger, R. M. (1982, 1996). *Gay and gray: The older homosexual man* (2nd ed.). New York: Harrington Park Press.

Berger, R. M., & Kelly, J. J. (1986). Working with homosexuals of the older population. *Social Casework: The Journal of Contemporary Social Work, 67,* 203–210.

Berger, R. M., & Kelly, J. J. (1996). Gay men and lesbians growing older. In R. Cabaj & T. S. Stein (Eds.), *Textbook of homosexuality and mental health* (pp. 305–318). Washington, DC: American Psychiatric Press.

Brady, S., & Busse, W. J. (1994). The gay identity questionnaire: A brief measure of homosexual identity formation. *Journal of Homosexuality, 26*(4), 1–22.

Cannell, C., Oksenberg, L., Kalton, G., Bischoping, K., & Fowler, F. (1989). *New techniques for pretesting survey questions.* Survey Research Center, University of Michigan Ann Arbor.

Cass, V. C. (1979). Homosexual identity formation: A theoretical model. *Journal of Homosexuality, 4*(3), 219–235.

Catania, J. A., Osmond, D., Stall, R. D., Pollack, L., Paul, J. P., Blower, S., Binson, D., Canchola, J. A., Mills, T. C., Fisher, L., Choi, K. H., Porco, T., Turner, C., Blair, J., Henne, J., Bye, L. L., & Coates, T. J. (2001). The continuing HIV epidemic among men who have sex with men. *American Journal of Public Health, 91,* 907–914.

Cochran, S. D., & Mays, V. M. (2000). Lifetime prevalence of suicide symptoms and affective disorders among men reporting same-sex sexual partners: Results from NHANES III. *American Journal of Public Health, 90*(4), 573–578.

Coleman, E. (1982). Developmental stages of the coming out process. *Journal of Homosexuality, 7,* 31–43.

Dank, B. (1971). Coming out in the gay world. *Psychiatry, 34,* 180–197.

Davis, M., & Kennedy, E. L. (1990). Oral history and the study of sexuality in the lesbian community. In M. Duberman, M. Vicinus, & G. Chauncy, Jr. (Eds.), *Hidden from history: Reclaiming the gay and lesbian past* (pp. 426–440). New York: Meridian.

Davis, J. A., & Smith, T. W. (1992). The NORC General Social Survey: A user's guide. Newbury Park, CA: Sage.

Davis, J. A., Smith, T. W., & Marsden, P. V. (1999). *General Social Surveys, 1972–1998: Cumulative codebook.* Chicago: NORC.

Deevey, S. (1990). Older lesbian women: An invisible minority. *Journal of Gerontological Nursing, 16*(5), 35–37, 39.

DeMonteflores, C., & Schultz, S. J. (1978). Coming out: Similarities and differences for lesbians and gay men. *Journal of Social Issues, 34*(3), 59–72.

Ehrenberg, M. (1996). Aging and mental health: Issues in the gay and lesbian community. In C. J. Alexander (Ed.), *Gay and lesbian mental health: A sourcebook for practitioners* (pp. 189–209). New York: Harrington Park Press/Haworth Press.

Farrell, R. A., & Morrione, T. J. (1974). Social interaction and stereotypic responses to homosexuals. *Archives of Sexual Behavior, 3,* 425–442.

Fava, G. A., Pilowsky, I., Pierfederici, A., Bernardi, M., & Pathak, D. (1982). Depression and illness behavior in a general hospital: A prevalence study. *Psychotherapy and Psychosomatics, 38,* 141–153.

Francher, S. J., & Henkin, J. (1973). The menopausal queen. *American Journal of Orthopsychiatry, 43,* 670–674.

Friend, R. A. (1980). GAYging: Adjustment and the older gay male. *Alternative Lifestyles, 3,* 213–248.

Friend, R. A. (1987). The individual and the social psychology of aging: Clinical implications for lesbians and gay men. *Journal of Homosexuality, 14*(1/2), 307–331.

Friend, R. A. (1989). Older lesbian and gay people: Responding to homophobia. *Marriage and Family Review, 14,* 241–263.

Gilman, S. E., Cochran, S. D., Mays, V. M., Hughes, M., Ostrow, D., & Kessler, R. C. (2001). Risk of psychiatric disorders among individuals reporting same-sex sexual partners in the National Comorbidity Survey. *American Journal of Public Health, 91*(6), 933–939.

Gray, H., & Dressel, P. (1985). Alternative interpretations of aging among gay males. *The Gerontologist, 25*(1), 83–87.

Hammersmith, S. K., & Weinberg, M. S. (1973). Homosexual identity: Commitment, adjustment, and significant others. *Sociometry, 36,* 56–79.

Hencken, J. D., & O'Dowd, W. T. (1977). Coming out as an aspect of identity formation. *Gay Academic Union Journal: Gai Saber, 1*(1), 18–26.

Herdt, G., Beeler, J., & Rawls, T. W. (1997). Life course diversity among older lesbians and gay men: A study in Chicago. *Journal of Gay, Lesbian, and Bisexual Identity, 2*(3/4), 231–246.

Herdt, G., & Boxer, A. (1993). *Children of Horizons: How gay and lesbian teens are leading a new way out of the closet.* Boston: Beacon Press.

Herdt, G., & Boxer, A. M. (1996). *Children of Horizons: How gay and lesbian youth are leading a new way out of the closet* (rev., 2nd ed.). Boston: Beacon Press.

Herek, G. M., & Berril, K. (1990). Anti-gay violence and mental health: Setting an agenda for research. *Journal of Interpersonal Violence, 5*(3), 414–423.

Herek, G. M., Cogan, J. C., Gillis, J. R., & Glunt, E. K. (1998). Correlates of internalized homophobia in a community sample of lesbians and gay men. *Journal of the Gay and Lesbian Medical Association, 2,* 17–25.

Herman, D. B., Susser, E. S., & Struening, E. L. (1994). Childhood out-of-home care and current depressive symptoms among homeless adults. *American Journal of Public Health, 84,* 1849–1851.

Jacobs, J. A., & Tedford, W. H. (1980). Factors affecting self-esteem of the homosexual individual. *Journal of Homosexuality, 5,* 373–382.

Kehoe, M. (1986a). A portrait of the older lesbian. *Journal of Homosexuality, 12,* 157–161.

Kehoe, M. (1986b). Lesbians over 65: A triple invisible minority. *Journal of Homosexuality, 12,* 139–152.

Kehoe, M. (1989). *Lesbians over 60 speak for themselves.* New York: Haworth Press.

Kelly, J. J. (1977). The aging male homosexual: Myth and reality. *The Gerontologist, 17,* 328–332.

Kelly, J. (1980). Homosexuality and aging. In J. Marmor (Ed.), *Homosexual behavior: A modern reappraisal* (pp. 176–193). New York: Basic Books.

Kimmel, D. C. (1978). Adult development and aging: A gay perspective. *Journal of Social Issues, 34,* 113–130.

Kimmel, D. C. (1979). Life history interviews of aging gay men. *International Journal of Aging and Human Development, 10,* 239–248.

Kimmel, D. C. (1992). The families of older gays and lesbians. *Generations, 17*, 37–38.

Laner, M. R. (1978). Growing older male: Heterosexual and homosexual. *The Gerontologist, 18*, 496–501.

Laner, M. R. (1979). Growing older female: Heterosexual and homosexual. *Journal of Homosexuality, 4*, 267–275.

Laumann, E. O., Gagnon, J. H., Michael, R. T., & Michaels, S. (1994). *The social organization of sexuality: Sexual practices in the United States*. Chicago: University of Chicago Press.

Lee, J. A. (1977). Going public: A study in the sociology of homosexual liberation. *Journal of Homosexuality, 3*, 49–78.

Lee, J. A. (1987a). What can homosexual aging studies contribute to theories of aging? *Journal of Homosexuality, 13*(4), 43–71.

Lee, J. A. (1987b). The invisible lives of Canada's gray gays. In V. W. Marshall (Ed.), *Aging in Canada: Social perspectives* (pp. 138–155). Markham, Ont.: Fitzhenry & Whiteside.

Lee, J. A. (1991). Foreword. In J. A. Lee (Ed.), *Gay midlife and maturity*. New York: Haworth Press.

Levy, N. J. (1979). The middle aged male homosexual. *Journal of the American Academy of Psychoanalysis, 7*, 405–418.

Lipman, A. (1986). Homosexual relationships. *Generations, 10*, 51–54.

Lyness, J. M., Noel, T. K., Cox, C., King, D. A., Conwell, Y., & Caine, E. D. (1997). Screening for depression in elderly primary care patients: A comparison of the Center for Epidemiologic Studies Depression Scale and the Geriatric Depression Scale. *Archives of Internal Medicine, 157*, 449–454.

McDonald, G. J. (1982). Individual differences in the coming out process for gay men: Implications for theoretical models. *Journal of Homosexuality, 8*(1), 47–60.

Minigerode, F. A. (1976). Age-status labeling in homosexual men. *Journal of Homosexuality, 1*(3), 273–275.

Minigerode, F. A., & Adelman, M. R. (1978). Elderly homosexual women and men: Report on a pilot study. *Family Coordinator, 27*, 451–456.

Plummer, K. (1975). *Sexual stigma: An interactionist account*. London: Routledge & Kegan Paul.

Quam, J. K., & Whitford, G. S. (1992). Adaptation and age-related expectations of older gay and lesbian adults. *The Gerontologist, 32*(3), 367–374.

Radloff, L. S. (1977). The CES-D Scale: A self-report depression scale for research in the general population. *Applied Psychological Measurement, 1*, 385–401.

Raphael, S., & Robinson, M. (1984). The older lesbian: Love relationships and friendship patterns. In T. Darty & S. Potter (Eds.), *Women-identified women* (pp. 67–82). Palo Alto, CA: Mayfield.

Ryan, C., & Bradford, J. (1993). The National Lesbian Health Care Survey: An overview. In L. D. Garnets & D. C. Kimmel (Eds.), *Psychological perspectives on lesbian and gay male experiences. Between men—between women: Lesbian and gay studies* (pp. 541–556). New York: Columbia University Press.

Sandfort, T. G. M., de Graaf, R., Bijl, R. V., & Schnabel, P. (2001). Same-sex sexual behavior and psychiatric disorders: Findings from the Netherlands mental health survey and incidence study (NEMESIS). *Archives of General Psychiatry, 58*(1), 85–91.

Schmitt, K. P., & Kurdek, L. H. (1987). Personality correlates of positive identity and relationship involvement in gay men. *Journal of Homosexuality, 13*(4), 101–109.

Troiden, R. R. (1979). Becoming homosexual: A model of gay identity acquisition. *Psychiatry, 42*(4), 362–373.

Turk, D. C., & Okifuji, A. (1994). Detecting depression in chronic pain patients: Adequacy of self-reports. *Behavior Research and Therapy, 32*, 9–16.

Vacha, K. (1985). *Quiet fire: Memoirs of older gay men.* Trumansburg, NY: Crossing Press.

Wahler, J., & Gabbay, S. G. (1997). Gay male aging: A review of the literature. *Journal of Gay and Lesbian Social Services, 6*(3), 1–20.

Weeks, J. (1983). The problem of older homosexuals. In J. Hart & D. Richardson (Eds.), *The theory and practice of homosexuals* (pp. 177–185). London: Routledge & Kegan Paul.

Weinberg, M. S. (1970). The male homosexual: Age-related variations in social and psychological characteristics. *Social Problems, 17*, 527–537.

Weinberg, M. S., & Williams, C. J. (1974). *Male homosexuals: Their problems and adaptations.* New York: Oxford University Press.

CHAPTER 6

Old, Gay, and Alone? The Ecology of Well-Being Among Middle-Aged and Older Single Gay Men

Andrew J. Hostetler

In the popular imagination, to be an older gay or lesbian person has long been synonymous with being alone. Although a growing body of research and the increasing visibility of older gay role models have helped to dispel such harmful misperceptions about LGBT elders, the specter of the lonely, aging homosexual still looms large in minds of many younger gays and lesbians contemplating their futures. Such fears can be partially attributed to internalized homophobia and ageism, but no stereotype is without a basis in truth. Although the language of statistical averages can be a powerful weapon against stereotypes, it too often precludes a critical consideration of the unique strengths and vulnerabilities of particular groups, including older gays and lesbians.

At least one statistic makes it difficult to ignore the specific vulnerabilities of older gay individuals: According to the best available estimates, somewhere in the vicinity of 40% to 60% of all gay men describe themselves as single (i.e., without a same-sex partner) at any given time (Hostetler, 2001; Herdt, Beeler, & Rawls, 1997; Kurdek, 1995;

Bell & Weinberg, 1978; Harry, 1984), a figure significantly higher than for heterosexual and lesbian counterparts.[1] Although singlehood should be assumed to be neither involuntary nor necessarily lonely (Hostetler, 2001; Lee, 1987; Stein, 1976, 1978, 1981), single (i.e., never married, widowed, or divorced) older adults as a group are at increased risk for a variety of mental and physical health problems. And while many single gay and lesbian adults create alternate support networks or "families of choice" (Weston, 1991), the meaning and organization of American friendship, which is based on voluntary participation, mutually shared interests, and limited obligations, make these bonds difficult to sustain across time and space (Bellah et al., 1985; de Tocqueville, 1988/1969). Taken together, this state of affairs suggests that a substantial proportion of gay men (as well as lesbians) is facing or will face the prospect of being "old and alone."[2]

The problem with both stereotypes and "risk groups," of course, is how little they actually reveal about individual behaviors, adaptations, and outcomes—a fact long recognized by AIDS researchers and the many other contributors to the growing body of knowledge about the richly varied lives of LGBT individuals. However, I believe that a sociocultural psychology of gay and lesbian lives demands attention to both the structural resources and constraints (including but not limited to prejudice and discrimination) as well as the agentic contributions of individuals that together shape "differential developmental pathways" (Savin-Williams, 1998). To that end, this paper offers an ecologically grounded analysis (Bronfenbrenner, 1979) of the well-being of middle-aged and older single gay men. Drawing from my own research, I critically examine some of the roadblocks single gay men encounter, and the resources at their disposal, on the pathway to well-being and "successful" aging.

SEARCHING FOR SINGLE LIFE IN GAY AGING RESEARCH

In the almost 30 years since the declassification of homosexuality as a mental illness, research on gay and lesbian development has flour-

---

[1]Although most studies have found that more lesbians than gay men are in relationships at any given time, some evidence suggests that lesbians have higher "breakup" rates and that gay male partnerships tend to be of longer duration. This could mean that the difference in singlehood rates flattens out over time, such that a roughly equal proportion of gay men and lesbians are single in later life.

[2]It remains unclear how the increasing cultural integration of gays and lesbians will affect partnership and child-rearing trends.

ished. However, academic interest in gay and lesbian aging appears to have peaked in the late 1970s and early 1980s and fallen off thereafter (in contrast to the relatively steady stream of research on adolescence, young adulthood, and "coming out"). This is particularly baffling given that the large and influential baby boom cohort is now well into midlife. Moreover, gay aging research only inconsistently acknowledges vulnerability and the interplay of risk and resilience in the adaptation of LGBT individuals. More attention is typically paid to gay/straight similarities or even to the special strengths of the older gay person. Indeed, a defensive tone and a selective focus characterize much of the research on LGBT lives.[3] In the words of Christopher Carrington (1999, pp. 175–176):

> Many lesbian and gay authors feel the need to present ourselves, and our communities, to the dominant culture in ideal terms, a feeling that I have often shared. These portrayals, as opposed to empirical realities, often reflect the efforts of lesbigay people to provide a respectable image of ourselves in a society often bent on devaluing and marginalizing us. . . .

One manifestation of this defensiveness, I believe, is the general invisibility of gay singles in the research literature (Hostetler, 2001; Hostetler & Cohler, 1997). Although same-sex partnership is the subject of a growing body of social-scientific inquiry, the experience of being gay or lesbian and single—across the life course or at any particular point—has been almost entirely neglected. This is an unfortunate and somewhat puzzling oversight, given that somewhere in the vicinity of 50% of gay men are single and therefore at increased risk for a variety of physical and psychological problems in later life. But despite the fact that gay singles have been pushed into the background and, in some cases, scapegoated for certain social and developmental problems facing the LGBT community, the literature also strongly implies that gays and lesbians might be ideally suited for single life. Unfortunately, the posited sources of gay strength and resilience are not necessarily any more reflective of "empirical realities."

---

[3]Research on gay adolescents is a notable exception. The vulnerability of gay adolescents is more often addressed, I believe, because they are more easily portrayed as relatively defenseless victims, bombarded by negative messages, isolated from potential allies, and generally unable to mobilize the necessary resources to combat homophobia and heterosexism. It is somewhat more difficult to attribute the adjustment problems of "out" and agentic gay adults solely to external forces. On a similar note, it is considerably less difficult to acknowledge pain and difficulty from a position of "survivorship," as in the case of gay adults who study adolescence. In contrast, most gay researchers have not yet successfully "survived" their adulthood.

None of this is to suggest that the growing body of important research on gay aging has been unobjective. Indeed, the earliest non-clinical studies of gay aging were a necessary response to a long and inauspicious history of biased research that, according to Lee (1987, p. 52), "focused on the special burdens of being homosexual . . . [including] a lonely and miserable old age lacking in marriage and family pleasures." Berger's (1984, p. 57) review of the early literature reveals a similar portrait of the stereotypical older gay man, who, in addition to being lonely, depressed, and without social support, is also believed to be an effeminate pedophile. Even into the early and mid-1970s, researchers continued to characterize the lives of middle-aged and older gay men in terms of isolation and depression (Laner, 1978).

Given the pervasiveness of this stereotype, the lonely old homosexual has long been the straw man of gay aging research, and the first gay-positive studies go to great lengths to promote more positive images. As Lee (1987, p. 52) has noted, "gay liberation produced a tendency to contradict earlier research, sometimes by shock tactics that took a totally opposing view." Many of these studies simply refute antigay stereotypes by providing counter examples, often ignoring cases that conform to conventional assumptions. For example, Berger (1984) emphasizes the modal characteristics of his sample of 18 homosexual men and women, the majority of whom were in committed relationships, had regular contact with their families, had both homosexual and heterosexual friends (usually in nonoverlapping groups), and were engaged in civic and/or religious activities. However, he chooses *not* to draw attention to the fact that half of the gay men he interviewed were single or that a full third of the sample did not participate in any religious, social, or civic organizations.

Kehoe (1986, p. 139) more explicitly evinces a desire to combat the invisibility of older lesbians, who are commonly assumed to have either succumbed to "alcoholism, suicide or social diseases" or to have been "cured" by the time they reach seniority, and yet the portrait that emerges from her study is not always flattering. She accents the diversity of older lesbians throughout her report, but then concludes that the average or "composite" lesbian in her sample is single, lives alone involuntarily, and has very little contact with other lesbians (among other more positive characteristics). Similarly, Kimmel (1979, p. 239) acknowledges that the happiest of his research participants had long-term partners, and yet gives only passing reference to the fact that 10 out of 14 men lived alone. In general, while researchers might acknowledge that single older gays and lesbians are at increased risk for social isolation, depression, and other problems, they typically deny that singlehood is itself a common phenomenon within LGBT communities.

As part of the same selective and somewhat defensive approach, single gays and lesbians—and particularly single gay men—are sometimes blamed for the social ills believed to afflict the community, such as "accelerated aging." According to the accelerated aging hypothesis (Simon & Gagnon, 1967; Gagnon & Simon, 1973; Minnegerode, 1976; Laner, 1978; Friend, 1980), gay men are subject to dramatically constricted age norms that make them "old before their time." The evidence in support of this theory is somewhat mixed (see Simon & Gagnon, 1967; Gagnon & Simon, 1973; Weinberg & Williams, 1974; Friend, 1980; Kelly, 1977; Minnigerode, 1976). For example, while Friend (1980) and Kelly (1977) both report that gay subjects describe themselves as "old" at significantly younger ages than heterosexual men, Minnigerode (1976) found no such differences. In an effort to explain away findings in support of accelerated aging and to resolve the controversy, Friend (1987, p. 322) attributes gay/straight differences to the overrepresentation of single gay men in previous research, since "single people in general are more likely to place a greater value on youthfulness and physical characteristics."

Other researchers resist the tendency to deny the prevalence of gay singlehood or cast it in uniformly negative terms, but their efforts to promote more positive images of single gays and lesbians come up short and leave many questions unanswered. In her review of Adelman's (1987) *Long Time Passing*, Cruikshank (1991, p. 84) alludes to differences between "couple-oriented" and "more autonomous" lesbians, but she does not clarify this distinction and leaves the impression that these two lifestyles are equivalent in terms of their impact on well-being and adjustment. Lee (1987), a sociologist, offers one of the most sophisticated treatments of gay singlehood to date. He is one of the few researchers to directly acknowledge the prevalence of singlehood among older gay men, who, he notes, are somewhat more likely to be living without a partner than with one. He also raises the possibility of voluntarily chosen singlehood, and reminds us that "loneliness is not the same thing as aloneness" (pp. 59–60). He further speculates that "the ability of some single older homosexual men to maintain their satisfaction with life without activity in a family or even 'support group' may hold important lessons for aging in general"

(p. 45). Unfortunately, he does not further explore this provocative idea, nor does he clarify the role of choice in singlehood. Given existing research, he ultimately concedes that partnered older gay men tend to be happier than their single counterparts.

Although singlehood is rarely referred to in positive terms, several researchers have identified special strengths and forms of resilience that gays and lesbians may develop, some of which are particularly relevant for single life. Kimmel (1977, 1979) suggests that gay men may be more self-sufficient and therefore better able to live alone and/ or adjust to the loss of a partner as compared to their straight male counterparts, who have likely depended on their wives for care throughout most of their adulthood. On a similar note, gay men and lesbians are presumably less constrained by traditional gender roles, and may therefore be able to draw from a broader and more flexible behavioral repertoire (Kimmel, 1979; Dawson, 1982; Francher & Henkin, 1973; Friend, 1980, 1987). In the words of one of Kimmel's (1979, p. 244) participants, "The preparation for old age is much better among gays than it is among heterosexuals. Because you've always been that way—you haven't expected anyone to take care of you except your-self."

Dawson (1982) likewise proposes that gays and lesbians are better equipped to deal with the difficulties of aging because fears of familial abandonment prompt a greater degree of planning and preparation. Among the other advantages believed to accrue from being outside the traditional family structure is the gradual accumulation of a large network of friends (Friend, 1987; Francher & Henkin, 1973; Bell & Weinberg, 1978), who become a second family or "family of choice" (Weston, 1991). Additionally, older gays and lesbians are said to be sustained by the "presence of an empowering [LGBT] community" (Friend, 1987, p. 312).

Unfortunately, many of these proposed gay-specific resources turn out to be seductive ideas without much demonstrated basis in empirical fact. For instance, new evidence suggests that the presumed gender role flexibility and egalitarianism of gays and lesbians reflect ideology more than reality. While research based on self-reports indicates a more equal and less specialized division of domestic labor among same-sex couples (Kurdek, 1995; Peplau, Veniegas, & Campbell, 1996), Carrington's (1999) careful ethnographic study reveals that what gay and lesbians partners say (i.e., in surveys) and what they do are not always the same. He finds that the perception of "fairness" rarely reflects true equality, and that the differential contributions of same-sex partners tend to fall along familiar (and sometimes gendered) lines of power and prestige. Hence, it is not always the case that gays and lesbians, and particularly those who have been in long-term relationships, will have acquired a "lifetime of practice in self-sufficiency."

Nor is it the case that gays and lesbians are necessarily more prepared for their later years. For example, Mock (2001) finds a lower degree of financial planning for retirement among lesbian couples as compared to gay male and heterosexual couples. In line with previous research, he concludes that gender is the more potent predictor of retirement planning. Finally, although gay men and women often have more close friends than their heterosexual counterparts (Friend, 1987; Bell & Weinberg, 1978; Saghir & Robins, 1973; Cotton, 1972), my own research suggests that "families of choice" remain an unobtainable ideal for many gays and lesbians (Hostetler, 2001; see below), and social commentators from de Tocqueville (1988/1969) to Bellah et al. (1985) have pointed to the difficulty of sustaining friendship bonds across time and space.

It is not my intention to deny that older gays and lesbians, whether single or partnered, may possess material and/or symbolic resources that their heterosexual contemporaries lack. Rather, in keeping with Lee's (1987) critique, I believe that any consideration of the strengths, vulnerabilities, resources, and constraints that together shape the experience of "gay aging" must be grounded in systematic empirical research. Research on gay aging must further move away from static, essentialist (if often implicit) conceptions of group difference, which I believe are partially responsible for the defensive tone that characterizes much of the earlier research tradition. To that end, gay/straight (male/female, white/black, etc.) similarities and differences in aging should be approached from an ecological perspective (Bronfenbrenner, 1979) that addresses the broader social, cultural, and historical contexts of development.

Of course, the importance of context is far from a novel concept to most life-course researchers, and scholars of gay aging are no exception. However, although scholars of gay development generally have a keen, if not fully articulated, appreciation of the social and cultural forces that shape lives, psychological discourse has a way of translating important aspects of the ecological context into discretely analyzable, "independent," and often intrinsic variables. Paradoxically, psychological research also tends to produce an impoverished portrait of individual actors, who may or may not possess certain adaptive traits but who are otherwise relatively powerless to change either themselves or their environments. (In general, quantitative research paradigms make it difficult to portray the complexity of actors, contexts, and their interactions, and for that reason I draw on both quantitative and qualitative research below.) The individualization and essentialization of group difference contribute, I believe, to defensiveness on the part of those who study minority groups. For example, to acknowledge that ageism exists in the gay community or that singlehood is more pronounced than in the general population is to identify an intrinsic difference or inherent weakness characteristic of gay people—a concession that gay scholars are understandably reluctant to make.

For many researchers, the way around this seemingly unavoidable conflation of the sociocultural and individual levels is to limit an analysis of the sociocultural context to the impact of discrimination and prejudice, which clearly cannot be blamed on their intended "victims." More specifically, several researchers attribute instances of less-than-successful gay aging to the insidious consequences of homophobia and heterosexism, and the internalization of these negative societal images and stereotypes. In a similar vein, failures to adapt in midlife and later life are frequently traced to a more fundamental failure to "come out" (which reflects societal dysfunction at least as much if not more than individual weakness). For example, Berger (1984) argues that the acceptance of (a post-Stonewall) gay identity is an important predictor of adaptation and well-being in later life. As reviewed in Cruikshank (1991, p. 79), he attributes the problems of older gay men to institutional policies, discrimination, and neglect by social service agencies and the medical establishment. Similarly, Kimmel (1979) blames the loneliness, isolation, and unhappiness of certain older gay men on the experience of antigay oppression and their unfortunate alienation from their families of origin.

Friend (1991, pp. 103–104) posits two options for the older gay man: He can either accept a homophobic self-definition or reconstruct the meanings of being old and gay, or he concludes that "those older gays who conform to stereotypes of being lonely, depressed and alienated are the ones who internalize homophobia." Adelman finds (1987, p. 11) an inverse relationship between psychosomatic complaints and self-acceptance in her sample of older lesbians, and she asserts that "the most important factor for determining psychological well-being in lesbians in later life is the level of homophobia in society and ourselves." Indeed, as is evident from Cruikshank's (1991) review, *most* authors attribute the adaptation problems of gay elders to homophobic, external sources.

I do not mean to deny the pervasive and often devastating effects of stigma and discrimination on the lives of gays and lesbians. Rather, I take issue with the tendency to neglect aspects of the sociocultural context that are not directly related to antigay prejudice, an oversight I believe is related to a broader failure in the psychologically oriented literature to distinguish between cultural differences (i.e., grounded in shared meanings and experience) and the individual phenotypical expression of essential group differences.[4] Such distinctions would be at the center of a sociocultural psychology of gay aging (Herdt, Beeler, & Rawls, 1997). In keeping with this perspective, I dedicate the rest of this chapter to an ecological analysis (relying on within-group comparisons) of the risks encountered and the resources employed by single middle-aged and older gay men in their too often ignored efforts to maintain happy, healthy lives.[5]

AT RISK: RELATIONAL STATUS AND WELL-BEING

Despite being generally ignored by researchers, existing statistics are not encouraging for singles. A long history of research has established significant relationships between marital status and a variety of physical and psychological health outcomes. The physical health benefits of marriage include more activated immune systems (Kennedy, Kiecolt-Glaser, & Glaser, 1990), longer lifespans (Johnston & Eklund, 1984), longer survival rates for heart disease (Williams et al., 1992), and decreased risk of recurrence following a heart attack (Case et al., 1992). The benefits to mental health are even more dramatic. Study after

---

[4]I believe the failure to make this critical distinction is not specific to research on gays and lesbians, but rather is at the heart of current social-scientific debates about how best to address difference in general—an insight I owe partially to Andrew Harlem (personal communication).

[5]In keeping with a socio-cultural perspective, I do not assume categorical differences between gays and straights, or between gay men and lesbians. I chose to focus on single gay men because of their disproportionately high numbers, and because there was good reason to believe that there are (sub)culturally-specific forms of adaptation to single life, such as might be embodied in "families of choice" and/or gay forms of community life. Given the lack of a comparison group, I am obviously unable to draw any conclusions about gay/straight differences.

study has demonstrated higher levels of happiness, well-being, and life-satisfaction among the married (Bradburn, 1969; Bradburn & Caplovitz, 1965; Knupfer, Clark, & Room, 1966; Gurin, Veroff, & Feld, 1960; Glenn & Weaver, 1979; Gove, 1972a, 1972b; Gove, Style, & Hughes, 1983, 1990; Veroff, Douvan, & Kulka, 1981; Campbell, 1981; Johnson & Eklund, 1984; Haring-Hidore et al., 1985; Inglehart, 1990; Mastekaasa, 1994; Veenhoven et al., 1994). Setting aside important differences between marital and other types of primary relationship (Blumstein & Schwarz, 1983), several studies suggest a similar relationship between relational status and psychological well-being among gays and lesbians (Bell & Weinberg, 1978; Berger, 1982/1996; Schmitt & Kurdek, 1987; Wayment & Peplau, 1995; O'Brien, 1992).

Notwithstanding these consistent and highly significant findings, the power of marital/relational status to predict any given physical or mental health outcome remains modest at best. On average, marriage accounts for only 14% of the variance in well-being across all studies (Diener et al, 1999; Andrews & Withey, 1976; Schwarz & Strack, 1999; Argyle, 1987), indicating a high degree of within-group variance. In other words, not all single gay men are unhappy, and where there is risk there is also resilience and a great deal of individual variability.

SINGLE GAY MEN: WHO ARE THEY, AND HOW ARE THEY DOING?

As a first step toward filling the research void in the area of gay singlehood, I carried out a two-part study of psychological well-being and adjustment among single gay men 35 and older. First, I recruited a convenience sample of 94 self-identified single gay men to complete the *Survey of Gay and Lesbian Adulthood* (SOGALA),[6] and then I conducted follow-up life-history interviews with 20 of these men.[7] Table 6.1 shows some demographic and social characteristics of my sample.

---

[6] I would like to thank Todd W. Rawls, Samantha Bergmann, Christine Glover, Gilbert Herdt, and Bertram Cohler, with whom I collaborated on the construction and pilot-testing of SOGALA.

[7] All self-defined single gay (or bisexual) men were eligible for the survey study, with the additional stipulation that they had not been in a committed relationship for the last six months. Life-history participants were selected to represent the diversity of the larger sample with respect to age, race, and satisfaction with single status. A more detailed description of sample and methods appears in the appendix.

TABLE 6.1 Demographic Characteristics of SOGALA Single Gay Men

Median age	52
% White	69.10%
% Nonwhtie	30.90%
Median years of education	16
Median income	$35–40K
% "Out" to all family members	35.10%
% "Out" to all friends	70.20%
% Participate monthly in LGBT social activities	36.10%
% Participate monthly in LGBT political activities	26.60%
% Participate monthly in LGBT volunteer activities	37.30%
Median number of "really close" relatives	2
Median number of "really close" friends	5
Median number of lifetime same-sex relationships	4

Despite the widely noted limitations of convenience sampling (Myers & Colten, 1999), my research participants nevertheless represented a wide spectrum of experiences and adaptations to single life. Not surprisingly, however, the men were predominantly middle class and generally highly educated, as indicated in Table 6.1. And although I made a concerted effort to recruit men of color, the racial breakdown is far from representative of Chicago in general (the population of which has been estimated to be more than half nonwhite). Specifically, 69.1% of the sample was Caucasian, while 17% was African American, 9.6% was Latino, and 4.3% was Asian. Participants had to be at least 35 years old to qualify for inclusion, of course, and they ranged in age from 35 to 82, with a median age of 52 and a relatively even distribution up to the age of 70.

As is also typical of convenience samples of urban-dwelling gay men and lesbians (Myers & Colten, 1999), the men are generally very open about their sexuality and highly involved in the public life of the lesbian and gay community. More than 70% of respondents had disclosed their sexual orientation to all of their friends, but only half that many had told all of their family members. In terms of their community involvement, more than a quarter of the men participated at least monthly in political activities in the LGBT community, and well over a third participated at least monthly in social and volunteer activities.

Most respondents reported a moderate to high degree of social support from family, and particularly, friends, both in terms of quantity and of quality. Respondents listed an average of 6.5 "really close" friends (with a median of 5) and an average of 3.7 "really close" relatives (with a median of 2). However, the large standard deviations for these figures, 4.8 and 4.0, respectively, indicate a high degree of variability. Finally, with respect to their previous relationship histories, only 7.4% of the men were ever heterosexually married, but all but 5 (94.7%) reported at least one significant same-sex relationship in the past. On average, respondents had 2.8 significant opposite-sex relationships excluding marriages (SD = 3.9; median = 2) and 5.8 significant same-sex relationships (SD = 6.9; median = 4).

Despite many demographic and social similarities, my research participants exhibited varying levels of life satisfaction, psychological well-being, and adjustment to being single. Mental health/well-being indices and a measure of the "integration of single status," designed for the study, all showed high degrees of variance.[8] Regarding whether or not they are "single by choice," a topic discussed at greater length below, 34% of the men strongly agreed that they were, 24.5% agreed, 20.2% neither agreed nor disagreed, 11.7% disagreed, and 9.6% strongly disagreed. The men similarly ran the gamut with respect to fears and concerns about growing older. However, as Table 6.2 indicates, 63% of the men were at least somewhat concerned about growing old in general, and similar percentages were at least somewhat concerned that they would become isolated and lonely in their old age, that no one would care for them, and that they would require the services of a long-term care facility.

So, what predicts psychological well-being and positive attitudes toward aging among single gay men? Perhaps not surprisingly, a summary measure of aging concern, constructed from the four items presented in Table 6.2 (with high scores indicating a high level of concern; alpha = .87), was significantly correlated with measures of well-being and mental health at the .01 level. Pearson coefficients ranged from −.38 (for overall psychological well-being) to .44 (for overall symptomatology). Given these intercorrelations, we might expect similar factors

---

[8]These measures are described in the appendix. Given that research participants are likely no less sensitive to or defensive about gay stereotypes than researchers, I suspect that well-being scores are somewhat inflated and symptomatology is somewhat underreported. However, assuming uniformly distributed pressure toward socially normative responses, the within-group variance appears to be real.

TABLE 6.2   SOGALA Single Gay Men's Concerns About
                          Growing Older

	Not at all	Not very	Some-what	Very
How concerned about becoming isolated/lonely?	14.90%	28.70%	42.60%	13.80%
How concerned that no one will care for you?	13.00%	26.10%	45.70%	15.20%
How concerned about being in a retirement or nursing home?	9.90%	35.20%	40.70%	14.30%
How concerned about growing older in general?	12.10%	25.30%	49.50%	13.20%

to predict both psychological well-being and aging concerns, and this was partially the case. Linear regression analysis[9] (not presented here) revealed that high integration of single status (including the perception of being single by choice)[10] was the single most potent predictor of well-being and (low) mental health symptomatology, followed by social support from family and social support from friends (Hostetler, 2001). Together these variables accounted for between 25% and 30% of the variance in these scores across models. Age was negatively associated with well-being scores at the .01 level but was not a significant predictor of symptomatology.[11]

Table 6.3 shows results for the regression of aging concern on social support, community involvement, and integration of single status (controlling for demographic variables). As expected, those men who

---

[9]Residual analysis supported the use of linear regression analysis, despite the fact that mental health/well-being data are not typically normally distributed.

[10]This measure includes both satisfaction and preference questions, the latter of which serve to distinguish it from the outcome measures. According to diagnostic analysis based on the Rasch model, overall scores indicated that overall scores on the measure were driven primarily by variance on the preference items (and the satisfaction items distinguished the least between respondents). In other words, issues of simultaneity and discriminant validity do not appear to pose a major problem.

[11]The Brief Symptom Inventory (BSI), the measure of symptomatology used in this study, yields a t-score based on age-specific population norms. In other words, age is already controlled for in these scores given positive associations between age and certain types of symptoms.

TABLE 6.3   Regression Models for Aging Concern

	Model 1	Model 2	Model 3
Demographic variables			
Age	0.032	0.034	0.023
	(.031)	(.031)	(.031)
Nonwhite race	.217	0.359	.445
	(.800)	(.795)	(.748)
Household income	0.028	0.054	0.108
	(.081)	(.081)	(.075)
Social support and integration			
Social support from friends		−0.062	−0.022
		(.044)	(.042)
Social support from family		−0.040*	−0.035
		(.024)	(.022)
LGBT community involvement		0.056*	0.056*
		(.032)	(.029)
Feelings and attitudes about being single			
Acceptance of/satisfaction with single status			−0.079**
			(.020)
Perceived likelihood of future partnership			−0.360
			(.482)

**p < .001.
*p < .10.

were the most comfortable with their single status had the least amount of concern about aging, but social support and aging concerns were surprisingly unrelated. More unexpectedly, a high level of community involvement was associated with having more concerns about aging (p = .06). This finding appears to support a subcultural social comparison hypothesis (Bennett & Thompson, 1991) indicating that internalized ageism is more pronounced among those who have the most contact with the LGBT community (i.e., those who use other gay men as their primary reference group). As the regression models indicate, neither age nor any other demographic variables offer much predictive value. The variables in the final model only account for 18% of the variance in aging concerns (with 17.3% of the total variance being accounted for by integration of single status and community involvement).

Although these findings are relatively modest, they offer some important points of departure in my efforts to understand the experiences and well-being of single gay men. First, even within my well-educated, middle-class sample, there is a great deal of variability in the level of adjustment to single life and in general life satisfaction and well-being. Clearly, then, not all single gay men are unhappy about being single or about their lives in general. Second, social support is not surprisingly associated with higher levels of well-being, although it is not as powerful a predictor as I expected, and it does not appear to be related to fears and concerns about aging. Third, involvement in the lesbian and gay community does not necessarily have positive consequences, and may be related to a more negative evaluation of aging. Finally, as we might expect, the happiest men are also the most comfortable and satisfied with their single status, but this finding does not speak to the meaning of being "single by choice." Taken together, these results suggest the need for further investigation. In the final part of this chapter, I attempt to contextualize the quantitative findings, further exploring the meaning and experience of community, "chosen families," and being "single by choice."[12]

AGEISM AND THE CONTRADICTIONS OF COMMUNITY

Above and beyond their disproportionate numbers, I chose to focus on single gay men because I surmised that the secret to happy singlehood might lie in gay-specific forms of family and community life, a belief with a basis in previous research. More precisely, I hypothesized that involvement in a supportive community, one that has historically embodied alternative ideals about relationships and the purpose of adult life (Wittman, 1972; Bawer, 1993), would provide a buffer against the potentially negative consequences of "living single." However, I also wondered if the increasing ideological emphasis on same-sex relationships and families (Warner, 1999; Vaid, 1995) signaled broader changes in the sociocultural context, changes that might imperil the well-being of single gay men and women. I further suspected, given research findings on ageism and "accelerated aging," that feelings and attitudes about the LGBT community would be highly depen-

---

[12]Space limitations obviously preclude a detailed analysis of all the ecological factors relevant to an understanding of the lives of single gay men. Most notably absent from this chapter is a consideration of the wide-ranging impact of cohort/historical change and the AIDS epidemic on men's expectations for their lives and their experiences of being single.

dent on age. I was nevertheless somewhat surprised by the finding, reported above, that involvement in the LGBT community is associated with a higher degree of concern about aging. In order to shed more light on the meaning and experience of "community" in the lives of middle-aged and older single gay men, I offer a more thorough consideration of the dynamics of gay ageism.

As most researchers have recognized, the issue of ageism in the LGBT community is rather thorny. When I broached the topic in the life-history interviews, many of my research participants seemed reluctant to confirm stereotypes about the gay community, but at the same time they were eager to share hurtful experiences of being devalued because of their age. The survey results also suggest a somewhat mixed picture. More than half of my participants agreed that gays and lesbians under 30 do not appreciate their more mature counterparts, 44% reported feeling ignored in the community because of their age, and 42% told me that gay and lesbian social service agencies are not doing enough for people over 60. However, more than two thirds believed that there are plenty of opportunities for someone their age to get involved in the LGBT community.

Above and beyond the defensiveness of research participants and other methodological issues (e.g., whether questions are framed positively or negatively), it can be a challenge to achieve more than a tenuous grasp on the dynamics of gay ageism. Many researchers and several of my own respondents deny that ageism is any more prevalent in the gay community than in the general population, pointing to the relative lack of respect paid to elders in the contemporary West and the "looksism" and "youthism" inherent to consumer culture. Others locate the problem not in sexual orientation but in gender, or more specifically in the objectifying tendencies of men (Friend, 1987; Francher & Henkin, 1973). More relevant to present purposes is the (often implicit) scapegoating of gay singles and gay sexual culture. As we saw above, Friend (1987) argues that rumors of gay ageism are greatly exaggerated due to an overabundance of single people—slaves to the sexual marketplace—in research based on convenience samples.

While these are all valid, if not wholly satisfying, explanations, I believe they evade more fundamental questions. In fact, I am convinced that the problem has less to do with ageism, per se, and more to do with the meaning of community, the structure of gay intergenerational relationships, and unstated norms of the gay male life course. First, while Friend (1987) is correct to single out gay singles culture, he underestimates the extent to which the gay community, in its public and institutional incarnations, centers around the needs of its (young) single citizens. Despite the vast proliferation of lesbian and gay social, political, and professional organizations over the last 30 years, bars and other sexualized venues remain the focal point of gay community life to a remarkable extent. In the words of one of my research participants: "Unfortunately, in the gay community, most of the visibility comes through the bar scene. It's the most public, it's the most accessible to everybody" (Martin, 46-year-old white male).

Given the centrality of bars and other singles-oriented public spaces and organizations, partnered men may not always experience a sense of belonging in the gay community: "I think the sad thing is that we are not a part of the gay community once you're in a long-term relationship. You're in a small segment of your own . . . you no longer need to run to the bars" (Robert, 67-year-old white male).

Of course, the experience of community is highly variable even within the population of gay singles, reflecting divisions of age, race, class, etc. Age-related divisions are exacerbated by the nature of intergenerational contacts in the gay community, which do not typically follow the heterosexual, extended-family pattern but rather involve strangers and nonkin interacting in bars and similar venues. Ideally, the absence of predefined roles and of an inflexible, hierarchical kinship structure should provide opportunities for a wider range of relationships to develop, including sexual, romantic, platonic, and kinlike. Not surprisingly, then, large age differences between romantic partners seem more common and raise fewer eyebrows within the gay community. Above and beyond expanded possibilities for breaking down generational barriers, the structure of gay intergenerational relationships could promote a version of community that extends beyond the narrow, privatized (and ultimately individualistic) confines of the family.

Unfortunately, this promise remains largely unrealized. As Friend (1987) implies, the sexualized atmosphere of bars and similar environments can heighten the possibility for slights, misunderstandings, and intergenerational tensions. Cohort differences in the expression of homosexual or gay identity can further inflame these tensions. But ageism and generational bias are only part of the story. I would argue that to understand the ecology of gay intergenerational relationships and the workings of community is also to reveal the internal logic of the expectable gay male life course. More precisely, my interviews and participant observations of gay bar culture and community life suggest a "natural," age-graded progression not unlike the heterosexual life course. After sowing some wild oats in their 20s and early 30s, most of the gay men with whom I have spoken hope, or had hoped, to find permanent partnership and domestic bliss and leave the scene mostly behind (and thereby graduate to mature adulthood): "[Going out all the time] was fun. But, like everything else, you've got to put things aside as you grow up each stage of the way. You leave your childhood toys and you pick your adult toys and move on from each of those steps. It's the same thing here. I'm, I'm in my forties and I feel myself a professional and I try to conduct myself as such" (Antonio, 48-year-old Latino male).

For many gay men, the spectacle of an older man in a gay bar (or at least a bar with a primarily younger clientele) provides a cautionary tale about developmental failure. But it is not just the unwanted reminder of age's inevitable march that inspires fear and loathing; it is the very real possibility of being old, alone and pitifully looking for love in the wrong places, and eventually becoming the target of the same kind of derisive comments and attitudes. And it is the fear of reflecting back this reality, I believe, that led many of my research participants to distance themselves from the "lounge lizards" who remain in the bar scene too long and who can't "quit pretending they're still hot." In fact, several men commented on this age-related dynamic at length:

> "[When I was young] there weren't a lot of people my [present] age hanging out in the bars. It's not something you do at 45. Or, if you do it at 45, it's time you gave up the ghost" (Martin, 46-year-old white male).

> "I do recall, for as old as I was when I entered gay life in my late 30s/early 40s, seeing the occasional bar-goer who was then the age I am now. I would say I thought that was kind of pathetic that this old man was out hunting in this youth ground. . . . I hate bars. . . . I wouldn't want to walk into one because some young guy is going to think I'm after him when in fact my preference is older men" (Tom, 65-year-old white male).

> "[T]he single people [in my social network], except for maybe one or two, are past all that, trying to make out in bars and all that stupid stuff. The ones who are not are considerably younger and they *should* be interested in going out to bars and stuff" (Henry, 61-year-old white male).

> "Boystown [gay neighborhood in Chicago] is very nice when you're young and cute and gay, and maybe not so nice if you're not so young and

cute . . . maybe I was wrong, but I was assuming it was pretty much over for me in that area" (Dean, 58-year-old white male).

"Older folks . . . are always left out. . . . If they are alone, it's going to be hell because if they go to a bar, oh, look at him, he should be, you know, in a—walking with a walker, or something like that, you know. You know, imagine an old man in a disco. That's why I swear that, when I'm old, I'm not going out" (41-year-old Latino male).

Given this pervasive attitude, many older gay men, not surprisingly, avoid the bars, clubs, and cafes in which younger gay men congregate. Unfortunately, this pattern of avoidance severely limits the community involvement of these men; with some notable exceptions, there remain relatively few other public spaces in which mature gay men and women can just socialize or "sit and talk in a group." In the words of one 56-year-old, "In your fifties it's hard to meet a gay man. . . . There are fewer spaces where you can go at that age. . . . I don't know where to go." Although some men expressed the hope that things are changing with the aging of the baby boom cohort and the maturing of the gay and lesbian movement, others were of the belief that ageism and exclusion are here to stay. And without the benefit of a viable community life, it is extremely difficult to articulate and enact a cultural template for satisfying single adulthood. As a 30-something single friend recently said to me, older single gay role models do not (yet) exist.

The point of this discussion is not to suggest that ageism is more pronounced in LGBT communities, or that gay community life is particularly impoverished. It is my intention, rather, to highlight the specific structural and symbolic arrangements that make gay ageism so problematic and antithetical to community. I further wish to draw attention to the discrepancy between, on the one hand, the idealized version of community promoted in political rhetoric and academic research, and the longing for a more fulfilling community life among many middle-aged and older single gay men, on the other.

LONERS, "ALONERS," AND THE LIMITS OF FAMILIES OF CHOICE

In addition to being surrounded by a supportive and empowering community, older gays and lesbians are supposed to draw emotional sustenance from a large, dense network of friends gradually accumulated over the years (Weston, 1991; Nardi, 1999; Weeks, Heaphy, & Donovan, 2001). In the absence of a life partner, this friendship network or "family of choice" should ideally be sufficient to provide for most socioemotional needs. Those gay singles who lack such support may simply be more independent, or they may even be loners who don't require extensive contact with others in order to maintain a happy and healthy life. This, anyway, is the portrait that emerges from the research literature.

However, as we have already seen, the public spaces and institutions that constitute the gay and lesbian community are not always a welcoming place for older single gay men. Nor does there seem to be a well-articulated cultural template for life as an older single gay man. But what about other forms of social support? Do single gay men find adequate support in their chosen families of friends (in addition to or in the absence of support from their families of origin)?

The survey findings are again somewhat difficult to interpret. As indicated above, social support from family and social support from friends were both significantly associated with psychological well-being. However, these relationships were not as strong as I expected, and were likely depressed by the relatively small degree of variance on the social support measures. Specifically, most respondents were clustered near the upper end of the social support scales, suggesting measurement error attributable to socially normative responses and/or the inadequacy of the measures themselves. Responses to one item in particular led me to believe that normative pressure was at least partially responsible for the inflated social support scores. The item in question asked respondents if they had "a close circle of friends that [they] think of as family, or what some might call a family of choice." The concept of "chosen families" (Weston, 1991) has recently received considerable attention in the gay media, but I was nevertheless taken aback that 82% of respondents agreed that they have a family of choice, largely irrespective of the density of their social network. Indeed, despite the fact that the overwhelming majority of respondents embraced this term, more than half (53.8%) stated that none of their three closest friends were also friends with one another. Of the possible friendship pairings among these three closest friends, 27.5% reported a single pair of mutual friends, 4.4% reported two pairs, and 14.3% reported three. These findings suggest either that respondents define "families of choice" in a different way (i.e., network density is not an important criterion), or that they provided the answer they felt was expected of them (e.g., gay men are *supposed* to have a family of choice).

The life-history interviews provide further evidence of the inadequacy of the social support measures. Even among those who indicated a relatively high degree of social support on the survey, desires for more emotional support and more friends "just to hang out with" were frequently voiced. More importantly, I did not find a clear-cut distinction between true "loners," who might have less need for extensive social contact, and those who were merely alone and lonely. Although many men in my sample possessed characteristics that might qualify them as loners, it was often unclear whether I was observing an enduring personality trait or a life pattern acquired as a result of many years spent alone. Hence, I distinguished between two groups of men, which I label the "loners" and the "aloners." A whopping 18 out of 20 respondents fall into one or the other category.

The "loners" (9 out of 20) believe that their single status (and in some cases social isolation) at least partially reflects a long-standing dispositional or temperamental characteristic, which they trace throughout their adult lives if not back to childhood. These men may see themselves as "too independent," as "control freaks," or they may even be self-defined loners. The "aloners" (9 out of 20) also fear that they may be temperamentally unsuited for long-term relationships, but, in addition, they report an increasing pattern of social isolation with age that extends beyond the romantic and sexual realms. Hence, it is difficult to determine—perhaps for them as well as for me—which came first, the experience of social isolation or the posited personality trait. In other words, most of the men in my interview sample experienced a degree of social isolation, and it wasn't always clear how and when this pattern was acquired, or whether it was voluntary or involuntary.

Despite this ambiguity, several of the men were quite articulate concerning the difficulty of maintaining a satisfying social life as one aged, and about the limitations of friendship networks. For example, Marc (56, white) had always had an active social life and was shocked to find how few people he could actually count on following a serious and debilitating accident: "It's very frightening when this happens to you because you realize how alone you are and how you have to have somebody to help you . . . you can't really rely on somebody unless they're your mother or your son or daughter, or lover hopefully."

He also described his efforts to make new friends as increasingly problematic. Bennett (77, white) expressed a similar sentiment: "So I [used to know] a lot of people, of course now a lot of them are dead. So it was a very full day, full week, with knowing lots of people. Now I don't." But it was Tom (58, white) who was perhaps the most eloquent in reflecting on his diminishing contact with others, and I quote him at length:

> . . . I realized that my life has come down to a very isolated, very small numbers, and very isolated, so I don't even have anybody that I could ask to join me on a trip.
> . . . [I]s it that I'm at a point in my life where there just aren't those people? Have I pushed them away? Did they die? There's certainly some of that. You know, lots of the folks that when, I mean not so much self-consciously building a community, you find people who are interested in things. Well, nearly all the people who are interested in the various things I'm interested in are gone. So now it's a question, well, do I spend a lot of energy trying to find replacement people or just do I go and do those things on my own. Well, mostly I just do them on my own.
> I've got dozens and dozens and dozens of people on my email list, but I can go weeks, where except for maybe my brother or a couple other people call. There are no messages on the telephone, nobody calls me, I might as well live in Florence. I mean, I don't have a life here at some level. And yet, at another level I just know so many hundreds of people that its hard to go out anywhere without seeing somebody I know, but there's absolutely no, no engaged life. So I float along as an independent person, sort of like Velcro, or whatever, lots of little things that catch, snags of others, but nothing is linked, chain-link fence or something.

Although Tom experienced an unusually high degree of isolation, and most of the men I interviewed could count on at least two to five friends for regular social interaction and emotional support, this pattern of increasing difficulty in maintaining a satisfying social life was nearly universal among those over 50. Even one 61-year-old who boasted the "busiest social calendar in the Midwest" lamented that so many of his closest friends had relocated to more temperate climes. The blurry boundary between the "loners" and the "aloners," or between those who claim to have chosen a more solitary lifestyle and those who simply drifted into one, illustrates the relative precariousness of voluntary, nonkinship bonds, and further obscures the meaning of "choice." Indeed, if many loners are made and not born, and if community and friendship ties are so fragile, then how are we to understand the meaning of voluntary singlehood? I turn to this topic in the final section of the chapter.

PERSONAL CONTROL AND BEING "SINGLE BY CHOICE"

My interest in the psychological well-being of single gay men quickly led me to the concept of voluntary singlehood, and my central research questions focused on its meaning, measurement, and relationship to well-being. Peter Stein (1975, 1976, 1978, 1981) was one of the first social scientists to address the possibility of being "single by choice," and his typology of (heterosexual) singles included a voluntary-involuntary dimension. In the gay aging literature, Lee (1987) offers the strongest defense of singlehood in midlife and later life, and reminds us of the crucial distinction between loneliness and being alone. Unfortunately, these and other treatments have done little to clarify the meaning of voluntary singlehood or the best means by which to assess it.

As already indicated, the SOGALA survey included several items (17 total) addressing satisfaction with single status and preferences for being single or in a relationship. Of the men in my sample, 58.5% agreed at least somewhat with the statement "It is my choice to be single." But what does this mean in practical terms? In the course of developing a summary measure through the application of Rasch analysis,[13] I uncovered some surprising (non)answers to this question. Specifically, responses to the "choice" item offered little predictive value with respect to the overall pattern of responses. In other words, among those who agreed that they were single by choice, there was a large amount of variation in levels of satisfaction with and adjustment to being single.

The life-history interviews provided further opportunities to explore the meaning of voluntary singlehood. Having previously asked participants whether or not they considered themselves single by choice, I

---

[13]Rasch analysis is a "method for obtaining objective, fundamental, linear measures (qualified by standard errors and quality-control fit statistics) from stochastic observations of ordered category responses" (Linacre & Wright, 2001, p. 1). It produces "weighted" measures that takes into account both item difficulty and individual ability or attitude on a unidimensional scale (typically with WINSTEPS software) using a logit-based probability scale (with the mean set at or near 50).

did not repeat the question in the life-history interviews, nor did I directly ask participants to define voluntary singlehood, since I wanted to know whether or not they would spontaneously employ the concept. I did ask several questions about their experiences being single, and later coded their responses for themes relevant to issues of choice.

When used in common parlance, *choice* usually signifies a deliberate selection from two or more viable options. In the psychological literature, the ability to shape a course of action is referred to as "primary control" (Rothbaum, Weisz, & Snyder, 1982; Heckhausen & Schulz, 1995). It seemed unlikely to me, in a cultural context in which marriage and partnership are highly socially normative if not obligatory, that many individuals could or would choose singlehood—in the sense of primary control—as a potentially permanent life option. But despite a growing relationship ethic in LGBT communities (Warner, 1999; Hostetler, 2001; Hostetler & Cohler, 1997), there is also a long history of antimonogamy and antimarriage sentiment, part of a larger counter-cultural belief structure that could provide ideological cover for a single lifestyle. Perhaps more importantly, gays and lesbians allegedly have access to unique forms of social and community support that might constitute a viable alternative to more traditional relationship and family forms.

However, as the preceding analysis indicates, the promise of a rewarding social and community life remains unfulfilled for most of the men in my study. And as further evidence that the men "drifted" into singlehood, the life-history interviews show relatively few signs of primary control, with the notable exception of certain younger men (primarily under 40) who have chosen to be temporarily single following the dissolution of a previous long-term relationship. In fact, none of my participants explicitly described themselves as voluntarily single or spontaneously embraced the term *single by choice*. Nor did they express countercultural convictions or cite principled protest as a factor motivating their decision to be single. In general, voluntary singlehood does not appear to provide the basis for either a salient personal or a collective identity. So, among those who had told me in the survey that they were satisfied with their relational status and who had agreed that they were single by choice, what did they mean?

Although I was hard pressed to find examples of primary control, the theme of choice nevertheless reverberated throughout the interviews. More specifically, for many of the men being single by choice operated as a form of "secondary control" (Rothbaum, Weisz, & Snyder, 1982;

Heckhausen & Schulz, 1995), which refers to efforts to "fit in with the world and to 'flow with the current' " (Rothbaum, Weisz, & Snyder, 1982, p. 8) when primary control fails. One example of secondary control is "interpretive control" (Rothbaum, Weisz, & Snyder, 1982), through which individuals make meaning out of essentially uncontrollable events in order to accept them. Among the men who saw themselves as happily and perhaps permanently partnerless, voluntary singlehood is best conceptualized as a developmental and narrative strategy—a way of reading the past, present, and future—through which they convince themselves that things are as they were meant to be. For instance, they may express a preference for a relationship in an ideal world while conceding that their personal history and/or personality has rendered them "not the relationship type." They may also find evidence in their past of direct and indirect choices that have led up to the current state of affairs. Martin, a 46-year-old white male, provides a perfect example of this: "I've come to the realization that I'm single because that's what I wanted. . . . Over the years there were a lot of choices I made that sort of insured that I wound up single. Lots of choices."

In short, permanent, voluntary singlehood is neither a salient group identity nor an example of deliberate, "planful" action. Instead, it appears to reflect the necessities of ego-integrity (Erikson, 1950/1963) and the tendency of individuals, in the words of Bourdieu (1988, p. 216), "to collaborate with their destinies." Although this may seem like the illusion of control, it is nevertheless an adaptive strategy, an example of resilience and personal agency that protects self-esteem, minimizes loss, and provides "a pathway from loss of control back to primary control" (Heckhausen & Schulz, 1995, p. 286) in other life domains. At the same time, to the extent that it does not provide the basis for a collective identity but rather remains tied to the individual life history, it remains a relatively fragile strategy.

DISCUSSION

At the beginning of this chapter, I echoed the comments of Lee (1987), Carrington (1999), and others in my criticism of the sometimes overzealous efforts of researchers to cast gays and lesbians in a positive light. As I hope is already apparent, it is certainly not my intention to compensate for any perceived shortcomings in the research literature by airing the community's "dirty laundry," as other like-minded individuals have been accused of doing (Carrington, 1999). Indeed, such a characterization would miss the mark entirely. I would argue instead that the take-home message of this chapter has at least as much to do with the common concerns and shared problems of single gays and straights as it does with gay/straight differences. Despite political rhetoric and the assertions of certain researchers, gay and straight singles likely encounter many of the same problems in their efforts to forge satisfying social and community lives. Building strong families (of origin, procreation, and/or choice) and vibrant communities is a goal most Americans share, and I am far from the first to address the ways in which current social and cultural arrangements can frustrate our best efforts to realize these goals.

For singles, such aspirations may seem particularly unobtainable. The gradual insulation of the private, domestic realm from public life and the isolation of the nuclear family, so well documented by Bellah and his colleagues (1985), have paradoxically made single adult lifestyles both possible and, for many, extremely difficult. These historical developments also contributed to the emergence of modern gay and lesbian communities and identities, as well as a political movement that increasingly gauges its own success by the extent to which homosexuals are able to retreat from both public scrutiny and civic participation into "sentimental couplehood" and the safe, sanitized, and hermetically sealed domestic unit (Warner, 1999). Perhaps it is not so surprising, then, that gay men are not necessarily specially equipped for the challenges of single life. For gay and straight alike, the process of building a happy single life and/or becoming "voluntarily single" is likely idiosyncratic and solitary, requiring a good deal of individual agency.

At the same time, there are important differences to consider in understanding the lives of mature single gay men, differences grounded more in social, cultural, and historical circumstances than in essential group characteristics. First and foremost, and for reasons beyond the scope of this paper, gay men are disproportionately represented among the single. Even assuming a lower percentage of single gay men than has been found using convenience samples, their exclusion from social-scientific research is neither warranted nor justified. In light of the best available estimates of gay singlehood rates and the well-established relationship between marital/relational status and well-being, a relatively high percentage of gay men may be at risk for isolation, depression, and a variety of physical and psychological problems in middle and later life.

However, even in the absence of political rhetoric and the claims of researchers, the large number of unattached gay men might also lead us to expect high participation rates in a rich and satisfying community life. Unfortunately, the case of single gay men proves to be particularly effective in illuminating the glaring inadequacies of American community life. The sexualized nature of so much of gay public life, paired with ageism and the fear of becoming (or being seen as) "old, gay, and alone," turns out to be a powerful deterrent to community. Finally, the unfortunate alienation of many gays and lesbians from their families of origin, particularly among older generations, means that middle-aged and older single homosexuals may be even more socially isolated than some of their heterosexual counterparts. Nevertheless, comparative research is clearly needed before *any* gay/straight (or gay male/lesbian) differences can be established.

CONCLUSION

Three decades of research on gay and lesbian aging have effectively countered many pernicious stereotypes, demonstrating that being old and gay does not preclude being happy and healthy. In contrast to the clinically based research of previous generations, these studies offer a more *emic* or inside perspective on gay aging, providing gay elders with some of their first opportunities to speak in their own voices. Fortunately, the voices of mature single gays and lesbians are also beginning to be heard. This history of important scholarship has laid the groundwork for a new generation of research on gay and lesbian aging—represented in the present volume by both seasoned scholars and relative newcomers—that seeks to situate an analysis of commonality and difference, risk and resilience in an ecological framework that integrates social, cultural, and individual levels of analysis. As evidenced by the contributions to this volume, this research comes in many forms, is often interdisciplinary, and frequently combines quantitative and qualitative methods. Perhaps most importantly, it preserves the commitment of the earlier tradition to represent the diverse experiences of older gays and lesbians—including those who are single—while also promoting a higher quality of gay life for both present and future generations.

APPENDIX: METHODS

Data

The findings reported in this chapter are based on quantitative and qualitative data collected in Chicago's gay and lesbian community in three phases. The first phase involved a pilot survey study of psychological well-being and adjustment among a convenience sample of 60 gay men and women, 35-years and over. Of the 32 men in the pilot study, 18 described themselves as currently single (i.e., without a primary relationship). In the second phase of the research, an additional 76 surveys were administered to self-identified single gay men (with the stipulation that they had not been in a serious relationship for at least six months). A total sample of 94 single gay men, diverse with respect to age and race, completed face-to-face structured interviews covering a variety of topics, including developmental history and milestones in the gay identity formation process, social and political attitudes, social support and resources, history of sexual and romantic relationships, LGBT community involvement, experiences with violence and harassment, mental and physical health, and adjustment to aging. In the third and final phase, 20 men from the original sample were selected to participate in an in-depth, life-history interview based on a semi-structured protocol.

Measures

Independent variables included social support and resources, LGBT community involvement, integration of homosexual identity, and integration of single status. Five measures were constructed using the Rasch model of analysis (Linacre & Wright, 2001; see footnote 13): the Social Support from Family Measure (SSFam), the Social Support from Friends Measure (SSFrnd), the LGBT Community Involvement Measure (CIM), the Integration of LGBT Identity Measure (IIM), and the Integration of Single Status Measure (ISSM). In addition to those items composed by the research group, items for the SSFam and SSFrnd measures were adapted from the General Social Survey, from Pearlin and Lieberman's (1979) modification of Bott's (1957) instrument, and from the measure of Social Provision (Mancini & Blieszner, 1992; Weiss, 1974). CIM and IIM items were adapted from Weinberg and Williams (1974), Bell and Weinberg (1978), Berger (1982/1996), and Herdt and Boxer (1993/1996). Most items for the Integration of Single Status Measure (ISSM) were constructed by the research group. Reliability estimates for the other measures ranged from .93 to .96.

The dependent variable, mental health and psychological well-being, was assessed with three widely used measures: the Brief Symptom Inventory (BSI) (Derogatis et al., 1974; Derogatis & Spencer, 1982; Derogatis & Melisaratos, 1983; Derogatis, 1993), which includes nine subscales and three summary scores that assess symptomatology; the 18-item version of the Ryff Well-Being Questionnaire (Ryff, 1989; Ryff & Keyes, 1995), which includes six subscales assessing global well-being; and the Bradburn Affect Balance Scale (ABS) (Bradburn, 1969; Bradburn & Caplowitz, 1965), which consists of ten yes/no items designed to assess general mood and morale, and includes both positive and negative affective dimensions. Internal consistency and test-retest reliability coefficients for these measures are high and have been well documented.

Analysis

Survey data were analyzed using SPSS. Relationships between independent and dependent variables were preliminarily assessed with scatterplots and Pearson correlation coefficients, and then by linear regression analysis. Analysis of the life-history interviews was guided by what Mishler (1990) has called an inquiry-guided perspective, which highlights the means by which individuals maintain a sense of continuity over time, construct identities, and manage tensions in personal and social life, and by Strauss and Corbin's (1990) open coding methodology. Each life history was read, reread, analyzed, and hand-coded on its own terms, with the primary purpose of identifying the major themes that characterize each individual's understanding of his single status. In the second phase of analysis, I employed a content analysis approach (Lieblich, Tuval-Masiach, & Zilber, 1998). I searched for common themes in the men's understandings of their single status, and then coded the interviews with the application of Nudist Vivo, or NVIVO (Richards, 1999), a qualitative analysis software program.

REFERENCES

Adelman, M. (1987). *Long time passing: Lives of older lesbians.* Boston: Alyson.
Andrews, F. M., & Withey, S. B. (1976). *Social indicators of well-being: Americans' perceptions of life quality.* New York: Plenum Press.

Argyle, M. (1987). *The psychology of happiness*. London: Routledge.

Bawer, B. (1993). *A place at the table: The gay individual in American society*. New York: Poseidon Press.

Bell, A., & Weinberg, M. (1978). *Homosexualities: A study of diversity among men and women*. New York: Simon and Schuster.

Bellah, R. N., et al. (1985). *Habits of the heart: Individualism and commitment in American life*. Berkeley: University of California Press.

Bennett, K. C., & Thompson, N. L. (1991). Accelerated aging and male homosexuality: Australian evidence in a continuing debate. *Journal of Homosexuality*, 20(3/4), 65–75.

Berger, R. M. (1982/1996). *Gay and gray: The older homosexual man* (2nd ed.). Binghamton, NY: Harrington Park Press/Haworth.

Berger, R. M. (1984). Realities of gay and lesbian aging. *Social Work*, 27, 236–242.

Blumstein, P., & Schwartz, P. (1983). *American couples: Work, money, sex*. New York: Morrow.

Bott, E. (1957/1971). *Family and social network* (2nd ed.). London: Tavistock.

Bourdieu, P. (1988). *Homo academicus* (P. Collier, Trans.). Stanford, CA: Stanford University Press.

Bradburn, N. M., with Noll, C. E. (1969). *The structure of psychological well-being: National Opinion Research Center monographs in social research*. Chicago: Aldine.

Bradburn, N. M., & Caplowitz, D. (1965). *Reports on happiness: A pilot study of behavior related to mental health*. Chicago: Aldine.

Bronfenbrenner, U. (1979). *The ecology of human development: Experiments by nature and design*. Cambridge, MA: Harvard University Press.

Campbell, A. (1981). *The sense of well-being in America: Recent patterns and trends*. New York: McGraw-Hill.

Carrington, C. (1999). *No place like home: Relationships and family among lesbians and gay men*. Chicago: University of Chicago Press.

Case, R. B., Moss, A. J., Case, N., McDermott, M., & Eberly, S. (1992). Living alone after myocardial infarction: Impact on prognosis. *Journal of the American Medical Association*, 267, 515–519.

Cotton, W. L. (1972). Role playing substitutions among male homosexuals. *Journal of Sex Research*, 8, 310–323.

Cruikshank, M. (1991). Lavender and gray: A brief survey of lesbian and gay aging studies. *Journal of Homosexuality*, 20(3/4), 77–87.

Dawson, K. (1982, November). Serving the older gay community. *SEICUS Report*, 5–6.

de Tocqueville, A. (1988/1969). *Democracy in America*. New York: Harper & Row.

Derogatis, L.R. (1993). *Brief Symptom Inventory: Administration, scoring, and procedures manual* (3rd ed.). Minneapolis, MN: National Computer Systems, Inc.

Derogatis, L., et al. (1974). Neurotic symptom dimensions. *Archives of General Psychiatry*, 24, 454–464.

Derogatis, L. R., & Melisarators, N. (1983). The Brief Symptom Inventory: An introductory report. *Psychological Medicine*, 13(3), 595–605.

Derogatis, L. R., & Spencer, P. M. (1982). *Brief Symptom Inventory*. Baltimore: Clinical Psychometric Research.

Diener, E., Suh, E. M., Lucas, R. E., & Smith, H. L. (1999). Subjective well-being: Three decades of progress. *Psychological Bulletin, 125*(2), 276–302.

Erikson, E. H. (1950/1963). *Childhood and society* (rev. ed.). New York: Norton.

Francher, S. J., & Henkin, J. (1973). The menopausal queen. *American Journal of Orthopsychiatry, 43*, 670–674.

Friend, R. A. (1980). GAYging: Adjustment and the older gay male. *Alternative Lifestyles, 3*, 213–248.

Friend, R. A. (1987). The individual and the social psychology of aging: Clinical implications for lesbians and gay men. *Journal of Homosexuality, 14*(1/2), 307–331.

Friend, R. A. (1991). Older lesbian and gay people: A theory of successful aging. *Journal of Homosexuality, 20*, 99–118.

Gagnon, J. H., & Simon, W. (1973). *Sexual conduct: The social sources of human sexuality.* Chicago: Aldine.

Glenn, N. D., & Weaver, C. N. (1979). A note on family situation and global happiness. *Social Forces, 57*, 960–967.

Gove, W. R. (1972a). Sex, marital status, and suicide. *Journal of Health and Social Behavior, 13*(2), 204–213.

Gove, W. R. (1972b). The relationship between sex, marital roles, and mental illness. *Social Forces, 5*(1), 34–44.

Gove, W. R., Hughes, M., & Style, C. B. (1983). Does marriage have positive effects on the psychological well-being of the individual? *Journal of Health and Social Behavior, 24*, 122–131.

Gove, W. R., Style, C. B., & Hughes, M. (1990). The effect of marriage on the well-being of adults: A theoretical analysis. *Journal of Family Issues, 11*, 4–35.

Gurin, G., Veroff, J., & Feld, S. (1960). *Americans view their mental health.* New York: Basic Books.

Haring-Hidore, M., Stock, W. A., Okun, M. A., & Witter, R. A. (1985). Marital status and subjective well-being: A research synthesis. *Journal of Marriage and the Family, 47*, 947–953.

Harry, J. (1984). *Gay couples.* New York: Praeger.

Heckhausen, J., & Schulz, R. (1995). A life-span theory of control. *Psychological Review, 102*(2), 284–304.

Herdt, G., Beeler, J., & Rawls, T. (1997). Life course diversity among older lesbians and gay men: A study in Chicago. *Journal of Lesbian, Gay, and Bisexual Identities, 2*, 231–246.

Herdt, G., & Boxer, A. (1993/1996). *Children of Horizons: How gay and lesbian teens are leading a new way out of the closet.* Boston: Beacon.

Hostetler, A. J. (2001). *Single gay men: Cultural models of adult development, psychological well-being, and the meaning of being "single by choice."* Doctoral dissertation, University of Chicago, Chicago.

Hostetler, A. J., & Cohler, B. J. (1997). Partnership, singlehood, and the lesbian and gay life course: A research agenda. *Journal of Gay, Lesbian, and Bisexual Identity, 2*, 199–230.

Inglehart, R. (1990). *Culture shift in advanced industrial society.* Princeton, NJ: Princeton University Press.

Johnson, M., & Eklund, S. (1984). Life-adjustment of the never-married: A review with implications for counseling. *Journal of Counseling and Development,* 63(4), 230–236.

Kehoe, M. (1986). Lesbians over 65: A triple invisible minority. *Journal of Homosexuality, 12,* 139–152.

Kelly, J. J. (1977). The aging male homosexual: Myth and reality. *The Gerontologist, 17,* 328–332.

Kennedy, S., Kiecolt-Glaser, J. K., & Glaser, R. (1990). Social support, stress and the immune system. In B. R. Sarason, I. G. Sarason, & G. R. Pierce (Eds.), *Social support: An interactional view* (pp. 253–266). New York: Wiley.

Kimmel, D. C. (1977). Psychotherapy and the older gay man. *Psychotherapy: Theory, Research and Practice, 14,* 386–393.

Kimmel, D. C. (1979). Life history interviews of aging gay men. *International Journal of Aging and Human Development, 10,* 239–248.

Knupfer, G., Clark, W., & Room, R. (1966). The mental health of the unmarried. *American Journal of Psychiatry, 122,* 841–851.

Kurdek, L. (1995). Lesbian and gay couples. In. A. R. D'Augelli & C. Patterson (Eds.), *Lesbian, gay and bisexual identities over the lifespan: Psychological perspectives* (pp. 243–261). New York: Oxford University Press.

Laner, M. R. (1978). Growing older male: Heterosexual and homosexual. *The Gerontologist, 18,* 496–501.

Lee, J. A. (1987). What can homosexual aging studies contribute to theories of aging? *Journal of Homosexuality, 13*(4), 43–71.

Lieblich, A., Truval-Mashiach, R., & Zilber, T. (1998). *Narrative research: Reading, analysis and interpretation.* Thousand Oaks, CA: Sage Publications.

Linacre, J. M., & Wright, B. D. (2001). *A user's guide to Winsteps, Ministep, and Bigsteps Rasch—Model Computer Programs.* Chicago: MESA Press.

Mancini, J., & Blieszner, R. (1992). Social provision in adulthood: Concept and measurement in close relationships. *Journal of Gerontology: Psychological Sciences, 47,* 14–20.

Mastekaasa, A. (1994). Marital status, distress, and well-being: An international comparison. *Journal of Comparative Family Studies, 25,* 183–205.

Minnigerode, F. A. (1976). Age-status labeling in homosexual men. *Journal of Homosexuality, 1*(3), 273–275.

Mishler, E. (1990). Validation: The social construction of knowledge—A brief for inquiry-guided research. *Harvard Educational Review, 60,* 415–442.

Mock, S. (2001). Retirement intentions of same-sex couples. Working paper, Bronfenbrenner Life Course Center, Cornell University, Ithaca, NY.

Myers, I. H., & Colten, M. E. (1999). Sampling gay men: Random digit dialing versus sources in the gay community. *Journal of Homosexuality, 37*(4), 99–110.

Nardi, P. M. (1999). *Gay men's friendships: Invincible communities.* Chicago: University of Chicago Press.

O'Brien, K. (1992). Primary relationships affect the psychological health of men at risk for AIDS. *Psychological Reports, 71,* 147–153.

Pearlin, L., & Lieberman, M. (1979). Social sources of emotional distress. In R. Simmons (Ed.), *Research in community and mental health* (Vol. I, pp. 217–248). Greenwich, CT: JAI Press.

Peplau, L., Veniegas, R., & Campbell, S. (1996). Gay and lesbian relationships. In R. Savin-Williams & K. C. Cohen (Eds.), *The lives of lesbians, gays, and bisexuals: Children to adults* (pp. 250–273). New York: Harcourt Brace College Publications.

Richards, L., and Qualitative Solutions and Research. (1999). *Using NVIVO in qualitative research* (Version 1.1). Thousand Oaks, CA: Sage Publications/Scalar.

Rothbaum, F., Weisz, J. R., & Snyder, S. S. (1982). Changing the world and changing the self: A two-process model of perceived control. *Journal of Personality and Social Psychology, 42,* 5–37.

Ryff, C. D. (1989). Happiness is everything, or is it? Explorations on the meaning of psychological well-being. *Journal of Personality and Social Psychology, 57*(6), 1069–1081.

Ryff, C. D., & Keyes, L. M. (1995). The structure of psychological well-being revisited. *Journal of Personality and Social Psychology, 69*(4), 719–727.

Saghir, M., & Robins, E. (1973). *Male and female homosexuality.* Baltimore: Williams & Wilkins.

Savin-Williams, R. C. (1998). *" . . . and then I became gay": Young men's stories.* New York: Routledge.

Schmitt, J. P., & Kurdek, L. A. (1987). Personality correlates of positive identity and relationship involvement in gay men. *Journal of Homosexuality, 13,* 101–109.

Schwarz, N., & Strack, F. (1999). Reports of subjective well-being: Judgmental processes and their methodological implications. In D. Kahneman, E. Diener, & N. Schwarz (Eds.), *Well-being: The foundations of hedonic psychology* (pp. 61–84). New York: Russell Sage Foundation.

Simon, W., & Gagnon, J. H. (1967). Homosexuality: The formulation of a sociological perspective. *Journal of Health and Social Behavior, 8,* 177–185.

Stein, P. (1975). Singlehood: An alternative to marriage. *The Family Coordinator, 24,* 489–503.

Stein, P. (1976). *Single.* Englewood Cliffs, NJ: Prentice-Hall.

Stein, P. (1978). The life styles and life chances of the never-married. *Marriage and Family Review, 1,* 2–11.

Stein, P. (Ed.) (1981). *Single life.* New York: St. Martin's Press.

Strauss, A., & Corbin, J. (1990). *Basics of qualitative research.* Newbury Park, CA: Sage.

Vaid, U. (1995). *Virtual equality: The mainstreaming of gay and lesbian liberation.* New York: Anchor Books.

Veenhoven, R., et al. (1994). *World database of happiness: Correlates of happiness.* Rotterdam: Erasmus University.

Veroff, J., Douvan, E. M., & Kulka, R. A. (1981). *The inner American.* New York: Basic Books.

Warner, M. (1999). *The trouble with normal: Sex, politics, and the ethics of queer life.* Cambridge, MA: Harvard University Press.

Wayment, H., & Peplau, L. A. (1995). Social support and well-being among lesbian and heterosexual women: A structural modeling approach. *Personality and Social Psychology Bulletin, 21,* 1189–1199.

Weeks, J., Heaphy, B., & Donovan, C. (2001). *Same sex intimacies: Families of choice and other life experiments*. London & New York: Routledge.

Weinberg, M. S., & Williams, C. J. (1974). *Male homosexuals: Their problems and adaptations*. New York: Oxford University Press.

Weiss, R. S. (1974). The provision of social relationships. In Z. Rubin (Ed.), *Doing onto others* (pp. 17–26). Englewood Cliffs, NJ: Prentice Hall.

Weston, K. (1991). *Families we choose: Lesbians, gays, kinship*. New York: Columbia University Press.

Williams, R. B., Barefoot, J. C., Califf, R. M., Haney, T. L., Saunders, W. B., Pryor, D. B., Hlatky, M. A., Siegler, I. C., & Mark, D. B. (1992). Prognostic importance of social and economic resources among medically treated patients with angiographically documented coronary artery disease. *Journal of the American Medical Association, 267,* 520–524.

Wittman, C. (1972). A gay manifesto. In K. Jay & A. Young (Eds.), *Out of the closets: Voices of gay liberation*. New York: Douglas/Links.

CHAPTER 7

Lesbian Friendships at and Beyond Midlife: Patterns and Possibilities for the 21st Century

Jacqueline S. Weinstock[1]

I n the year 2000, those born between 1935 and 1961 were between the ages of 40 and 65, ages that typically represent middle adulthood. Lesbians of these birth cohorts and the ones immediately preceding them in the United States have witnessed tremendous changes in the images of and possibilities for living as lesbians. Midlife lesbians spent their younger years in a prefeminist and pregay libera-

[1]Jacqueline S. Weinstock is Associate Professor in the Human Development and Family Studies Program at the University of Vermont. An earlier version of this paper was published. The author would like to thank her friends, colleagues, and students who have shared in many wide-ranging and thought-provoking conversations about lesbians, midlife, late adulthood, friendships, lover relationships, parenting, and the development of nurturing communities. She would especially like to thank the following friends and colleagues for their contributions to her midlife development and to the ideas upon which this chapter is based: Marcy Adelman, Eileen Blackwood, Lynne Bond, Michelle Clossick, Dani Comey, Diane Felicio, Dorothy Forsyth, Anne Ghitman, Lynn Goyette, Kristi Hannan, Betsy Hinden, Josie Juhasz, Esther Rothblum, and Karen Wasserman. The author may be reached by post at the University of Vermont, C-150 Living & Learning Center, 633 Main St., Burlington, VT 05405, or by e-mail at Jacqueline.Weinstock@uvm.edu.

tion era, moved through young adulthood during the rise of the current feminist and gay liberation movements, and subsequently entered into midlife in the wake of the changes brought about by these movements. These combined historical and developmental contexts shaped midlife lesbians' conceptions and experiences of friendships. My aim for this chapter is to turn the spotlight on conceptions and experiences of friendship among some white, middle-class, midlife lesbians in the United States today and to consider their implications for lesbians' middle and late adulthood. In particular, I present and examine three diverse patterns of "friends as family": (a) friends as substitute family members; (b) friends as a challenge to the core family structure; and (c) friends as in-laws.

Much of the available literature on lesbians in general and lesbians' friendships in particular has concentrated on the period of young adulthood. When friendships have been examined, the focus has been directed to the impact of friendships on lesbians' lover relationships. Little attention has been paid to examining the realities and possibilities of lesbians' friendships at midlife. Yet this phase of life may bring with it particular challenges to and perspectives on friends, family, and friends as family. Directing the spotlight onto lesbians' friendships at midlife may contribute to the construction of new frameworks for thinking about and working with lesbians, their friends, and their families that may better recognize and honor the many varied, overlapping, and often central roles that both friends and family may play in midlife lesbians' lives.

In constructing the three conceptions of "friends as family" outlined in this chapter, I have drawn upon a combination of resources, including theoretical analyses, empirical research, published personal reflections, and a small sample of interviews with self-identified lesbians in or nearing midlife, conducted as part of a larger study of the friendships of lesbians, gay men, bisexual women and men, and transgender persons (LGBTs). All of these sources draw upon and most accurately reflect the experiences of young adult, white, middle-class lesbians in the United States who are publicly associated, at least to some extent, with LGBT cultural or political events and/or feminist movements. My own particular circumstances also reflect these experiences.

The patterns of friendship presented in this article and their presence in midlife lesbians' lives today clearly reflect a select population and a particular intersection of historical time and cohort. The stories of friendship focused upon in this article are also most reflective of a particular pattern of lesbian life, where identification as a lesbian occurs in the transition to adulthood, without prior long-term heterosexual involvement or children from such involvement; the young adult years are marked by engagement in lesbian community and multiple lesbian relationships; and as the era of young adulthood ends and midlife begins, issues arise related to the establishment and maintenance of a long-term committed relationship and the decision to raise children. By focusing on this one pattern of lesbian life, individual differences in relationship and family circumstance, coming-out histories, and the meanings attached to claiming a lesbian sexual identity are, along with race, ethnicity, socioeconomic backgrounds, gender identities, and physical appearance and abilities, of necessity glossed over. Yet such differences likely impact conceptions and constructions of lesbians' friendships. The patterns described in this article are offered as a beginning for more closely considering just how some lesbians at midlife today from one particular background may conceptualize and experience friendships.

LESBIANS AT MIDLIFE

To understand midlife lesbians' friendships, it is important to first consider midlife itself as experienced by lesbians. Although more and more heterosexual women may be choosing to remain child-free, the midlife structure for white heterosexual women typically has been organized around reproduction and child-rearing; these organizational structures continue to dominate both the lives and the societal images of women at midlife (Gergen, 1990; Levinson, 1996). Yet these structures are less pervasive as organizing frameworks for lesbians (Kirkpatrick, 1989). This is not to say that midlife lesbians are not engaged in reproduction and child-rearing. Indeed, some are raising children borne in the context of relationships with men during young adulthood. Furthermore, midlife as well as young adult lesbians today are increasingly choosing to have and raise children as out lesbians—and typically with life partners (for more on lesbians as parents and lesbian families, see, e.g., Demo & Allen, 1996; Laird, 1993, 1999; Patterson, 1995; Slater, 1995). But lesbian culture does not itself center on these activities. While the culture is adapting to incorporate these realities of lesbians' lives, that culture also includes attention to political activism, lesbian community, and lesbian friendships. Indeed, as Lewin (1996) argues, lesbians often seek to consciously highlight in their commitment ceremonies their resistance as well as accommodation to marriage and norms of heterosexuality. While children are becoming more a part of lesbians' lives through a diversity of pathways and across a wide range of ages, there remains to date great variability in the extent to which children are present in the lives of midlife and late-life lesbians, and in the roles that they play.

There is also variability among lesbians with regard to participation in long-term romantic partner relationships. Yet such a relationship—be it real or desired—may be the most common organizing structure for midlife and late-life lesbians today. Rothblum, Mintz, Cowan, and Haller (1995) point out that lesbians at midlife typically are in—or are striving for—long-term partnerships. It seems that many, if not most, adult lesbians anticipate growing old with a partner (Bell & Weinberg, 1978; Blumstein & Schwartz, 1983; Bryant & Demian, 1994; Kurdek, 1995; Loulan, 1991; Peplau, 1993; Saghir & Robins, 1973; Savin-Williams, 1995; Slater, 1995; Tully, 1989; see Gabbay & Wahler, 2002, for a review). As Rose (1996) argues, the dominant cultural script for lesbians is the romance script—lesbians move through courtship toward the goal of establishing a permanent relationship. The predominant script for lesbians, as for heterosexual women, appears to be a couple relationship that continues as a long-term partnership. The extent to which alternative patterns of relationships are accepted and respected varies across lesbian communities and friendship groups. Many who study and theorize about lesbians' families note that alternative family forms do exist; still, most if not all of their attention is on those families comprising a monogamous partner and now, increasingly, children.

Midlife may be a particularly significant time for lesbians' family development in a context of heterosexism. Heterosexism alters lesbians' individual and family life cycles (see, e.g., Kimmel & Sang, 1995; Kurdek, 1995; Reid, 1995; Slater, 1995; Slater & Mencher, 1991), not only by limiting lesbians' rights to raise children, but also by not recognizing, validating, and supporting lesbian romantic partnerships and long-term commitments. At midlife, however, lesbian identity may have more room to maneuver and lesbians' lovers may gain a different status (Loulan, 1991). There may be a decrease in efforts on the part of parents to change a child in midlife compared to young adulthood; there may also be more acceptance of a child's sexuality as parents recognize, finally, that it is not just a phase (Rothblum et al., 1995). Because of ageism, there is also a decreased likelihood that people will look at a midlife or late-life lesbian couple and think about sex. This, combined with the years of familiarity one's family of origin may have with a lesbian's long-term partner, may make the relationship more acceptable and accepted. Alternatively, for those lesbians beginning a new relationship at midlife, Loulan (1991) suggests that families of origin simply may be happy to see that their daughter is no longer alone. In other words, at midlife, one's family of origin may be more used to and accepting of the idea of their daughter as a lesbian. The introduction of children also may bring families of origin back into the picture and may even help to reduce their heterosexism (see Patterson, 1996; see also Slater, 1995).

Renewed or strengthened connections with families of origin may be validating for lesbians, particularly those who are engaged in partner relationships and parenting activities that reflect closely the norms of these families of origin (besides the difference in sexual identities). But such connections—and the expectations that may go with them— may be problematic for midlife and late-life lesbians who bring different values and structures to their relationships and who are seeking to create alternative family forms that do not easily fit into the family forms their families of origin wish to validate. Similarly, for lesbians who share many values with their families of origin, it may still be that to remain in or be able to return to these families, lesbians have to follow certain rules and patterns of behavior that may not be good for their individual health and development, nor for their partner relationships and families of creation (Brown, 1995; see also Brosnan, 1996). For example, Brown (1995) notes that some lesbians may be asked to remain closeted in their families of origin, at least to some members; or perhaps they may be known as lesbians and thus expected to be grateful for being allowed to continue to participate in family events with their partners—as long as they are not affectionate in front of anyone. Judy MacLean (1995, p. 23) reflects the question Brown (1995) is raising when she says, "As a lesbian, I've been so busy trying to get *into* the family circle that I forgot to ask whether I would be interested in what goes on inside it." There may be a great tradeoff with respect to emotional health and validation of their own families of creation for some lesbians who seek to remain in—or return to—their families of origin; there also may be a great tradeoff with respect to time and energy for friendships—a point further explored shortly. These tensions may become more evident—and more in need of re-examination—at midlife.

For those lesbians who reach midlife after living as lesbians through young adulthood, the process of self-development may be more continual than for heterosexual women at midlife who have followed a traditional life course. It may also involve a wider range of options for healthy, successful adulthood and aging. While many developmental theories and the larger society posit marriage and parenting as the markers of true adulthood or at least well-being (Demo & Allen, 1996; Smolak, 1993), lesbians at midlife are likely to have discovered for themselves their own ways of entering into and moving through adulthood that may or may not include—and are less likely to be restricted only to—the roles of partner and parent. Indeed, among current LGBTs in late adulthood, available research evidence suggests that they are more likely than their heterosexual age-peers to live alone (see, e.g., Cahill, South, & Spade, 2000).

In addition to heterosexist models of development, lesbians at and beyond midlife also face, along with heterosexual and bisexual women, the stigma of aging that predominates in an ageist society. This stigma may be more shocking to white heterosexuals than to white lesbians, lesbians of color, and heterosexual women of color, because the latter groups are more likely to have had to deal with and adjust to societal stigma by the time they reach midlife. Furthermore, growing older for lesbians may provide greater freedom for being out as lesbians, less pressure to date men, and/or less of a need to live a double life (Kirkpatrick, 1989; Loulan, 1991). Indeed, lesbians at midlife and beyond may find themselves free of the pressures to marry and to parent—either because others have stopped putting on the pressure or because they have come to recognize that these are not the only markers for healthy adulthood. On the other hand, there may be added concerns that health care providers and retirement options may be inadequate to meet the needs of lesbians (see, e.g., Butler, 2002a; Cahill et al., 2000; Gabbay & Wahler, 2002; Tully, 1989). This may be of particular concern to lesbians who have not raised children, who are not in partner relationships, and/or who have not remained a part of their families of origin. But it also may, for these women, highlight and reinforce the importance of friendships.

Lesbians enter and move through midlife in a diversity of contexts. Some may be in long-term partnerships, others may be newly partnered or newly single, and still others may choose to be single. Among these, some may have children from prior heterosexual relationships, from a currently ongoing lesbian relationship, or from a prior lesbian relationship that is ongoing as friends and coparents. Furthermore, relationships with families of origin may have been severed for years, while for others, relationships may be ongoing but there is either no knowledge or limited acceptance of the lesbian's identity or family of creation. Additionally, some lesbians at midlife may find themselves drawn back to the family of origin because of the needs of aging parents or their desires to connect with their nieces and nephews; similarly, families of origin may find themselves seeking to reconnect or improve connections with their lesbian family members for the same reasons. Along with the historical changes described earlier in this paper, each of these contexts shapes the midlife experience in particular ways. Each also shapes the manner in which friendships at midlife are imagined and conducted.

LESBIANS' FRIENDSHIPS

Only a very few researchers have concentrated their research attention on examining lesbians' experiences in and perspectives on friendships (see, e.g., Hall & Rose, 1996; Nardi & Sherrod, 1994; O'Boyle & Thomas, 1996; Stanley, 1996; see also Weinstock, 1998, for a review). Relatively speaking, there is more published theorizing and personal reflections (see, e.g., Card, 1995; Daly, 1996; Hoagland, 1988, 1992; Kitzinger, 1996; Kitzinger & Perkins, 1993; Raymond, 1986, 1990; Weinstock & Rothblum, 1996a, 1996b). Supplementing the limited availability of direct, explicit research and reflection upon lesbians' friendships, much of what we know about lesbians' friendships has been gleaned from studies focused on other issues related to their experiences—for example, lesbians' experiences with partners, families of origin, and children (see, e.g., Hetrick & Martin, 1987; Kurdek, 1988, 1995; Kurdek & Schmitt, 1987; Lewin, 1993); lesbians' and bisexual women's attitudes toward bisexuality and bisexual women (Rust, 1995); historical examinations of various lesbian communities (see, e.g., Faderman, 1991; Kennedy & Davis; 1993); and examinations of lesbians' mental, emotional, and social supports (see, e.g., D'Augelli, 1989b; D'Augelli, Collins, & Hart, 1987). Furthermore, the focus of available research and theorizing about lesbians' lives in general and lesbians' friendships in particular has typically been on young adult women with race, education, and economic privilege who self-identify as lesbians and who are participants in established gay and lesbian activities and organizations. Most studies have also been based on relatively small samples.

One theme that has received attention is *sexual tensions in lesbians' friendships*; while sometimes explored from a political perspective—the role of sex in friendships might be examined, as Esther Rothblum does (e.g., Rothblum, 1994, 2000; see also Diamond, 2002), in a manner that seeks to expand or alter the meaning of friends and lovers, sex and sexual activity—oftentimes such issues involve consideration of lesbians' friendships as they may impact upon lesbians' lover relationships. For example, friendships as precursors to lover relationships and/or as alternatives to such relationships have been considered (e.g., Rose, 1996; Rose & Zand, 2002; Rothblum & Brehony, 1993; Vetere, 1982). But more often, attention has been paid to the role of friends as validators and supports for lesbian couple relationships or, conversely, as threats to or possible distractions from the demands (e.g., time and attention) and/or difficulties of such relationships (see, e.g., Clunis & Greene, 1988; Kurdek, 1988; Slater, 1994; Stanley, 1996). The tendencies for many lesbians to consider their lovers to be their best friends and to remain friends with ex-lovers also have been frequently highlighted (e.g., Clunis & Greene, 1988; Peplau, 1993; Shumsky, 1996; Weinstock, in press) and occasionally researched (e.g., Becker, 1988; Stanley, 1996). Some attention has been paid as well to the presence and qualities of lesbians' friendships with heterosexual and bisexual women (see e.g., O'Boyle & Thomas, 1996; Palladino & Stephenson, 1990; Rust, 1995; Weinstock & Bond, 2002).

By far, as with heterosexual friendships, the theme that has received the greatest empirical attention has been that of *describing* lesbians' friendships—particularly with whom lesbians are friends—and *identifying* the roles friends play in supporting lesbians' individual health and development (see, e.g., Bradford, Ryan, & Rothblum, 1994; D'Augelli & Hart, 1987; Grana, 1989; Kurdek & Schmitt, 1987). Lesbians, like their heterosexual counterparts (see, e.g., Blieszner & Adams, 1992; O'Connor, 1992), tend to be friends with similar others on a multiplicity of dimensions, including race, age, sex, socioeconomic class, current relationship circumstance, and sexuality (see Weinstock, 1998, for a review). That is, while there are exceptions, lesbians tend to be friends with other lesbians like themselves (see, e.g., D'Augelli, 1989a; Rust, 1995).

As for the roles friends play in lesbians' lives, most research has concentrated on exploring the roles of friends in fostering lesbians' psychosocial and social well-being. Much less attention has been paid to friends' roles in fostering the development of lesbian communities, feminist alliances, or other political actions. Drawing upon what has been studied, it does appear that friendships for lesbians are typically positive sources of both support and satisfaction. They also appear to play an important role in lesbians' positive experiences of themselves as lesbians and to be important in the process of lesbians' claiming and sustaining a positive lesbian identity and a sense of belonging (see, e.g., D'Augelli, 1989a; D'Augelli & Hart, 1987; D'Augelli et al., 1987; Stanley, 1996; see Weinstock, 1998, for a review).

FRIENDS AS FAMILY

In the 1970s, a time when the modern lesbian, gay, bisexual, and transgender movements were emerging in the United States, LGBT people were defined—and oftentimes came to define themselves—as outside the family, indeed, antithetical to family. LGBT people were viewed as uninterested in and incapable of family relationships. While privately, LGBT people formed their own families, these were typically hidden from public view, as were LGBT identities themselves. But the last few decades have evidenced a rise in public attention to families by LGBT persons who began to claim their rights to families of creation in part by using the language of "family" in general and "families of choice," "friends as family," or "family/friend" in particular to highlight the existence and importance of families to LGBT people. The use of this language helped to shift both private and public images of LGBT persons as somehow separate from families. Indeed, the act of naming family as composed of chosen members—including friends—was a powerful personal and political strategy for LGBT persons (Weston, 1991/1997; see also Nardi, 1992; Shumsky, 1996; Weeks, Heaphy, & Donovan, 2001). Today, these phrases are familiar; a diversity of researchers, theorists, and social service providers have noted the tendency for LGBT persons to rely upon their friends in ways that heterosexuals typically rely upon traditional family members (see, e.g., de Vries & Hoctel, in press; Friend, 1989; Nardi, 1992, 1999; Shumsky, 1996; Weeks et al., 2001; Weston, 1991/1997). For example, Nardi (1992) noted that lesbians' and gay men's friends are a form of family, and Kimmel (1992, p. 38) identified three roles that gay men and lesbians can play in families: (a) long-term partners; (b) caretakers, financial supporters, and other special roles in families of origin, due to their presumably "single" status and/or lesser likelihood of being a part of a traditional family of creation; and (c) members of "self-created networks of friends, significant others, and selected biological family members that provide mutual support of various kinds, as family systems might do." Similarly, several writers (e.g., Kus, 1991; Laird, 1993; Nardi, 1982; Shernoff, 1984; Shumsky, 1996; Weston, 1991/1997) have argued that therapists, theorists, and/or researchers ought to expand the traditional meaning of "family" to include nontraditional important others. That is, these authors argue, in the course of theorizing, research, therapy, and other work with lesbian and gay clients, that it is important to include current friendship families.

Little is known, however, about the extent of—and reasons for—conceptualizing and creating friends as family among individual LGBT persons today. The construct itself may have developed among LGBT people in response to their anticipated and/or real exclusion from their families of origin (see Weston, 1991/1997, 1996; see also Nardi, 1999), as well as limited legitimization and support for families of creation with partners and children (see Patterson & Redding, 1996). But most of the theorizing and research on lesbians' friends and families have focused on young adulthood and on previous historical contexts. In the remainder of this chapter, I consider lesbians' friendships at midlife today, with particular attention to the ways that historical context and developmental period may interact in the construction and prevalence of one of three conceptualizations of friends as family.

LESBIANS' FRIENDS AT MIDLIFE

Given the limited attention paid to date to midlife lesbians and to lesbians' friendships in general, it is not surprising that research on and theorizing about lesbians' friendships at midlife also are quite limited. Drawing upon what is available, including published personal reflections and the small sample of interviews I have conducted as part of my ongoing study of midlife lesbians' friendships, it does appear that friendships play an important role in the lives of midlife lesbians today. In an exploratory study by Tully (1989) of a sample comprising mostly white, professional, midlife lesbians, respondents reported high involvement with friendship networks; they also noted that women friends were especially likely to provide caregiving support: "women relatives (n = 38, 52%), and more specifically, women friends (n = 65, 89%), were identified as the ones from whom these midlife lesbians sought and received the most support" (Tully, 1989, pp. 96–97). These women also reported that they turned first to their lovers or emotionally close women friends for caregiving, and that emotional support and personal care from other women as well as ongoing companionship from other women—especially from lesbians their own age—were "vitally necessary" (p. 97). In addition, Kirkpatrick suggests that the high value lesbians place on intimacy "fuels and helps maintain the supportive network of friendships characteristic of many older lesbians" (quoted in Kirkpatrick, 1989, p. 141). Furthermore, in their review of midlife lesbians' relationships, Kimmel and Sang (1995, p. 197) note that both single midlife women and those who are partnered "tended to derive support and a sense of connection from friends, family, and the lesbian community." They also tended to spend their social time with and receive support from other lesbians their own age—including lovers, ex-lovers, and friends—or to engage in mixed lesbian and gay activities (see, e.g., Bradford & Ryan, 1988, 1991; Sang, 1991). Strikingly, in Sang's (1991) questionnaire study of 110 midlife lesbians, 38% of the respondents noted that they derived both meaning and satisfaction from their friendships, 47% from their intimate relationships, and 12% from their children. While there were additional categories of responses, other family relationships were not identified.

The tendency for lesbians to maintain ties—and often close friendship ties—with ex-lovers as well as the larger lesbian community has been frequently noted (see, e.g., Becker, 1988; Kirkpatrick, 1989; Rothblum et al., 1995; Shumsky, 1996). Rothblum et al. (1995, p. 68) note that midlife may bring with it "a renewed sense of the importance of friends." This may be particularly true among those lesbians who do not have the support of their families of origin and those who currently have or anticipate an increased need for caregiving support because of their physical health; because of heterosexism, lesbians may not anticipate finding sufficient support from formal caregiving service systems (see, e.g., Bradford & Ryan, 1991; Butler, 2002a; Cahill et al., 2000; Gabbay & Wahler, 2002; Pred, 1986/1996; Tully, 1989). Similarly, Kirkpatrick (1989, p. 141), reflecting on lesbians in middle adulthood, noted that "lesbians tend to have a close network of friends which may substitute for estranged family and kin." Close friendship ties may be especially likely when lesbians are not out to their families of origin or when these families react negatively to their daughters' lesbian identity (Lipman, 1986). The importance of friendship networks frequently has been identified as one consequence of heterosexism (see, e.g., Butler, 2002b; Kimmel, 1992; Kurdek & Schmitt, 1987; Lipman, 1986; Raphael & Robinson, 1984). Indeed, the first meaning of friends as family, described next, closely reflects this context of heterosexism.

Friends as Substitute Family Members

Many lesbians in midlife today came out in a context in which lesbianism was constructed as a deviant identity and being a lesbian meant that one would not be accepted in one's family of origin nor likely be supported in forming long-term romantic partnerships or relationships with children. In such a context, friendships might be expected to hold tremendous importance. Indeed, friends may have been the only family some of the lesbians of this era were able to form and sustain. A diversity of individual lesbians, empirical researchers, theorists, and social service providers who work with lesbians (see, e.g., Kirkpatrick, 1989; Kurdek, 1988; Weston, 1991/1997) have emphasized the role of friends as substitute family members. Consider, for example, the conclusion offered by Nardi and Sherrod, after conducting their questionnaire study of lesbians' and gay men's friendships; they wrote: "friends provide gay people with an identity and a source of social support that are not often available in a heterosexual, sometimes hostile culture" (Nardi & Sherrod, 1994, p. 197; see also Nardi, 1999). In an earlier work, Nardi (1982) argued that one way to conceptualize lesbian and gay "families" is as an extended family of close gay friends. Nardi also noted the likelihood of such a family developing as a consequence of being gay in a heterosexual world. This actually leads gay men and lesbians to form a network of close gay and lesbian friends; it is these friends who help the gay or lesbian person develop and maintain a positive gay or lesbian identity. Thus, in contrast to a network of close heterosexual friends, the gay network of friends/family

arises out of a need to find role models and identity in an oppressive society. The heterosexual friendship group for heterosexuals may be close and important, but it occurs as an option in the context of a heterosexually dominant society. However, the gay person must create, out of necessity, a meaningful friendship group to cope with threats to identity and self-esteem in a world of heterosexual work situations, traditional family systems, and stereotyped media images. (Nardi, 1982, p. 86)

Carol, a white lesbian in her 50s whom I interviewed, reflected a similar theme when she said: "I think friendships are particularly important in the lesbian and gay community because I think oftentimes families do reject [us]. Or they may not; they verbally say they accept, [but] there is a lot of tension. And so I think extended family is particularly important in the lesbian and gay community." Asked what she means by "extended family," she goes on: "I mean just really close friends who can be really supportive and almost be as family members, as blood relatives would be in situations of crisis and whatever. I think it's particularly important in our community to have those friendships."

Another white lesbian, Rosemary, in her early 40s, explicitly notes the replacement role friends play as family because of not being as secure in her family of origin:

"You know, if I was to say who my best friends are right now, it would be my partner, it would be my ex-partner. I mean, if I had to categorize friends, those are my best friends in the whole wide world, and they know more about me than anybody else knows about me. So friendships have played an important part in my life, and friends are important to me. And more important to me now, because of family relationships not being as solid as they have been in the past. So kind of doing what I, I guess we call in the gay, lesbian, bisexual, transgender community, the family of choice versus the family of origin."

The approach reflected in these comments and much of the research, theoretical, and autobiographical literature, involves viewing friends from the perspective of substitute family members—replacements for the loss of access to or support from traditional families of origin and/or limited opportunities and supports for creating families with partners and children. While it is certainly a political act for lesbians to claim and create families of their own, whatever the underlying motivation or need, the conceptualization of "friends as family" just described appears to emerge from and reflect the limited support lesbians may receive from family and the limited support they anticipate receiving from social service providers, and thus their greater need for friends to fulfill traditional family functions (e.g., Cahill et al., 2000; D'Augelli, 1989b; D'Augelli et al., 1987; Gabbay & Wahler,

2002; Grana, 1989; Weston, 1991/1997). This construction of friends as family may have emerged from and most closely reflects the prior, pre–gay liberation, pre–feminist historical era, when most if not all lesbians had to be closeted and lesbians themselves were conceptualized as unacceptable members of families of origin as well as families of creation with partners and children. It also may most closely reflect the developmental time period that involves initial separation from family of origin, entry into adulthood, and the claiming of a lesbian identity. Yet this pattern has relevance for midlife and late-life lesbians today, particularly those who continue to be rejected by or isolated from their families of origin and extended family members who do not know, understand, or accept them as lesbians, and/or those who are not partnered and raising children. Even as these lesbians may continue or renew their connections with their families of origin, their friendships and, for those who are partnered, their partners, may be what sustains them and functions like family in their day-to-day lives.

Indeed, among those midlife and late-life lesbians with partners, friends may be specifically experienced as substitute extended family members, while one's partner is viewed and experienced as immediate family. For some lesbians at midlife, making such a distinction may be particularly important as a means of sustaining and supporting their romantic partner relationship. For example, Carol, introduced earlier, says, when asked who her closest friend is:

> "Beth [her partner] is my closest friend. . . . I suppose that may not always be true for people, but certainly without question she is my dearest and closest friend, in addition to being my partner. All of those things that I mentioned that identify close friends are double pluses for her. It would be very hard for me to name anybody that even came close. . . . I think for me it's probably a matter of degree. The degree to which I have those things with Beth, I don't think I could ever have with anybody else. Some of those things are present with other people. I think I have some really fine friends who are very caring, who are good listeners, who have the same kinds of feelings that I do about a number of issues, who like some of the same kinds of things that I do, but it's a matter of degree I think. I just really don't feel that I have another friend that even comes close."

Carol also talks about and distinguishes between friendships formed as a couple and friendships that one member of a couple forms with a single woman. The latter, she notes, might be weird; it is better to have couple friends because, she says:

" . . . if one of the people starts to form a strong friendship with somebody outside of the relationship, if that strong friendship is formed with somebody who's free and single, then there's doubt on the partner's part about what that relationship really is. Whereas if the two of you are forming a relationship with two other people who have a stable relationship, then there is no jealousy, no concern about what is really going on here. So sure, I think it's easier for a couple to form a relationship with another couple."

Similarly, Fran, another white woman in her 40s whom I interviewed, noted that after having an affair with one of her friends, at a time when she and her long-term partner were having problems, she is more careful about the friendships she develops. She doesn't want to become attracted to a friend again, or have a friend attracted to her because, as she puts it, "my relationship with Andrea [partner] is too important to me to allow anything to interfere with that." Like Carol, she considers her partner to be her best friend as well as her partner. Other friends are clearly important, but they function more as substitutes for extended family members than as immediate family. And there is a clear line between partner/best friend and other friends. Similarly, both Fran and Carol remain in touch with their ex-lovers, and some of these are friends, but they are not close friends.

Friends as a Challenge to the Core Structure of the Family

In the above conceptualization of friends as family, the emphasis is on choosing and developing family relationships with friends, especially as substitutes for extended family members. The structure or concept of the family itself is not identified as problematic. In contrast, some lesbian activists, researchers, and theorists have focused on friends as family specifically as a challenge to the nuclear structure of the family (see, e.g., Brosnan, 1996; Jo, 1996). There are several challenges that friends might pose to the family structure; the one I focus on here involves a challenge to the centering of one's partner in favor of the creation of families based on shared political as well as personal commitments to other lesbians. This challenge frequently involves—or implies—the placement of lesbians' friendships rather than lesbians' lover relationships at the center of family life. "Friends as family," from this perspective, represents a challenge to the organizing structure of the modern Euro-American traditional nuclear family, based as it is on a primary, sexual, and romantic partnership between two adults.

Some theorists and activists who pose this challenge actually reject the phrasing of "friends as family" because they see it as continuing to center and privilege both the family and heterosexuality (see, e.g., Jo, 1996; Weston, 1991/1997; see Weinstock, 1998, for a review). By naming family, it keeps our attention on family, and it also treats family as something to which friends ought to aspire. In contrast, these writers are more interested in centering friends and claiming the specialness and importance of friends—not as family—but as friends. They focus on identifying and considering the personal and political challenges that arise when friendships are placed at the center of lesbians' lives (e.g., Card, 1995; Kitzinger, 1996; Kitzinger & Perkins, 1993; Strega, 1996). At the same time, there is a push to honor our friendships by developing our own terminology to describe our distinct experiences in these relationships (see, e.g., Jo, 1996; Weston, 1991/1997). While these women reject the phrase *friends as family*, they share with those who rely upon it the goal of building lesbian friendships and community and breaking away from the automatic privileging of lover and family relationships over friendships.

This pattern of friendship seems to most closely reflect the era of lesbian feminism, when lesbians' allegiances were more likely to other lesbians and to lesbian community, and not (yet) to a specific partner and the raising of children, and there were limited expectations for relationship longevity. This pattern also may reflect the developmental period of young adulthood, especially the 20s. Still, it is a pattern that continues in the lives of some lesbians today (see, e.g., Jo, 1996; Strega, 1996) who seek to "create our own culture of love and closeness and commitment" (Jo, 1996, p. 290) and who view lesbian friendships as "the building blocks of lesbian communities and politics" (Kitzinger, 1996, p. 298; see also Card, 1995). It also exists among some lesbians who place equal—or greater—value on friendships than on couple relationships (see Rose, 1996; Weinstock & Rothblum, 1996a). For example, Elizabeth, a white lesbian in her 30s in a fairly new romantic relationship, had this to say: "I still see my primary support system as my friendship network, more so than my relationship." When asked if she felt that that would change over time if the relationship continued, she said, "I think they will probably become equal, I would hope so, but I don't see it superseding my relationships with my friends." Furthermore, when asked what her ideal for herself was around family, she said: "I've got a T-shirt somewhere that says, you know, 'a family is a circle of friends that loves you.' I love that. And I guess by and large that's on-target for me. "

It is important to note that Elizabeth is not currently in a committed, long-term partner relationship, nor has she yet entered midlife. It is possible that she will sustain her commitment to the centrality of friendships even as she enters midlife and even in the context of a long-term partner relationship. Yet it is also possible that, as both contexts change, Elizabeth may find herself, like other midlife lesbians, prioritizing her romantic partnership. Indeed, Elizabeth anticipates this occurrence when she continues to describe her ideal for herself around family in the following manner:

I would like to have a significant relationship, a long-term relationship with someone, which would, in my mind, sort of constitute my real, sort of primary family. And sort of see very closely around that long-term friends with whom I've got a lot of shared history and connection and that I would share holidays and significant times and events with. And some of those people might be blood relationships or family of origin, or whatever we want to call those, and some of those are, are friends of real significance and depth and substance.

For Elizabeth, then, friends are currently her primary supports, and she anticipates they will continue to be central. Yet when envisioning a significant, long-term relationship, she continues to view friends as very close and significant, but she also appears to view them as "very closely around" the partner relationship but not exactly part of her "real, sort of primary family." With this statement, Elizabeth begins to appear not to be challenging the centrality of lover relationships as much as seeking to sustain their centrality and the centrality of her friendships; this idea begins to reflect a third way of thinking about "friends as family," described shortly.

Kath Weston (1991/1997), in a participant observation and in-depth interview study with lesbians and gay men, also identified similar conceptions of "families we choose" (so did Nardi, 1999, with respect to gay men). Most of her interviewees spoke of building families of friends as a political challenge to the family as we know it, especially the centrality and privileging of biological ties and heterosexuality. A small minority of her sample reflected the perspective that friends as family was really a substitute for unavailable family forms, an alternative born of oppression rather than a revolutionary challenge to the status quo. For these individuals, like the "friends as substitute family" pattern already described, lesbians and gay men "choose" and "create" families of friends not because they seek to challenge the status quo but because the status quo has historically denied and/or limited their family possibilities (see also Weston, 1996). In a context of oppression, this is both a political and a personal feat.

Friends as In-Laws—Negotiating a Place in Between Friends and Lovers

The question arises: What will become of the notion of "friends as family" as lesbians are no longer viewed as or view themselves as antithetical to family, and as "family" issues are claimed as part of lesbians' political and personal agendas? Today, young adult and mid-life lesbians are increasingly having and coparenting children with romantic partners, domestic partnerships and other supports for part-ner relationships are becoming more available, and legal marriage appears a possibility. While these movements into the mainstream indicate progress, it is important to consider the potential losses as well. Specifically, as more and more lesbians construct families of procreation and are less marginalized by their families of origin and society as a whole, what might happen to lesbians' ways of conceptual-izing families and friendships? Will there be less of an impetus for lesbians to build lesbian friendship families and communities?

It does appear that there is, now, less of a need for friends to serve as substitutes for families, and that there is also less of a political push by lesbians in general to develop alternative family forms based on friendships rather than romantic partnerships. However, friends them-selves continue to hold great value (see, e.g., Shumsky, 1996; Wein-stock, 1998). This valuation of friendships may be reflected in a third way of conceptualizing friends as family that does not appear to be articulated in the literature to date. Indeed, it may be more observable now that midlife lesbians are increasingly and publicly in romantic partner relationships and/or raising children, and are seeking to negoti-ate their own ways of balancing the multiple demands, responsibilities, and desires of this time period. Specifically, some lesbians who speak of their friends as family appear to be seeking to negotiate a place in between a challenge to the core, central adult relationship that typi-cally organizes families—the lover relationship—and the temporary substitute value of friends when this relationship and/or supportive family of origin relationships are unavailable. These lesbians appear to view a partner/lover relationship as "primary," yet at the same time they wish to sustain their intimate and in some ways also primary friendships. Indeed, it appears that "friends as family" may be a means for lesbians at and beyond midlife to negotiate having both a partner and close friends with whom one is very intimate. It may be a means by which midlife and late-life lesbians negotiate the feelings of jealousy, insecurity, and the sense of being left out that both a lover and close friends may feel. It may be a means as well for lesbians to negotiate sexual feelings, attractions, and tensions among friends and lovers. Indeed, "friends as family" may be a strategy that enables lesbians to negotiate sexual tensions in friendships and, more broadly, to negoti-ate multiple, close, intimate relationships—only one of which is likely to be genitally sexual, but all of which are passionately experienced.

In explaining this way of viewing "friends as family," it is important to mention the tendency, noted in the literature and among my small sample, for lesbians with partners to view these partners as their closest friends and for those who do not currently have but who desire partners to envision these partners being their closest friends. Furthermore, there is a tendency for lesbians to wish to remain friends with their ex-lovers (see, e.g., Becker, 1988; Hite, 1987; Nardi & Sherrod, 1994; Shumsky, 1996; Slater, 1995; Stanley, 1996; Weinstock, in press; Weinstock & Rothblum, in press). Also important to mention is that a common pattern by which lesbians become lovers is through friendship (the friendship script; see Rose, 1996; Rose & Zand, 2002; see also Grammick, 1984; Vetere, 1982). For example, Fran, intro-duced earlier, noted that she and her long-term partner were friends before becoming involved in their romantic relationship, and that they remain friends. Indeed, as she put it, "Thinking of my partner not being my best friend is something that doesn't compute. . . . I wouldn't want it any other way." The course of development from friends to lovers, however, is not necessarily a clear one; these two forms of relationships are themselves intertwined for many lesbians (see, e.g., Diamond, 1997; Futcher & Hutchins, 1996; Munson, 1996; Vetere, 1982; Weinstock & Rothblum, in press).

For lesbians at midlife, there may be an increased need or desire to reexamine and reorganize the balance constructed among one's commitments, including to a lover and to friends, as well as to one's family of origin and the larger community. Most of the available literature on midlife and the transition to midlife suggests this is a time for reorganizing important aspects of one's life and the self (see, e.g., Levinson, 1978, 1996; Stewart & Gold-Steinberg, 1990), often motivated by a new awareness of one's location in the life course and one's relationship to the aging process. For some current midlife lesbians, it also may be a time of return to, as well as reconciliation with, one's family of origin. Some midlife lesbians' parents may require caretaking as they age; some siblings and parents may make renewed attempts to learn about and understand the lesbian's life and identity; and some siblings may recognize their desire for their own children to know their aunts. Additionally, some lesbians may make renewed efforts to be a part of their families of origin, and to be known and accepted as lesbians within them. And for some midlife lesbians, this may be just the time they adopt or bear children of their own, while others may be focusing on building—or changing—careers. With all these possibilities—and realities—coupled with the changing perspective often brought about by the recognition of one's midlife location itself, there may be an increased need to reconsider priorities as well as to alter or resolve long-standing patterns or issues so as to make room for new desires and life balances.

The extent to which one effects or responds to changes in the midlife structure by shifting priorities among friends, partners, families of origin, children, and careers depends on a diversity of factors. Yet the practical need for negotiating among multiple relationships at this busy time of life cannot be overstated. What I turn to now is a particular kind of balance that midlife and late-life lesbians may strike among the multiple relationships in their lives—one that seeks to find a way to center both a partner and close friends.

Rosemary, a white lesbian in her 40s, spoke during an interview I conducted with her about the struggle to negotiate her continued connection with her ex-partner, her own relationship with her partner, and her ex-partner's current lover relationship. For Rosemary, the struggle is twofold (at least). On the one hand, Rosemary has had to work with her current partner to help her partner accept and honor the relationship she has with her former partner; similarly, her ex-partner has to work with her new partner to accept their ex-lover, friendship relationship. As Rosemary put it, her ex-partner's current partner "doesn't know quite what to do with me or our relationship." She goes on:

> [My ex-lover, Helen] is still a very important part of my life, but she has a partner in her life now, and, you know, her partner is very resentful and

jealous of me and doesn't understand how we can still be in this relationship. And we understand that, but it's kind of like, you know, you get Helen, you get a package deal because you get Rosemary along. And if you get Rosemary, you get a package deal because you get Helen along with it.

And, with respect to her own current relationship, she notes that

calling my ex-partner my best friend, that was a real struggle for my present partner, not understanding that. Like, where does best friends stop and where does previous partner, you know. And we have not been sexually involved with each other at all. If you ask me if I love Helen, I love her dearly. And so, you know, it sounds like a fine line but it's a very clear line for me, very clear line for [Helen], and, and Mary, my present partner is as much my best friend, and probably more, you know.

This example does not easily fit into the two conceptualizations of friends as family described thus far and typically offered by lesbian friendship researchers, theorists, and service providers. Rosemary appears to be engaged in an effort to negotiate the centrality of friendship relationships—in this case an ex-lover friendship—in a way that keeps a "very clear line" between friend and partner and at the same time blurs the line in certain respects. Indeed, the negotiation seems to involve an effort to hold her partner as central at the same time as recognizing and holding firm to the importance and in some manner centrality of close friendships. What I suggest here is that "friends as family" may in fact be a strategy by which lesbians in committed, monogamous relationships at and beyond midlife make close, intimate friendships feel safer to their current partners, their friends' current partners, and to themselves than they might be if they remained conceptualized as friends but not family.

More broadly speaking, "friends as family" may be a strategy by which lesbians at midlife create and negotiate their own type of in-law relationships, where in-laws are friends rather than biological family. As family, these friends come with a lesbian into a new romantic relationship, and remain a part of the family over time. Furthermore, as family, those friends who were previously romantic partners or whose relationships currently involve sexual attraction need not be a threat (or as much of a threat) to partner relationships. Reliance upon the notion of family—particularly a notion of family that makes room for a special and unique place for both partners and close friends—helps to place a friend more clearly and firmly outside the realm of possible romantic interest but inside the family. And, over the continued course of a romantic partnership, it also helps each lesbian keep her friends on her own "side" of the family, at the same time as it provides added impetus to acknowledge and—with more or less success—accept the partner's friends as part of the family.

This same strategy for negotiating boundaries between friends and lovers may prove useful for a diversity of friendships—including those among single lesbians and those where there is little sexual interest but great emotional attachment, as well as friendships where both sexual and emotional interest are present. As an example, Jan, a white lesbian in her late 30s who describes herself as "approaching 40," is not currently in a partner relationship. During my interview with her, Jan noted that one of her two closest friends is someone for whom she has strong emotional feelings, and for whom she has had sexual feelings and attractions as well. She describes her current way of thinking about this friendship as "like us being sisters, in a blood sense. That, she is to me, like a sister. I mean, you know we confide in each other, we cry together, we laugh together, we do things that sisters would do and we know just about everything about each other."

Jan explains that this conception of close friends as sisters emerged from her struggle to make sense of her strong feelings for her friend, including her sexual feelings, that were not reciprocated to a similar degree. As Jan put it, conceptualizing this friend as a sister has "been helpful in separating the sexual part out in a healthy way." As sisters, she feels she will be less able and willing to view the friendship in anything other than friendship terms. At the same time, the reference to sister, to this friend as family, helps Jan to feel assured of "the depth of commitment to the relationship." As she put it, "A sister is someone who really stays there through it all. Whereas a friend can come and go, they may blow me off, you know, if they just don't have the energy, or they're just not as invested."

It is this meaning of friends as family that has not typically been attended to in the research or theoretical literature—as a strategy for negotiating undesired sexual feelings, jealousy, and possessiveness in lesbians' friendships. That this is a strategy used by some lesbians in negotiating friendships is not surprising given that the most frequently mentioned concern raised by the lesbians who participated in Jeanne Stanley's (1996, p. 53) focus group research was "the potential threat of a friend becoming romantically involved with one member of the couple." Naming friends as family may be a strategy lesbians use to sustain important friendships, including ex-lover friendships; it may ease one's own and one's partner's concerns about the closeness of these relationships at the same time as it creates a structure within which such friendships are recognized as part of one's family that comes along into any new family form. It may not be easy to negotiate these in-law relationships, but as Rosemary put it, "it's a package deal." If you get her, you get her ex-lover; that is what happens with in-laws.

To summarize, "friends as family" may reflect a strategy lesbians use to make a place at the family table for both friends and lovers, a place that recognizes the importance and centrality of both forms of relationships and that seeks to negotiate the tensions that arise or may arise between these relationship forms, or within ourselves in relation to these relationships. Sometimes, of course, these negotiations do not work, and lesbians give up or withdraw some intimacy from friendships to preserve partner relationships; at times, the reverse occurs. Yet it may be that "friends as family" is a concept that provides a framework that pushes current partners to work harder than they might like at times to find a place for their partners' close friends in their new family of creation together—just as they would do with the more typical blood in-laws. It may also be a strategy that pushes lesbians to continue to prioritize their friendships, even as they engage in raising children of their own, maintaining and building connections with members of their families of origin, and/or pursuing new interests, including careers. Indeed, this pattern may fit well into the current historical era where, rather than there being one primary alliance—typically, in the era of lesbian feminism, to lesbian identity—it seems more accurate to say that lesbians recognize multiple alliances (Stein, 1997). Some lesbians at and beyond midlife today may create friends as family as one means by which they might sustain multiple alliances—to friends as well as to partner, children, family of origin members, and/or other individual interests, including careers.

By including friends in their conceptions of families, even as they may build families with partners and children and seek to sustain ties with family of origin members, lesbians place themselves in a position to continue to challenge the definition of family, not only with respect to sex composition but also with respect to the emphasis on biological ties and "the relative weight given to friendships as well as blood relatedness" (Laird, 1993, p. 297; see also Nardi, 1992; Shumsky, 1996; Weinstock, in press; Weston, 1991/1997). With friends as a model for acceptance, respect, and appreciation—and as an option toward which they might turn for validation and support—lesbians may be more likely to demand similar treatment in their families of origin, leave such families when this treatment is not forthcoming, and create new families constructed upon these givens.

CONCLUSIONS

Lesbians today are entering into and moving through midlife and late adulthood in a historical time of increased engagement in and legitimacy for same-sex partner and parenting relationships; meanwhile fewer lesbians now meet with automatic rejection from families of origin. As a result, the time and energy available for friends may decrease and the necessity for friends to be as family may lessen. At the same time, the remembrance and continued presence of heterosexism in families of origin and the larger society, and the sense of familiarity, shared perspective, and shared experience among lesbian friends, may contribute to the continuing prioritization of lesbians' friendships among midlife and late-life lesbians. At this historical juncture, it appears that friends as family may be conceptualized by lesbians at and beyond midlife in at least the three diverse ways described in this paper. It also appears that the first two of these patterns may be in decline; the extent to which the third pattern prevails depends upon a diversity of factors, some of which are addressed next.

Research

"Friends as family" has been a phrase often heard in the daily discourse of lesbians' lives and relied upon in the writings of researchers and theorists of lesbians' lives. Yet we know very little about the intended meaning of this phrase by those lesbians who use it (for an important examination of this issue for gay men, see Nardi, 1999). It is important, then, that we attend more closely to individual lesbians' meanings of this phrase. As we study these meanings, however, it is critical that we begin to identify and study specific parameters that may influence the meanings of and possibilities for "friends as family." Current age, historical cohort, and age at time of coming out all warrant additional attention. We need as well to attend to the particular patterns of "friends as family" among lesbians in a couple relationship compared with those unintentionally or chosen single, whether they have or desire to have children, and whether and how they have sustained relationships with their families of origin. Most important, we need to take a longitudinal approach to the study of lesbians' friendships, as well as more consistently examine friendship patterns across a diversity of cohorts. It may be that the patterns of conceptualizing friends as family that I have described here are the result of movement through the adult developmental life course and a corresponding movement toward acceptance and consolidation of a positive lesbian identity. On the other hand, it may be that historical changes and adult development patterns have coincided for the cohorts of lesbians in midlife today such that for many, friends were initially experienced and constructed as substitute families in the early years of young adulthood and post–World War II. But this conception shifted to friends as a challenge to the family in the later years of young adulthood and the early years of the current feminist and lesbian liberation movements, and finally, it now reflects midlife lesbians' efforts, in the post-Stonewall, lesbian parenting boom era, to negotiate a place at the family table for friends, lovers, children, and families of origin.

In addition to examining cohort differences and developmental patterns over the course of adulthood, it is critical that we consider other aspects of lesbians' identities and experiences, such as race, class, sex, religion, and ability. What are the experiences and conceptions of friends and families across a diversity of cultural communities, and how do these influence lesbians' experiences and conceptions of friends as family? The images of friendships painted in these pages reflect most closely the experiences and perspectives of white, middle-class lesbians.

Theory, Public Policy, and Practice

When working with midlife and late-life lesbians and on issues relevant to their lives, it is important that theorists, policymakers, therapists, and other social service providers consider friendships as a legitimate central component in lesbians' lives. But in order to hear and support lesbians who view friendships as central or equal to if not more important than current partner, children, and family of origin, it may be necessary for those who work with lesbians to first consider and examine their own assumptions about the "proper" place of partner, friend, children, and family of origin and the "proper" structure and function of particular relationships (see also Shumsky, 1996; Weeks et al., 2001). Not all midlife and late-life lesbians conceptualize, experience, or desire their friendships to be central, of course, and in some cases, such a structure may not work. Yet for those who have sought and been satisfied with such life structures, support has been limited in both theory and practice. Therapists, policymakers, and theorists alike must consider the desires of lesbians themselves, as well as the origins of developmental models that prioritize marriage and family for women. Rather than impose the prioritization of partner and family over friends, it is important to look at the particular situation and goals of the lesbians involved. In other words, theorists and social service providers may need to take care not to project mainstream—and their own—models of family and friendship onto midlife and late-life lesbians, but instead recognize the possibility of alternatives and listen to and help support the development of these alternative models of friends, family, and friends as family toward which some of the lesbians with whom they work or study may be striving. At the same time, it is critical that providers and policymakers not make the assumption that LGBTs' friends will play the caregiving roles typically played by family members—and thus act as if they need not develop programs and policies to better meet the needs of aging LGBTs. In her preface to the ground-breaking report *Outing Age*, Urvashi Vaid (2000, p. v) notes that "This country's aging policies assume heterosexuality and close relationships with children and extended families to provide basic needs as we age." The salience of friendships and their centrality in lesbians' lives does not mean that aging policies need not change. What it does mean is that as we revise existing policies, we need to pay greater attention to the valuation that LGBTs may place on friends, and recognize that for some of us, friends are our families.

The current challenge, I believe, is not to enforce or value any one pattern over another, but rather to preserve for lesbians the right and freedom to choose the pattern that best reflects their personal desires and best fits within their particular life choices and structures. Those who work with lesbians can do much to ensure that these options remain both equally available and respected. We may only do so, however, if we recognize that just as a central commitment to one's family of origin leaves less room for commitment to other forms of family and to friendship, those who are centrally committed to their friendships likely have less time and energy for parenting, partnering, and families of origin. Midlife and late-life lesbians may desire and negotiate a variety of ways of balancing among these relationship forms and commitments, in addition to their careers and community involvements. Practitioners need to take care not to privilege one manner of balancing these multiple possibilities over another.

Finally, I would caution therapists and theorists alike to carefully consider just what is being offered to lesbians in their families of origin as compared to their friendships, and to examine the costs and benefits of devoting energy to each. At the very least, lesbians' friendship families, which provide a place where lesbians are accepted and respected as lesbians, ought to serve as a guide to what is possible—and acceptable—in lesbians' families of origin (see also Brown, 1995). Indeed, lesbians' conceptions and experiences of friends as family may provide a powerful model for lesbians' relationships to their families of origin as well as families of procreation: to hold these families up to the ideal of friendship, striving to build family as friends, in addition to the other way around.

REFERENCES

Becker, C. S. (1988). *Unbroken ties: Lesbian ex-lovers*. Boston: Alyson Publications.

Bell, A. P., & Weinberg, M. S. (1978). *Homosexualities: A study of diversity among men and women*. New York: Simon & Schuster.

Blieszner, R., & Adams, R. G. (1992). *Adult friendship*. Newbury Park, CA: Sage.

Blumstein, P., & Schwartz, P. (1983). *American couples*. New York: William Morrow.

Bradford, J., & Ryan, C. (1988). *The National Lesbian Health Care Survey: Final Report*. National Lesbian and Gay Health Foundation, Virginia Commonwealth University.

Bradford, J., & Ryan, C. (1991). Who we are: Health concerns of middle-aged lesbians. In B. Sang, J. Warshow, & A. J. Smith (Eds.), *Lesbians at midlife: The creative transition* (pp. 147–163). San Francisco: Spinsters Book Company.

Bradford, J., Ryan, C., & Rothblum, E. D. (1994). National Lesbian Health Care Survey: Implications for mental health care. *Journal of Consulting and Clinical Psychology, 62*, 228–242.

Brosnan, J. (1996). *Lesbians talk detonating the nuclear family*. London: Scarlett Press.

Brown, L. S. (1995). Are we family? Lesbians and families of origin. In K. Jay (Ed.), *Dyke life: From growing up to growing old. A celebration of the lesbian experience* (pp. 19–35). New York: Basic Books.

Bryant, S., & Demian (1994). Relationship characteristics of American gay and lesbian couples: Findings from a national survey. *Gay and Lesbian Social Services, 1*, 101–117.

Butler, S. S. (Ed.). (2002a). Geriatric care management with sexual minorities. *Geriatric Care Management Journal, 12*(3).

Butler, S. S. (2002b). Guest editor's message: Geriatric care management with sexual minorities. *Geriatric Care Management Journal, 12*(3), 2–3.

Cahill, S., South, K., & Spade, J. (2000). *Outing age: Public policy issues affecting gay, lesbian, bisexual and transgender elders.* Washington, DC: The Policy Institute of the National Gay and Lesbian Task Force.

Card, C. (1995). *Lesbian choices.* New York: Columbia University Press.

Clunis, D. M., & Green, G. D. (1988). *Lesbian couples: Creating healthy relationships for the '90s.* Seattle: Seal Press.

Daly, M. (1996). (Ed.). *Surface tension: Love, sex, and politics between lesbians and straight women.* New York: Simon & Schuster.

D'Augelli, A. R. (1989a). Lesbian women in a rural helping network: Exploring informal helping resources. *Women and Therapy, 8*(1/2), 119–130.

D'Augelli, A. R. (1989b). The development of a helping community for lesbians and gay men: A case study of community psychology. *Journal of Community Psychology, 17*, 18–29.

D'Augelli, A. R., Collins, C., & Hart, M. M. (1987). Social support patterns of lesbian women in a rural helping network. *Journal of Rural Community Psychology, 8*(1), 12–22.

D'Augelli, A. R., & Hart, M. M. (1987). Gay women, men, and families in rural settings: Toward the development of helping communities. *American Journal of Community Psychology, 15*, 79–93.

Demo, D. H., & Allen, K. R. (1996). Diversity within lesbian and gay families: Challenges and implications for family theory and research. *Journal of Social and Personal Relationships, 13*, 415–434.

de Vries, B., & Hoctel, P. (in press). The family-friends of older gay men and lesbians. In N. Teunis (Ed.), *Sexuality inequalities: Case studies from the field.*

Diamond, L. M. (1997, March). *Passionate friendships: Love and attachment among young lesbian, bisexual, and heterosexual women.* Invited paper presented the annual meetings of the Association for Women in Psychology, Pittsburgh, PA.

Diamond, L. M. (2002). "Having a girlfriend without knowing it": Intimate friendships among adolescent sexual-minority women. In S. M. Rose (Ed.), *Lesbian love and relationships* (pp. 5–16). Binghamton, NY: Harrington Park Press.

Faderman, L. (1991). *Odd girls and twilight lovers: A history of lesbian life in twentieth-century America.* New York: Columbia University Press.

Friend, R. A. (1989). Older lesbian and gay people: Responding to homophobia. *Marriage and Family Review, 14*, 241–263.

Futcher, J., & Hopkins, C. (1996). Heart like a wheel: A friendship in two voices. In J. S. Weinstock & E. D. Rothblum (Eds.), *Lesbian friendships: For ourselves and each other* (pp. 65–79). New York: New York University Press.

Gabbay, S. G., & Wahler, J. J. (2002). Lesbian aging: Review of a growing literature. *Journal of Gay and Lesbian Social Services, 14*(3), 1–21.

Gergen, M. M. (1990). Finished at 40: Women's development within the patriarchy. *Psychology of Women Quarterly, 14*, 471–493.

Grammick, J. (1984). Developing a lesbian identity. In T. Darty & S. Potter (Eds.), *Women identified women* (pp. 31–44). Palo Alto, CA: Mayfield.

Grana, S. J. (1989). *The friendship triangle: The relationship between expectations, experiences and satisfaction for dyadic and nondyadic heterosexual women and lesbians.* Unpublished doctoral dissertation, University of Nebraska, Lincoln, NE.

Hall, R., & Rose, S. (1996). Friendships between African-American and White lesbians. In J. S. Weinstock & E. D. Rothblum (Eds.), *Lesbians and friendship: For ourselves and each other* (pp. 165–191). New York: New York University Press.

Hetrick, E. S., & Martin, A. D. (1987). Developmental issues and their resolution for gay and lesbian adolescents. *Journal of Homosexuality, 14,* 25–43.

Hite, S. (1987). *Women in love: A cultural revolution in progress.* New York: Alfred A. Knopf.

Hoagland, S. L. (1988). *Lesbian ethics: Toward new value.* Palo Alto, CA: Institute of Lesbian Studies.

Hoagland, S. L. (1992). Introduction. In J. Penelope, *Call me lesbian: Lesbian lives, lesbian theory* (pp. xi–xvii). Freedom, CA: The Crossing Press.

Jo, B. (1996). Lesbian friendships create lesbian community. In J. S. Weinstock & E. D. Rothblum (Eds.), *Lesbian friendships: For ourselves and each other* (pp. 288–291). New York: New York University Press.

Kennedy, L. L., & Davis, M. (1993). *Boots of leather, slippers of gold: The history of a lesbian community.* New York: Routledge.

Kimmel, D. C. (1992). The families of older gay men and lesbians. *Generations, 17*(3), 37–38.

Kimmel, D. C., & Sang, B. E. (1995). Lesbians and gay men in midlife. In A. R. D'Augelli & C. J. Patterson (Eds.), *Lesbian, gay, and bisexual identities over the lifespan: Psychological perspectives* (pp. 190–214). New York: Oxford University Press.

Kirkpatrick, M. (1989). Lesbians: A different middle-age? In J. Oldham & R. Liebert (Eds.), *New psychoanalytic perspectives: The middle years* (pp. 135–148). New Haven, CT: Yale University Press.

Kitzinger, C. (1996). Toward a politics of lesbian friendship. In J. S. Weinstock & E. D. Rothblum (Eds.), *Lesbian friendships: For ourselves and each other* (pp. 295–299). New York: New York University Press.

Kitzinger, C., & Perkins, R. (1993). *Changing our minds: Lesbian feminism and psychology.* New York: New York University Press.

Kurdek, L. A. (1988). Perceived social support in gays and lesbians in cohabiting relationships. *Journal of Personality and Social Psychology, 54,* 504–509.

Kurdek, L. A. (1995). Developmental changes in relationship quality in gay and lesbian cohabiting couples. *Developmental Psychology, 31,* 86–94.

Kurdek, L. A., & Schmitt, J. P. (1987). Perceived support from family and friends in members of homosexual, married, and heterosexual cohabiting couples. *Journal of Homosexuality, 14,* 57–68.

Kus, R. J. (1991). Sobriety, friends, and gay men. *Archives of Psychiatric Nursing, 5,* 171–177.

Laird, J. (1993). Gay and lesbian families. In F. Walsh (Ed.), *Normal family processes* (2nd ed., pp. 282–328). New York: The Guilford Press.

Laird, J. (Ed.) (1999). *Lesbians and lesbian families: Reflections on theory and practice.* New York: Columbia University Press.

Levinson, D. J. (1978). *The seasons of a man's life.* New York: Ballantine Books.

Levinson, D. J. (1996). *The seasons of a woman's life.* New York: Alfred A. Knopf.

Lewin, E. (1993). *Lesbian mothers: Accounts of gender in American culture.* Ithaca, NY: Cornell University Press.

Lewin, E. (1996). "Why in the world would you want to do that?" Claiming community in lesbian commitment. In E. Lewin (Ed.), *Inventing lesbian culture in America* (pp. 105–130). Boston: Beacon Press.

Lipman, A. (1986). Homosexual relationships. *Generations: Quarterly Journal of the American Society on Aging, 10*(4), 51–54.

Loulan, J. (1991). "Now when I was your age": One perspective on how lesbian culture has influenced sexuality. In B. Sang, J. Warshow, & A. J. Smith (Eds.), *Lesbians at midlife: The creative transition* (pp. 10–18). San Francisco: Spinsters Book Company.

MacLean, J. (1995). An afternoon with my if-there-were-a-laws. In K. Jay (Ed.), *Dyke life: From growing up to growing old. A celebration of the lesbian experience* (p. 23). New York: Basic Books.

Munson, M. (1996). Celebrating wild erotic friendship: Marcia and Martha. In J. S. Weinstock & E. D. Rothblum (Eds.), *Lesbian friendships: For ourselves and each other* (pp. 125–132). New York: New York University Press.

Nardi, P. M. (1982). Alcohol treatment and the non-traditional "family" structures of gays and lesbians. *Journal of Alcohol and Drug Education, 27*(2), 83–89.

Nardi, P. M. (1992). That's what friends are for: Friends as family in the gay and lesbian community. In K. Plummer (Ed.), *Modern homosexualities: Fragments of lesbian and gay experience* (pp. 108–120). New York: Routledge.

Nardi, P. M. (1999). *Gay men's friendships: Invincible communities.* Chicago: University of Chicago Press.

Nardi, P. M., & Sherrod, D. (1994). Friendships in the lives of gay men and lesbians. *Journal of Social and Personal Relationships, 11,* 185–199.

O'Boyle, C. G., & Thomas, M. D. (1996). Friendships between lesbian and heterosexual women. In J. S. Weinstock & E. D. Rothblum (Eds.), *Lesbian friendships: For ourselves and each other* (pp. 240–248). New York: New York University Press.

O'Connor, P. (1992). *Friendships between women: A critical review.* New York: The Guilford Press.

Palladino, D., & Stephenson, Y. (1990). Perceptions of the sexual self: Their impact on relationships between lesbian and heterosexual women. *Women and Therapy, 9,* 231–253.

Patterson, C. J. (1992). Children of lesbian and gay parents. *Child Development, 63,* 1025–1042.

Patterson, C. J. (1995). Lesbian mothers, gay fathers, and their children. In A. R. D'Augelli & C. J. Patterson (Eds.), *Lesbian, gay, and bisexual identities over the lifespan: Psychological perspectives* (pp. 262–290). New York: Oxford University Press.

Patterson, C. J. (1996). Contributions of lesbian and gay parents and their children to the prevention of heterosexism. In E. D. Rothblum & L. A. Bond (Eds.),

Preventing heterosexism and homophobia (pp. 184–201). Thousand Oaks, CA: Sage.

Patterson, C. J., & Redding, R. E. (1996). Lesbian and gay families with children: Implications of social service research for policy. *Journal of Social Issues, 52,* 29–50.

Peplau, L. A. (1993). Lesbian and gay relationships. In L. D. Garnets & D. C. Kimmel (Eds.), *Psychological perspectives on lesbian and gay male experiences* (pp. 395–419). New York: Columbia University Press.

Pred, E. (1986/1996). Healing group. In M. Adelman (Ed.), *Lesbian passages: True stories told by women over 40* (pp. 51–57). Los Angeles: Alyson Publications.

Raphael, S., & Robinson, M. (1984). The older lesbian: Love relationships and friendship patterns. In T. Darty & S. Potter (Eds.), *Women-identified women* (pp. 67–82). Palo Alto, CA: Mayfield.

Raymond, J. G. (1986). *A passion for friends: Towards a philosophy of female affection.* Boston: Beacon Press.

Raymond, J. G. (1990). Not a sentimental journey: Women's friendships. In D. Leidholdt & J. G. Raymond (Eds.), *The sexual liberals and the attack on feminism* (pp. 222–226). London: Pergamon.

Reid, J. D. (1995). Development in late life: Older lesbian and gay lives. In A. R. D'Augelli & C. J. Patterson (Eds.), *Lesbian, gay, and bisexual identities over the lifespan: Psychological perspectives* (pp. 215–240). New York: Oxford University Press.

Rose, S. (1996). Lesbian and gay love scripts. In E. D. Rothblum & L. A. Bond (Eds.), *Preventing heterosexism and homophobia* (pp. 151–173). Thousand Oaks, CA: Sage.

Rose, S. M., & Zand, D. (2002). Lesbian dating and courtship from young adulthood to midlife. In S. M. Rose (Ed.), *Lesbian love and relationships* (pp. 85–109). Binghamton, NY: Harrington Park Press.

Rothblum, E. D. (1994). Transforming lesbian sexuality. *Psychology of Women Quarterly, 18,* 627–641.

Rothblum, E. D. (2000). Sexual orientation and sex in women's lives: Conceptual and methodological Issues. *Journal of Social Issues, 56,* 193–204.

Rothblum, E. D., & Brehony, K. A. (1993). *Boston marriages: Romantic but asexual relationships among contemporary lesbians.* Amherst: University of Massachusetts Press.

Rothblum, E. D., & Weinstock, J. S. (Eds.). (in preparation). *Lesbians' ex-lover relationships.* Binghamton, NY: Haworth Press.

Rothblum, E. D., Mintz, B., Cowan, D. B., & Haller, C. (1995). Lesbian baby boomers at midlife. In K. Jay (Ed.), *Dyke life: From growing up to growing old. A celebration of the lesbian experience* (pp. 61–76). New York: Basic Books.

Rust, P. C. (1995). *The challenge of bisexuality to lesbian politics: Sex, loyalty, and revolution.* New York: New York University Press.

Saghir, M. T., & Robins, E. (1973). *Male and female homosexuality: A comprehensive investigation.* Baltimore: Williams & Wilkins.

Sang, B. (1991). Moving towards balance and integration. In B. Sang, J. Warshow, & A. Smith (Eds.), *Lesbians at midlife: The creative transition* (pp. 206–214). San Francisco: Spinsters Book Company.

Savin-Williams, R. C. (1995). Lesbian, gay male, and bisexual adolescents. In A. R. D'Augelli & C. J. Patterson (Eds.), *Lesbian, gay, and bisexual identities over the lifespan: Psychological perspectives* (pp. 165–189). New York: Oxford University Press.

Shernoff, M. J. (1984). Family therapy for lesbian and gay clients. *Social Work, 29*, 393–396.

Shumsky, E. (1996). Transforming the ties that bind: Lesbians, lovers, and chosen family. *Psychoanalysis and Psychotherapy, 13*, 187–195.

Slater, S. (1994). Approaching and avoiding the work of the middle years: Affairs in committed lesbian relationships. *Women and Therapy, 15*(2), 19–34.

Slater, S. (1995). *The lesbian family life cycle.* New York: Free Press.

Slater, S., & Mencher, J. (1991). The lesbian family life cycle: A contextual approach. *American Journal of Orthopsychiatry, 61*, 372–382.

Smolak, L. (1993). *Adult development.* Englewood Cliffs, NJ: Prentice-Hall.

Stanley, J. L. (1996). The lesbian's experience of friendship. In J. S. Weinstock & E. D. Rothblum (Eds.), *Lesbian friendships: For ourselves and each other* (pp. 39–59). New York: New York University Press.

Stein, A. (1997). *Sex and sensibility: Stories of a lesbian generation.* Berkeley, CA: University of California Press.

Stewart, A. J., & Gold-Steinberg, S. (1990). Midlife women's political consciousness. *Psychology of Women Quarterly, 14*, 543–566.

Strega, L. (1996). A lesbian love story. In J. S. Weinstock & E. D. Rothblum (Eds.), *Lesbian friendships: For ourselves and each other* (pp. 277–287). New York: New York University Press.

Tully, C. (1989). Caregiving: What do midlife lesbians view as important? *Journal of Gay and Lesbian Psychotherapy, 1*, 87–103.

Vaid, U. (2000). Preface. In S. Cahill, K. South, & J. Spade (Eds.), *Outing age: Public policy issues affecting gay, lesbian, bisexual and transgender elders* (pp. iv–vi). Washington, DC: The Policy Institute of the National Gay and Lesbian Task Force.

Vetere, V. A. (1982). The role of friendship in the development and maintenance of lesbian love relationships. *Journal of Homosexuality, 8*(2), 51–65.

Weeks, J., Heaphy, B., & Donovan, C. (2001). *Same sex intimacies: Families of choice and other life experiments.* New York: Routledge.

Weinstock, J. S. (1998). Lesbian, gay, bisexual, and transgender friendships in adulthood: Review and analysis. In C. J. Patterson & A. R. D'Augelli (Eds.), *Lesbian, gay, and bisexual identities in families: Psychological perspectives* (pp. 122–153). New York: Oxford University Press.

Weinstock, J. S. (in press). Lesbian FLEX–ibility: Friend and/or family connections among lesbian ex–lovers. In J. S. Weinstock & E. D. Rothblum (Eds.), *Lesbians' Ex-Lovers: The Really Long-Term Relationships.* Binghamton, NY: Harrington Park Press.

Weinstock, J. S., & Bond, L. A. (2002). Building bridges: Examining lesbians' and heterosexual women's close friendships with each other. *Lesbian Studies, 6*(1), 149–161.

Weinstock, J. S., & Rothblum, E. D. (Eds.). (1996a). *Lesbian friendships: For ourselves and each other.* New York: New York University Press.

Weinstock, J. S., & Rothblum, E. D. (1996b). What we can be together: Contemplating lesbians' friendships. In J. S. Weinstock & E. D. Rothblum (Eds.), *Lesbian friendships: For ourselves and each other* (pp. 3–30). New York: New York University Press.

Weinstock, J. S., & Rothblum, E. D. (Eds.) (in press). *Lesbian ex-lovers: The really long-term relationships.* Binghamton, NY: Harrington Park Press.

Weston, K. (1996). Requiem for a street fighter. In E. Lewin (Ed.), *Inventing lesbian culture in America* (pp. 131–141). Boston: Beacon Press.

Weston, K. (1991/1997). *Families we choose: Lesbians, gays, kinship* (rev. ed.). New York: Columbia University Press.

CHAPTER 8

Saturday Night at the Tubs: Age Cohort and Social Life at the Urban Gay Bath[1]

Bertram J. Cohler

The study of sexuality across the course of life has led to renewed interest in the lives of middle-aged men and older men who seek sex with other men. However, the manner in which men realize their same-gender sexual desire cannot be understood except in the context of social and historical change (Elder, 1995, 1996). This chapter contrasts both the setting and patterns of social interaction of two generation-cohorts—older men and young adults—patronizing bathhouses in a midwestern city. This work is based on my ethnographic study of these two urban gay spaces over several years as an observing participant in each setting (Styles, 1979; Tedlock, 1991). My fieldwork has been informed by previous reports of gay baths and other public gay sex venues by other gay ethnographers studying these public gay spaces. However, these earlier reports have not generally been concerned with the interplay of aging and setting (Bolton, 1995; Leap, 1966, 1999; Styles, 1979).

[1]From the Committee on Human Development and the Evelyn Hooker Center for Gay and Lesbian Mental Health. Thanks to Tom Boellstorff, David Grazian, Erik Gregory, Gregory Horn, Andrew Hostetler, Dennis Shelby, Ben Shepard, and Ben Soares for their comments on earlier drafts of this paper.

SEXUALITY, COHORT, AND AGING AMONG MEN
WHO SEEK SEX WITH OTHER MEN

Following Mannheim (1923), Elder (1974, 1995, 1996) has shown that it is important to understand the manner in which persons make meaning in their own lives in terms of particular historical and social changes at particular ages. While, as Settersten (1999) emphasizes, there is also considerable intracohort variability in terms of life circumstances and outcomes, there are at least some ways in which members of a particular generation-cohort share common experiences and a common outlook on self and social life, including sexual identity (Boxer & Cohler, 1989). This chapter contrasts performance of same-gender desire within the public sexual setting of the urban bathhouse across two contrasting generation-cohorts, men presently in late middle and older age, and men who are presently young adults.

The older generation came of age in the time following the end of World War II. These men were already middle-aged by the time of the Stonewall Inn riots of 1969 and the emergence of Gay Liberation (Clendinen & Nagourney, 1999; Loughery, 1998). Many of these men had no name for their same-gender attraction. Our continuing study of these older urban residents has shown that they learned through word of mouth about particular settings, such as bars or bowling alleys, that were "safe" for finding others similarly seeking same-gendered relationships (Hostetler & Cohler, 1997). Political activity was difficult for this generation because homosexuality was often defined as illegal and was subject to criminal sanctions. Men in this generation were careful not to attract attention and avoided the larger community (Berger, 1982; Vacha, 1985).

Men who are presently young adults have come of age in the epoch following the emergence of gay rights and public recognition of minority sexual lifeways (Herdt, 1997; Hostetler & Herdt, 1998). These men often live in cities where legislation protects them from at least overt discrimination. They frequent visible public spaces such as bars and bathhouses in recognized gay neighborhoods. However, while enjoying enhanced tolerance and even legal protection for their same-gender desire, this generation has also borne the burden of knowing that sex with other men can lead to seroconversion, and they have been exposed to discussions about AIDS from the elementary school years to the present.

It is a commonplace in the gay community to assume that there is dramatic age segregation. Most men are presumed to value the beauty and vitality of youth; even with the aging of the baby boomers, comments from men with whom I have talked in several gay community settings suggest that 35 is still a transforming age when it is presumed that one is no longer attractive (Harry & DuVall, 1978; Weinberg, 1970). However, age segregation in the gay community may in some ways be an artifact of city life. In small towns there is simply not a large enough gay clientele to support more than one such gay venue in the community: there may be one gay bar on the outskirts of the town that attracts both gay men and women and both older and younger patrons.

THE CULTURE OF THE GAY BATH

In the literature on social deviance the gay bath has often been highlighted critically as an institution that turns sexuality into a commodity and promotes "unsafe" sex (Signorile, 1997; Rotello, 1997; Weinberg & Williams, 1975). However, gay baths have provided opportunity for both social and sexual camaraderie; the gay baths provide a space in which to enjoy the company of other gay men. The very success of the bathhouse in urban gay culture has led to the portrayal of this sexual venue as the source of much that was problematic with the gay community, including the spread of AIDS (Bérubé, 1996). Many cities took action against the gay bathhouse in an effort to close down those places where the HIV virus might be transmitted (Tattelman, 1999), although a study such as that of Henriksson (1995) suggests that such public sexual venues may actually be a means for safer sex education and do not directly contribute to the spread of sexually transmitted diseases.

While acknowledged as historically significant in the social organization of the gay community (Chauncey, 1994), there has been little ethnographic study of the gay bathhouse. Writing in the counterculture magazine *Rolling Stone*, Young (1973) reports on the normalization of the gay bath as a respectable space replacing the dingy and decrepit baths of an earlier time. During the 1970s, the café in New York's Continental Baths had become well known for the entertainment stars both on stage and in the audience at these performances. Most recently, Bolton and his colleagues (Bolton, 1995; Bolton, Vince, & Mak, 1994), Horn (1998), Styles (1979), and Tattelman (1999) all have shown that sociosexual transactions within these controversial settings may be quite complex.

This study is additionally complex because of the norm of silence that characterizes the social life of the gay bathhouse. Delph (1978) was particularly concerned with those nonverbal cues that elicit particular responses from another. Little has been written regarding modes of ethnographic study within settings in which speech is largely absent. Silence is a form of communication that conveys meanings in symbolic forms, reflecting a reciprocity of perspectives based on taken-for-granted reality and shared perspectives (Cicourel, 1964). Thus study of the social life of the bathhouse, with its norm of silence, requires more than the usual attention to gesture, posture, and other subtle aspects of nonverbal communication and is made all the more difficult because of the dark settings in which such communication must take place.

Over time, I became familiar with the meanings conveyed by these silent gestures and could read the meanings of a series of encounters carefully choreographed by participants sharing in the folkways of this silent erotic culture (Goffman, 1959). It was often possible to predict on the basis of posture and gaze in the preliminary phase of an encounter whether the participants would continue onward to sexual satisfaction or whether the encounter would be broken off. I have observed that if a man approached is without an erection, this is a turnoff and the man seeking an encounter will move on to another prospective partner. Sometimes men will pass by and feel one of the waiting men to see if they are erect, in which case there is a possibility of beginning an encounter. In a cubicle a man may be masturbating and trying to remain erect, seeking to entice a prospective partner; if the prospective partner is not acceptable, the man in the cubicle will often look away or cover himself with his towel. The entire encounter is silent and negotiated by glance and gesture.

The sequence of eye contact, touching, and subsequent aspects of the sexual encounter is to some extent scripted by gay culture (Simon & Gagnon, 1988), particularly the sexual stories of encounters printed in the gay male magazines (Plummer, 1995) and the ever present gay pornographic video (Burger, 1995). Consistent with Plummer's discussion of a dominant or master narrative and Simon and Gagnon's (1988) concept of a sexual script, this sequence has been repeated so often in gay fiction and videos (Burger, 1995) that it has become the dominant script for gay sexual encounters and plays an important role the sexual rhythm of the gay bathhouse and gay male sexuality more generally. It is the very dominance of this sexual script as portrayed in gay magazines and videos that facilitates the norm of silence. Each partner knows what is expected and what is to come next in this carefully scripted performance.

TWO BATHHOUSES: SEXUAL SPACES FOR YOUNGER AND OLDER MEN[2]

Brodsky (1993) observed that sexual venues operating within a market economy "demonstrated the power of culture and social organization to transform sensation and physiological response into erotic experience" (p. 249). The gay bath may be an ideal type of such transformation of sensation into erotic experience. Characteristically a setting including a wet area of steam room, whirlpool bath, and showers, most gay baths include both public spaces in which men may participate in a variety of sexual experiences and private cubicles with a television set for viewing gay pornographic movies and a bed for intimate sexual encounters in a more comfortable and private setting. The experience of sexual intimacy is most often understood as hidden or "private," as contrasted with a visible or "public" activity (Berlant & Warner, 1998; Friedl, 1994). The gay bathhouse represents a unique situation in which private becomes public and a unique opportunity for the organization of sexuality within bourgeois culture, for it is a setting in which that which is ordinarily private is turned into something public.

The Commodification of Sex: Frenetic Activity at the Stallion

The street lights shine brightly on Williams Street, illuminating a busy gay streetscape in which lighted pylons decorated in the colors of the gay rainbow celebrate a community or symbolically recognized public space organized around alternative sexualities. Most of the bars have

---

[2]The Stallion, the Man's Place, and the Man's Life are the three gay bathhouses in the city. The Man's Life is located in an ethnic neighborhood and is a part of what its owner describes as a "complete gay entertainment center," which also includes a bar where, on Saturday at midnight, male porn stars entertain patrons, a leather bar, and sponsorship of an Internet chat line. About 20% of the members of the Stallion are African American, very few African American men are found in the Man's Place, and about 40% of the patrons of the Man's Life are African American. While there is some variation in the range of ages of men visiting this third gay bathhouse, most patrons are of about the same age as those visiting the Stallion.

closed down at about two in the morning. Outside the Stallion, a line has formed, and patrons patiently wait to check in for a six-hour stay. The building facade has recently been remodeled; there are banners with the club's logo on the light pole in front of the club, big banners with the club's address, smaller banners with the club's logo, a stallion, and a sign of the stallion on the door. Bright lights illuminate the exterior, which features the industrial look popular in contemporary urban architecture, a motif emphasized throughout the club with metal wall panels, visible pipes, and other aspects of this stylish masculine decor.

The Stallion is essentially a younger man's club, with membership representing such occupations as flight attendants, lawyers, physicians, and computer types, mostly college graduates. Many of the members wear baseball caps bearing the name of prestigious colleges and universities. I have heard discussions in the locker room ranging from the structure of DNA to technical problems in the architecture of computer chips, and a detailed critique of a case recently argued before the Supreme Court. While the Stallion may not be the ideal place for meeting a prospective partner, I have seen many times when men have exchanged addresses and phone numbers, and on several evenings while waiting to check out I have seen men who came to the club singly and left in the company of another man.

The young men at the front desk greet members, many of whom are regulars, sometimes even former boyfriends, as members are carefully checked for legitimate identification and current membership cards, and against a list of patrons barred from entrance because of past drug use or threatening and stalking behavior toward another member. Bags are carefully searched for alcohol or illicit drugs. There is absolutely no hustling (sex for money) allowed. Members trade their valuables, carefully locked away in safe-deposit boxes, for their locker or room key, towels, and, for those renting a private room, linen and TV controller. Buzzed through the locked steel door separating the check-in area from the interior of the bathhouse, newly arrived patrons join the crowd of several hundred other generally young men enjoying the spotlessly clean two-story sauna and sex club.

With its industrial-styled exterior and interior, the Stallion exemplifies the commodification of gay male sexuality (Marx, 1867). Finding a partner for an anonymous sexual encounter becomes yet another market transaction, based on physical appeal. Men stand around in the hallway or display themselves in their cubicles, often with an

erection, inviting an encounter with an appropriately qualified (hand-
some, lean, and well-proportioned) partner in this sexual marketplace.
The sound of hip music played over a state-of-the-art sound system
pervades the club, which is known for its D.J.s and their good taste
in trendy music. Public areas, including the upstairs lounges and the
oral sex (glory hole) orgy room, have large television monitors playing
male porn videos characterized by young men engaging in varying
sexual activity. It is believed that looking at these videos fosters erotic
arousal and heightens preparation for engaging in sexual encounters.

At the Stallion, the cubicles, known as "rooms," are at a premium,
particularly on weekend nights. Sometime after eleven, the sign is
hung out at the check-in desk that there is a waiting list for rooms.
On nights when the rooms are full, some men take lockers but wait
for the opportunity to book a room as their locker number comes up
on the television monitors on each floor. The locker room serves as
a "liminal space" (van Gennep, 1909; Turner, 1974), marking the
transition from the outside world to the dimly lit, timeless, erotic
world beyond. For the men selecting a locker rather than a private
room, undressing in the bright light, checking their appearance and
adjusting their towels before the full-length mirror, this final action
before moving into the interior world of the club provides an opportunity for back-stage "face work" (Goffman, 1959, 1967) before going
front stage into the erotic areas of the bathhouse. Those men selecting
a cubicle, off one of the several hallways that are important spaces in
the search for erotic companions (Delph, 1978), face the problem of
moving from outsider to patron as they walk in street clothes to their
room, undress, open the door, and step directly into the dimly lit,
beckoning erotic world beyond.[3]

Leaving the locker room, members enter the club proper. As Weiss
(1985) has observed, the gay bathhouse has a timeless quality. The
always-darkened hallways and public spaces, the absence of any evidence of a clock except for the digital display on the television monitors
showing the list of lockers waiting for rooms, and the absence of
windows all contribute to this timeless quality. The intense search for

---

[3]While there are nights when there is a wait for rooms, I have not been able to determine
all the reasons why some men select lockers when there are rooms available. Some men
told me that the cost was a factor (rooms can cost up to three times the cost of a locker).
Other men are not sure how long they want to stay and don't want to invest in the cost
of a room. Other men enjoy cruising and sexuality in public spaces or are afraid of being
caught in a room alone with a partner who won't leave when asked.

a sexual encounter further enhances this quality, which pervades the bathhouse. Recent remodeling created an elaborate whirlpool with several semienclosed spaces where men may enjoy intimate moments together. The "water sports" room is hardly used but does provide a private toilet. The dry sauna and the steam room are both sites of sexual encounters.

The second floor is the major focus of sexual activities within the Stallion. The stairway is adorned with posters admonishing members to "wear your rubbers" and to remember that "oil and water don't mix" (a reminder of the fact that oil-based lubricants should not be used with latex condoms since they tend to dissolve the material). A lounge area with a television screen showing gay porn greets members climbing the stairs. It is an area about 20 feet square, and benches where members can watch both the television and the passing scene line the walls. A vending machine provides lubricant, dental dams for members engaging in oral sex and rimming or mouth-anal erotic activity and who wish maximum safety in their sexual activities, as well as hoses for watersports, and lubricant. I have never observed members using dental dams, although I did once observe two young men engaging in mutual oral sex but only after each had carefully, but with an erotic touch, put a rubber on his partner.

The ever present video screen shows gay pornographic videos with attractive, mostly young men having sex together, while a separate monitor lists room availability for those members with a locker but wishing to change to a room. The monitor carries safe-sex reminders and also lists times when HIV and other STD testing is available at a nominal cost. (After I had completed my fieldwork, the Stallion held a community seminar in the bathhouse to discuss the controversy regarding unprotected anal sex, or "barebacking," which is believed to be the chief means for the transmission of the HIV virus and which is assumed to be increasing after a decade of practicing "safer sex." This seminar, which was free and open to the community, was cosponsored by a local gay community health center and attracted well over 100 participants, who discussed measures within the gay community designed to foster safer sex. The Stallion also provides safer-sex demonstrations.)

The second-floor landing lounge is also the gathering place for those men known as "maids," who clean the cubicles between occupants. The maids and desk staff all wear t-shirts with the image of the Stallion on them. The maids and supervisory staff are supposed to monitor the club for evidence of unsafe sex, but I have never seen them intervene in an instance in which they observe risky sex taking place. The maids congregate, waiting for instructions for rooms to be cleaned and may themselves take part in some cruising activity before or after their shift.

The second floor contains three public spaces where sexual activity may be witnessed; the glory hole room, a video room showing gay porn, and a dark maze room with beds around which men congregate to watch and participate in spontaneous sexual encounters fostered by group contagion (LeBon & Mackay, 1897/1994). One owner of another bathhouse has told me that it is necessary to have such spaces in the 1990s; the fear of AIDS has led many men to give up sex with partners and to seek sexual satisfaction primarily from watching other men having sex. The room is directly off the second-floor landing lounge and is also about 20 feet square with a raised platform running along two sides of the room and two cubicles in the middle.

At the corner of this otherwise darkened room there is a lighted condom box ostensibly in readiness for possible sexual activity. The problem is that the risers and the space between where men stand and the wall is so crowded that it may be difficult to get to the condom box in the event that a condom is needed. Men may begin a sexual exchange and then move to the back of this very dark partitioned area to consummate their sexual activity. Other men show less concern with being observed. A group scene involving as many as 15 men may begin with the stimulation of watching two guys involved in a hot or passionate exchange. A third man will begin to fondle either or both partners, perhaps joined by a fourth or fifth. These men are then joined by others seeking to fondle them until a large number of men are involved in this group grope, which may end as suddenly as it begins when one of the initial participants moves away from the encounter.

Older men are present in this "glory hole" room to a greater extent than elsewhere in the club, with the exception of an area of the maze where they offer themselves as the recipient or "bottom" in anal intercourse. Younger men are willing to be serviced by older men; on occasion, if a younger man is servicing another younger man, a third or even fourth man will fondle the man providing this oral service, leading to a group activity sometimes including five or six men. Men worry about whether it is "safe" (safer sex) to "suck off another man" and, particularly, whether it is safe to "taste and swallow cum." I have often heard this topic debated at the Stallion, although not at the

Man's Place. While it is believed that saliva disarms the HIV virus, cases of seroconversion have been reported following oral sex.

Men wander back and forth between the glory hole room and two other adjoining spaces at the end of the hall. Late at night, certainly well after midnight, the halls are crowded with men in their 20s or 30s cruising for a sexual opportunity. Other men sit on their bed in their cubicle and play with themselves in order to maintain their erection and to attract other men, lie on their back, indicating their interest in oral sex, or on their stomachs, indicating their interest in anal sex. Potential partners for sexual encounters pass by and if attracted to the occupant, stop and watch, sometimes reciprocally playing with themselves and showing their erection, or opening their towels and showing off their bodies. If the occupant is interested, he continues to play with himself, showing his erection to the potential partner. Stallion members find another man's erection to be sexually stimulating; if a prospective partner does not have an erection, he is rejected even if otherwise very attractive. Less often, one man will try to stimulate another so that he will have an erection. If the occupant of the cubicle does not wish to proceed, he grabs for his towel; if the potential partner is particularly persistent, the occupant may shake his head no or wave the other man off. I have never seen an occasion in which a rejection led to any conflict. It is an understood and unwritten club rule that men are not to harass each other and are expected to respect each other's wishes. Club patrons are polite in this regard; most shrug off a rejection and move off to find another possible partner. Members realize that rejection is inevitable; at the same time there is some sense of disappointment with sexual interest not being reciprocated.

Older men are more likely to be rejected than younger men. Particularly early in the evening, when there is a larger proportion of older to younger men wandering the halls, older men may turn to each other for sexual pleasure although generally seeking younger partners. At other times, older men may be the subject of unflattering remarks. One of the common derogatory words for older men seeking to watch or be involved with younger men having sex is *troll*. A younger man may refer to an older man as a troll, meaning that he gets pleasure out of desiring younger men.

I had written in my fieldnotes . . .

> I was standing along the wall in the video orgy room, a U-shaped area with several levels of carpeted risers and a four-screen video monitor showing

all the channels presently available in the club. On one side of this room is a passageway leading to a maze in a darkened room beyond. Three younger men, perhaps in their late 20s, were getting it on with each other, alternately sucking each other off and fondling each other in the middle of the corridor (it is common when men meet and connect sexually for sexual activity to erupt in any part of the club). The youth, passion, and uncommon good looks of this three-way group of 20-somethings was very much like an Ambercombie and Fitch photograph advertisement, which helps to script both the dress and the demeanor of younger men with each other. One man turned to me, attempted to wave me away, and said, "We don't want any guys over 50 around here."

In addition to the glory hole room, the maze is another area in which older men may become involved in sexual activity. In an area of about 50 square feet, a series of plywood partitions has been constructed to form a maze through which men wander looking for sexual activity. In the middle of the maze, a platform has been constructed. Older men often sit or lie on this platform with their legs up, indicating their desire for anal sex. Younger men who otherwise might not welcome an older man for a sexual exchange are willing to participate in such an act with an older man. Indeed, it is not uncommon to find that the receptive partner in these maze-way encounters is an older man. This activity may, in turn, draw as many as 15 other men of different ages, all crowded into a small space.

Completing their stay at the Stallion, locker room patrons dress with less intensity than they undressed. Some members, smokers, visit their locker during the course of the evening for a cigarette, since it is difficult to carry around cigarettes while dressed only in a bath towel. Patrons turn in their towels, retrieve their valuables from the safe-deposit box, and exit by a different door from the entrance door. At the busiest time on a weekend night, there may be a rather lengthy line as members wait to retrieve the contents of their safe-deposit boxes. Members dressed and waiting to check out mingle with those wrapped in terrycloth towels waiting to exchange their lockers for rooms because they have come to the top of the waiting list.

Sexuality, Aging, and Marginal Urban Gay Culture: The Quiet Life of the Man's Place

Several miles north of the Stallion, located in the midst of a bustling neighborhood known as Boystown, facing a large cemetery, in a dimly lit marginal urban neighborhood of warehouses and taxicab garages, an unmarked door next to a car repair facility provides an entranceway with a buzzer to be admitted into the Man's Place. There is no long line at the Man's Place; there may be only three or four older men wandering about the dingy premises in a desultory manner. There is little formality associated with the check-in by a disgruntled employee, speaking broken English, who is often recruited from the nearby neighborhood, which is home to many first-generation residents from Central or South America or Southeast Asia. Membership is confirmed by a permanent plastic card good for a lifetime. There is no check of identification, little overt concern with possible illicit substances brought into the club, and just a generic key for a locker or cubicle. An aged safe-deposit box has fallen into disrepair.

Checking in at the Man's Place is an informal procedure. Patrons are buzzed in at an unmarked door between two car repair garages, where they show their permanent membership cards and pay a small amount for either a locker or a room. Since there is no formal check of identification, members can use assumed names. This is an advantage to some; several members noted that they are closeted at work and afraid that if they went to the Stallion and had to use their real names, in the event of a raid they would be "outed" when the membership list became public. Indeed, while most men at the Stallion expressed little concern about using their real names and were "out" at work and in the community, many more men at the Mans' Place had not disclosed their sexual identity and believed that the very anonymity of the Man's Place provided them with the protection they sought from possible public exposure of their sexual orientation.

The Man's Place offers about 40 private cubicles, most of which are never occupied, off a mazelike corridor, and a darkened room—the "orgy room"—as it is called by regular members, with a row of dirty, carpeted risers opposite carpeted benches arranged on opposite sides of the wall. The room is about 20 feet square, its stale air circulated by a noisy fan. On Saturday night after midnight, when there may be more than 200 men at the Stallion, there may be fewer than 10 at the Man's Place; the older patrons frequenting the Man's Place are likely to head for home sometime after ten. Lockers are arranged in three sections, each with a swinging wooden gate. Undressing and donning a towel, patrons using the lockers are usually drawn to the large, darkened orgy room, where visible sexual acts may be taking place. Earlier in the evening, two or three couples may be observed in the midst of a passionate embrace, apparently indifferent to their impact upon others watching them.

The contrast between these two gay baths, one centrally located in the middle of a recognized gay neighborhood (with about one third of residents self-identifying as gay or lesbian), advertising in the gay press, sponsoring safer-sex demonstrations, and decorating floats for the annual Gay Pride Parade, and the other, located in a socially marginal area, hidden away from public view, and poorly appointed, reflects two contrasting sociosexual spaces. Temporal rhythm makes an enormous difference in the social life of the bathhouse and in the age of the members frequenting the bathhouse at a particular time. For example, while some middle-aged and older men frequent the Stallion early in the evening, nearly all of these men have left the Stallion by midnight, while younger patrons may not arrive until two or three in the morning, after the bars have closed. The Man's Place is most active in the early evening, when men may arrive after work or after dinner, a time when there are very few patrons at the Stallion.

As contrasted with the upscale and spotless Stallion, the Man's Place is a depressing if predictable sociosexual space. It is not only the neighborhood, including the cemetery across the street, a grim reminder of the costs of missteps in the world of AIDS, but also the decor of this club and the demeanor of the patrons wandering idly about that lend a sense of quiet despair to the club. Many of the patrons are from working-class backgrounds. I have met primarily taxicab drivers, security guards, and electricians. While I have met some professional older men at the Man's Place, most of these middle-class men believe they need to remain "closeted" because of their work or because they are married. One patron lamented the change in the club after it moved from its former location. Another man in his 50s, a lawyer at a major law firm, noted that the nearly invisible locale and largely Eastern European ethnic membership at the club helped to ensure that his sexual orientation would not be detected. He insisted upon remaining "closeted," fearing that he would lose business if it was known that he was gay. As he sagely observed, it would be impossible even to find the club *with* the address.

The model club member attends more frequently than younger counterparts attending the Stallion. Many members told me they attend several nights a week and recognize other members, with whom they may also have had some sexual contact, although they do not know much about them. Visiting the Man's Place in the late afternoon, early evening, or later in the evening, I repeatedly met the same older men. There are never more than a dozen members sauntering about in torn towels and clogs over the filthy carpet. The very lack of traffic has made it easier for me to talk to members than at the Stallion. This may in part be due to the fact that I am closer to the age of the patrons than to the membership of the Stallion. However, many of the men who were resting in the TV lounge area or in the large hallway with benches outside the orgy room seemed pleased to have someone with whom to talk.

Most of these patrons report never having visited the Stallion. A few men have told me they regard it as a young man's club where older members would have difficulty finding company. Other men deny any knowledge of the Stallion. The regular patrons of the Man's Place appear to have little contact with the larger gay community. Even the staff has little contact with the larger gay community. As contrasted with the Stallion, there are few gay publications available at the Man's Place. When the Stallion was raided by the police in the midst of the time I was doing my fieldwork (the mayor then ordered that the police stay out of gay venues), the staff of the Man's Place denied knowing anything about this raid and appeared to know or care little about other gay venues in the city.

Revisiting the Man's Place after more than a year's absence, I noted a large stack of local gay publications; however, one club member observed that no one has any interest in these publications and they are usually thrown out after a period of a few weeks. I understand this lack of interest to reflect again the lack of interest and identification of these older club members, generally from the oldest cohort in early adulthood prior to the time of Stonewall and the emergence of Gay Liberation, with the gay community only a few miles distant and the two younger cohorts populating Boystown. Future study will show whether the life of the Man's Place reflects aging within a particular cohort or is more generally characteristic of the impact of growing older within the gay community, which is reflected in diminished interest in those sociosexual spaces frequented by younger men.

While at the Stallion there is a sense of erotic intensity with members hurrying about in an effort to find a sexual contact, life at the Man's Place is much less hurried. Club members lounge about, occasionally wandering in and out of the orgy room to check on possible sexual action that might be taking place. Most club members are well over the age of 45, with patrons with whom I have talked ranging in age into their 80s. I have seen only one or two younger men at the Man's Place; one younger visitor reported seeing a listing of the club in one of the national guides to gay venues (the Man's Place seldom advertises in the local gay media, while the Stallion has weekly ads). These younger men clearly felt out of place and soon departed. Even the videos, repeated across the evening, are old, faded videos of biker types performing rough sex. Most gay videos made since the late 1980s show men putting on condoms before anal penetration. However, because of their age few of the older videos have men taking such precautions for safer sex.

The present quarters, although remodeled when the Man's Place moved from its previous quarters in an ethnic neighborhood, have been permitted to run down to nearly the state of the former locale. The whirlpool is often broken, and the steam room is either so hot as to be unbearable or closed for lack of repair. There is considerable water damage and tile breakage where water from the steam room has leaked through the walls. The dry sauna has stopped working, and even the showers malfunction and are often out of soap. Bathrooms are often unkempt and on several occasions were stopped up but had not been cleaned or repaired. (In repeated visits at staggered times and days over the next several weeks the plumbing still had not been repaired; yellow and black construction tape indicated to patrons that the bathroom was out of order. A more recent visit to resolve some questions in reviewing field notes showed that some repairs had taken place, although both the dry and wet sauna remained out of order. The facility was somewhat better maintained than previously.)

Members of the Man's Place do not report dissatisfaction with the club's facilities or with management's lack of concern with cleanliness; they banter with the one regular bathhouse staff member, a member of an ethnic neighborhood adjacent to the club, working in a half-hearted manner to keep the bathhouse clean. Considering the run-down appearance and desultory atmosphere of the Man's Place, it is somewhat surprising that club members maintain their loyalty. Many club members with whom I have talked noted that this was a comfortable place. Several men did comment on the sorry state of the dry and wet saunas and the general state of disrepair, but they overlooked these problems because they felt safe and accepted by fellow club members and staff alike.

While at the Stallion condoms are readily available in all public areas, at the Man's Place there are no condoms accessible in places where men might need them. Indeed, there are evenings when there are not even condoms for sale at the check-in desk. There are few posters urging safer sex and little information available on safer sex. Club members have assured me that there is less need for worry about sexually transmitted diseases than at a club catering to younger men. As one man observed: "It's not like with younger guys. We've all made it this far. It's not likely that you can get AIDS when you're older. If you've lived long, the chances are that you're not [HIV] positive." This member's assertion that sex is safer among older men reflects the ethos of club members and management alike. For example, I observed one evening the front-desk clerk, no longer on duty, walk into the orgy room and initiate unprotected anal sex with a club member.

The private cubicles at the Man's Place are less often preferred spaces for sexual encounters than at the Stallion. Often, when there is a sexual encounter taking place in a private room, the participants will leave the door open and other members will gather around the entry or join in the encounter. At the Stallion it was much less common for men to leave their door open during such encounters. Particularly on less crowded nights, it is common for men at the Stallion to meet in a public space, make initial intimate contact, and then move off to the room of one or the other man to continue the encounter. This is less common at the Man's Place, where sexual encounters are more likely to be completed in the semidarkened orgy room. One or another older man may remain looking for an encounter, but by about ten in the evening the club is almost empty. During the week the club closes at two in the morning, while on weekends it is open around the clock. In contrast, the Stallion never closes and is busiest after the time at which the Man's Place has closed for the evening.

Typically, as the evening wears on, men drift in and out of the orgy room. Again, as at the Stallion, encountering men engaging in sexual acts stimulates other men to grope each other; as many as ten men may be involved in a group scene as the emotional contagion spreads among the on-lookers. Sometimes these encounters will attract a group of other men, who watch the encounter, become excited, and turn to their neighbors for joint sexual activity. One member may reach around and begin to caress another's body, reach for an erect penis to stroke, or turn around and begin a mutual caress. If the other observer is similarly excited, the pair begin sexual activity, which enhances group contagion and shared sexual activity. Similar scenes may be found at the Stallion, but generally only on weekend nights and only when private rooms are in short supply. Indeed, sex in public spaces within the club is more characteristic of the Man's Place than the Stallion.

Further, while Stallion participants may initially try to hide their activity from on-lookers, waving off the assembled crowd and attempting to keep their towels around themselves and their partners, or keeping their towel around them while kissing, caressing, or engaging in oral sex with their partners, the older men of the Man's Place show little such modesty. Towels are tossed aside as the sexual action begins. Indeed, while much of the group life of the Stallion consists of men standing around the halls and waiting to be approached by another, men at the Man's Place seldom stand around. They approach each other for sexual activity with much less hesitancy than at the Stallion and are less seldom rebuffed by their fellows. There is more visible sexual performance and less hesitancy about a public sexual display than at the Stallion.

Men resting after having realized orgasm generally move out of the orgy room to the area near the snack bar, where they watch television—most often tuned to sports programs—read the city daily newspapers, play pool, or lie down on one of the several benches in the safe, nonsexual lounges. Just as at the Stallion, some rooms are understood to be nonsexual spaces in which little "cruising" takes place. However, by about eleven in the evening the TV lounge has emptied out, and most men are on their way home.

Several members commented that men at the Man's Place are pretty relaxed about having sex or being able to find a partner for a sexual encounter. There is little pressure to show off one's body; finding a partner for a sexual encounter is less a consequence of having a great physique than at the Stallion, and there is much less concern with being rejected by a prospective partner. One markedly overweight man noted: "The thing about this place, I know that I can always find someone to have sex with. It's like we all come for the same reason. I'm at home here so why should I go to anyplace else?" Another club member noted that it was pretty hard for middle-aged and older gay men to meet other older gay men; the bars were difficult meeting places and, in any event, he didn't drink, which left the parks, tearooms,[4] and

---

[4]Bert Cohler writes as follows in defining tearooms: "Public places, particularly toilets, where anonymous sex between men is known to take place. The origin of this slang term is unknown but it is presumed to stem from the British slang for urine as tea, also to engage another person or go against traditions . . . "

the Man's Place. Claiming to be gay since childhood, he spoke with scorn of the suburban men who drive into the city, park in the beach parking lot, and seek a quick "blow job." He described these men as trying to have the best of both worlds, the typical suburban married man and the gay men seeking a quick sexual contact. This middle-aged gay man expressed the frustration that some middle-aged and older gay men feel about realizing some more enduring partnership that they both seek but feel they cannot realize. Other older men frequenting the Man's Place seek little more than a sexual outlet.

For many of these men, representing a cohort of what they self-describe as "homosexuals," much of their life has been closeted because of the impact of stigma and even possible criminal conviction simply as a consequence of their sexual orientation (Loughery, 1998). These men have long been accustomed to gay venues that are generally hidden from community scrutiny and dingy and uncomfortable; the physical setting of the Man's Place is consistent with such physical settings, which the men of this cohort have known since young adulthood. Requiring that their sexual orientation remain hidden, these men believed themselves fortunate to have even dingy places in which to meet.

The Man's Place offers a comfortable environment for its members. Many of the men have been attending over a period of a decade or more in both its former and present locales. These older men represent a cohort largely unconcerned with the political issues first posed in the wake of the Stonewall riots. Already in midadulthood at the time of Gay Liberation, they worked at jobs where their sexual orientation was not likely to be evident or in which they were expected to talk about their life off the job. Since they see themselves as men who have sex with other men, but not necessarily as homosexual or gay, the locale of the Man's Club, both socially and geographically distant from the gay community, is a virtue for them. These men seldom venture into the gay community, even to those bars in Boystown known to cater to older men, and show little interest in this larger gay community. They see the Man's Place as their community center.

Those men who have any familiarity with Boystown are wary of rejection by the younger gay men who frequent the bars and bathhouse and are uncomfortable with the more militant political stance of post-Stonewall cohorts demanding respect from workplace and community. For these older men, the Man's Place is a safe retreat from social change in the gay community, with which they feel little connection.

Those few men venturing into the lively world of the Stallion report feeling uncomfortable in the presence of so many young men with beautiful bodies, reminding them of their own aging. Enjoying the company of others sharing a similar lifestyle in the relaxed setting of the Man's Place, these men are tolerant of the problems posed by the club's chronic state of disrepair and little interested in alternative venues within the gay community.

It is possible that as the present generation of younger gay men moves into middle and older age, this cohort will maintain both greater awareness of sexual and social concerns within the gay community and will continue to frequent the Stallion and similar spaces explicitly catering to the needs of the gay community. Generally "out" since adolescence or early adulthood, these younger men see little reason for hidden gay spaces within their urban community. Self-identifying as gay, often wearing clothing with explicitly gay labels, men in this younger cohort presume visible spaces such as the Stallion for sociosexual encounters.

CONCLUSION

The present report on the social and sexual organization of the gay bathhouse was undertaken as part of a larger study of the interplay of social life and lived experience among middle-aged and older gay men and women in a large city. Together with settings such as bars, bookstores, churches, and volunteer organizations, the gay bathhouse is an important setting for men seeking other men as sexual partners. It is important that the study of particular lives be understood within the context of shared conceptions of sexuality and social change (Elder, 1974, 1996; Mannheim, 1923; Sadownick, 1997; Settersten & Hägestad, 1996). Within contemporary American and Western European bourgeois culture, there is also significant variability in both the realization and expression of sexual identity. While some older men report having been aware of same-gender sexual orientation from earliest childhood, other men report first awareness of gay sexual identity only in middle or later life. The meaning of a gay sexual identity is determined not only by cohort membership, but also by parental and own social status, together with such other cultural factors as ethnic background and both childhood and present geographic residence.

Accompanying cohort membership, there are particular social spaces that particular generations define as relevant. There was relatively little overlap between the older and younger generations in preferred venue for sociosexual satisfaction. The younger and middle-aged men found sociosexual satisfaction from visible sexual settings such as the well-advertised gay bathhouse located in the midst of the gay community. The older generation of men tended to prefer a gay bathhouse inconspicuous in a socially marginal area of the community. Indeed, older men had few criticisms against the Man's Place, even though it is not well maintained. Most of the middle-aged and older gay men with whom I talked were indeed from the cohort of men who had led the quiet, largely hidden gay life of the time before Stonewall and the emergence of Gay Liberation, and the Man's Place preserves that image.

The milieu of the Man's Place represented continuity of this less visible but also less commodified sociosexual world characteristic of this oldest cohort of men who see themselves either as homosexual or simply as men who enjoy sex with other men. While it might be assumed that the frequently claimed preference for youth within the gay community would lead older men to seek older men because of fewer chances for realizing sexual satisfaction in a bathhouse frequented primarily by younger men, most of the older men with whom I spoke at the Man's Place had little awareness or interest in going to the well-appointed and well-maintained Stallion bathhouse. Many of these older men did not venture into that area of the community known as Boystown. At the same time, these older men profess to be less concerned or even aware of the consequences of unsafe sex, in contrast to the younger cohorts of gay men, who have experienced the ravages of the AIDS pandemic and are more aware of the problems posed by unsafe sex.

It is difficult to know whether age differences in the patronage of these two different sociosexual venues was a consequence of aging as such or a consequence of membership in different cohorts with different understandings of self, other, and lived experience. Probably, as the present generations of younger and middle-aged men grow older, they are not as likely as the present generation of older men to prefer such social and geographic isolation from the larger gay community. The present cohort of older men seeking other men as sexual partners had attained midlife and a settled lifestyle prior to the Stonewall riots of 1969 and the emergence of Gay Liberation. Many of these older men feel uncomfortable describing themselves as "gay," relying upon terms such as *homosexual* or using no term at all and describing themselves in terms of their interest in other men as sexual partners.

This cohort of older men seeking other men as sexual partners has generally been little involved in the move for enhanced civil rights for gay men and women, although it has enjoyed some of the benefits of legal protection to the gay community. Among these benefits is the ability to socialize in an open manner and freedom from harassment in their lifestyle. Institutions such as the Man's Place, a bathhouse frequented primarily by older men, are able to offer facilities relatively free of worry regarding police raids. However, lack of interest in the larger gay community has particular costs, most notably lack of understanding of the threat posed by the AIDS pandemic and an accompanying lack of interest in realizing safer sex. These men did not read the gay press, did not attend or participate in the annual Gay Pride parade, and were also much less concerned with issues of safer sex than the cohorts of young to middle-aged gay men enjoying the facilities of the Stallion.

Failure to make condoms accessible in those public areas of the Man's Place where sexual activities might take place underscores the problems posed by this lack of contact with the larger gay community. It is important that management of settings such as the Man's Place take a more proactive role in promoting safer sex. Management of the Stallion has been particularly responsive to the issues posed by transmission of HIV and other STDs.

Ethnographic observation of two gay baths has suggested that there are significant differences across cohorts of men seeking sex with other men in both self-definition and use of community spaces. While an older cohort of men shuns such terms as *gay* and would bristle at begin called "faggots," even in jest, younger cohorts of gay men feel comfortable with this self-definition. Accompanying this acknowledgment of sexual identity, younger cohorts of gay men are both much more explicitly aware of the health problems posed by erotic encounters and also more likely to practice safer sex. The very isolation of the cohort of older gay men from the larger gay community prevents these men from education in safer sex. The belief of these men that AIDS and other sexually transmitted diseases are only a problem for young men further compounds the problem of safer sex education. The findings from this observational study suggest that public health education needs to be directed at this older population and that bars, baths, and other erotic venues frequented by older men should be more active than at present in education for safer sex.

REFERENCES

Berger, R. (1982/1996). *Gay and gray: The older homosexual man* (2nd ed.). New York: Harrington Park Press.

Berlant, L., & Warner, M. (1998). Sex in public. *Critical Inquiry, 24,* 547–566.

Bérubé, A. (1996). The history of gay bathhouses. In E. G. Colter, W. Hoffman, E. Pendleton, A. Redick, & D. Serlin (Eds.), *Policing public sex: Queer politics and the future of aids activism* (pp. 187–220). Boston: South End Press.

Bolton, R. (1995). Tricks, friends and lovers: Erotic encounters in the field. In D. Kulick & M. Willson (Eds.), *Taboo: Sex, identity and subjectivity in anthropological fieldwork* (pp. 140–167). New York: Routledge.

Bolton, R., Vince, J., & Mak, R. (1994). Gay baths revisited: An empirical analysis. *GLQ, 1,* 255–273.

Boxer, A., & Cohler, B. (1989). The life course of gay and lesbian youth: An immodest proposal for the study of lives. In G. Herdt (Ed.), *Gay and lesbian youth* (pp. 315–355). New York: Harrington Park Press.

Brodsky, J. I. (1993). The Mineshaft: A retrospective ethnography. In J. P. De-Cecco & J. P. Elia (Eds.), *If you seduce a straight person, can you make them gay? Issues in biological essentialism versus social constructivism in gay and lesbian identities* (pp. 233–251). New York: Haworth Press.

Burger, J. R. (1995). *One-handed histories: The eroto-politics of gay male video pornography.* Binghamton, NY: Harrington Park Press/Haworth.

Chauncey, G. (1994). *Gay New York: Gender, urban culture and the making of the gay male world, 1890–1940.* New York: Basic Books.

Cicourel, A. (1964). *Method and measurement in sociology.* New York: The Free Press of Glencoe/Macmillan.

Clendinen, D., & Nagourney, A. (1999). *Out for good: The struggle to build a gay rights movement in America.* New York: Basic Books.

Delph, E. W. (1978). *The silent community: Public homosexual encounters.* Thousand Oaks, CA: Sage Publications.

Elder, G. H., Jr. (1974/1998). *Children of the Great Depression: Social change in life experience.* Boulder, CO: Westview Press/Harper Collins.

Elder, G. H., Jr. (1995). The life-course paradigm: Social change and individual development. In P. Moen, G. H. Elder, Jr., & Kurt Lüscher (Eds.), *Examining lives in context: Perspectives on the ecology of human development* (pp. 101–139). Washington, DC: American Psychological Association.

Elder, G. H., Jr. (1996). Human lives in changing societies: Life course and developmental insights. In R. Cairns, G. H. Elder, Jr., & E. Costello (Eds.), *Developmental science: Multiple perspectives* (pp. 31–62). New York: Cambridge University Press.

Friedl, E. (1994). Sex the invisible. *American Anthropologist, 96,* 833–844.

Goffman, E. (1959). *The presentation of self in everyday life.* New York: Double-day-Anchor.

Goffman, E. (1967). *Interaction ritual: Essays on face-to-face behavior.* New York: Pantheon.

Harry, J., & DuVall, W. (1978). Age and sexual culture among homosexually oriented males. *Archives of Sexual Behavior, 7,* 199–202.

Henriksson, B. (1995). *Risk factor love: Homosexuality, sexual interaction, and HIV prevention.* Göteborg, Sweden: Göteborg University.

Herdt, G. (1997). *Same sex, different cultures.* Boulder, CO: Westview Press.

Horn, G. C. (1998). *"So that's what's goin' on!" Phenomenology and the negotiation of sexual interactions between men who have sex with men in sex-on-premises-venues.* Paper presented at "Health in Differences 2" conference. Melbourne, Australia.

Hostetler, A., & Cohler, B. (1997). Partnership, singlehood and the lesbian and gay life course: A research agenda. In G. Herdt, A. Hostetler, & B. Cohler (Eds.), Coming of age: Gays, lesbians, and bisexuals in the second half of life (W. J. Blumenthal, Ed.). *Journal of Lesbian, Gay and Bisexual Identities, 2,* 199–230.

Hostetler, A., & Herdt, G. (1998). Culture, sexual lifeways, and developmental subjectivities: Rethinking sexual taxonomies. *Social Research, 65,* 249–290.

Leap, W. L. (1996). *Word's out: Gay men's English.* Minneapolis: University of Minnesota Press.

Leap, W. L. (1999). Sex in "private" places: Gender, erotics, and detachment in two urban locales. In W. L. Leap (Ed.), *Public sex/gay space* (pp. 115–140). New York: Columbia University Press.

LeBon, G., & MacKay, C. (1897/1994). *The crowd: A study of the popular mind.* Greenville, SC: Traders Press.

Loughery, J. (1998). *The other side of silence: Men's lives and gay identities: A twentieth-century history.* New York: Henry Holt-Owl Books.

Mannheim, K. (1923/1952). The problem of generations. In K. Mannheim (Ed.), *Essays on the sociology of knowledge* (pp. 276–322). London: Routledge & Kegan Paul.

Marx, K. (1867/1978). *Capital* (Das Kapital) (Vol. 1). In R. C. Tucker (Ed.), *The Marx-Engels reader* (pp. 294–442). New York: W. W. Norton.

Plummer, K. (1995). *Telling sexual stories: Power, change, and social worlds.* New York: Routledge.

Rotello, G. (1997). *Sexual ecology: AIDS and the destiny of gay men.* New York: Dutton.

Sadownick, D. (1997). *Sex between men: An intimate history of the sex lives of gay men postwar to the present.* San Francisco: Harper.

Settersten, R. A., Jr. (1999). *Lives in time and place: The problems and promises of developmental science.* Amityville, NY: Baywood Publishing Company.

Settersten, R. A., Jr., & Hägestad, G. (1996). What's the latest ? Cultural age deadlines for family transitions. *The Gerontologist, 36,* 178–188.

Signorile, M. (1997). *Life outside: The Signorile report on gay men: Sex, drugs, muscles, and the passages of life.* New York: Harper-Collins.

Simon, W., & Gagnon, J. (1988). A sexual scripts approach. In J. H. Geer & W. T. O'Donoghue (Eds.), *Theories of human sexuality* (pp. 363–383). New York: Plenum.

Styles, J. (1979). Outsider/insider. *Urban Life, 8,* 135–152.

Tattelman, I. (1999). Speaking to the gay bathhouse: Communicating in sexually charged spaces. In W. L. Leap (Ed.), *Public sex: Gay space* (pp. 71–94). New York: Columbia University Press.

Tedlock, B. (1991). From participant observation to observation of participation: The emergence of narrative ethnography. *Journal of Anthropological Research, 47,* 69–94.

Turner, V. (1974). *Dramas, fields, and metaphors: Symbolic action in human society.* Ithaca, NY: Cornell University Press.

Vacha, K. (1985). *A quiet fire: Memoirs of older gay men.* Trumanburg, NY: Crossing Press.

van Gennep, A. (1909/1960). *The rites of passage* (trans. M. Vizedom & G. Caffee). London: Routledge & Kegan Paul.

Weinberg, M. S. (1970). The male homosexual: Age-related variations in social and psychological characteristics. *Social Problems, 17,* 527–538.

Weinberg, M. S., & Williams, C. J. (1975). Gay baths and the social organization of impersonal sex. *Social Problems, 23,* 124–136.

Weiss, P. (1985). Inside a bathhouse. *The New Republic.* December 2.

Young, P. D. (1973). "So you're planning to spend a night at the tubs . . . Here's some advice your mother never gave you." *Rolling Stone,* February 15.

CHAPTER 9

Narrating Past Lives and Present Concerns: Older Gay Men in Norway

Hans W. Kristiansen[1]

INTRODUCTION

"Turn down the lights!" Karl cries out to the young bartender who is busy distributing ashtrays and small multicolored candle-bowls on the mostly empty tables. Leaning toward me, he explains laughingly: "So that our wrinkles don't show." Shortly afterward the bright ceiling lights are turned down, and the bar is filled with the soft, dim light from candles. It is early afternoon and the Pub has just opened. I am sitting at a table together with Karl, who is in his early 70s, and Reidar, who is in his mid 60s. They both look considerably younger. Karl is dressed in a green blazer, carefully pressed trousers, and shining black shoes. Reidar is wearing a long, dark blue all-weather jacket with a sweater underneath and jeans. Through the one-way glass in the large

[1]The Norwegian Research Council supports the doctorate project upon which this paper is based. Besides the other contributors to the seminar on Adult Development, Aging and Well-being in LGBT Communities, San Francisco, October 26 and 27, 2001, the author is indebted to Kirsten Danielsen and Eduardo Archetti for useful comments on this paper.

basement window above our table I can see busy people passing by, most of them probably without even knowing that this dark and run-down basement locale has been Oslo's most frequented gay bar for nearly two decades. The regular after-work crowd, mostly men in their 50s and 60s, are syphoning down from the street above and finding their places at their regular tables and regular stools. A younger man, possibly a newcomer, is sitting alone by the bar. Almost everyone drinks beer from large 0.5-liter glasses. As the room is filled with cigarette smoke and the smell of beer, the conversation circles around news of the day and everyday topics and concerns. Other regulars come over to say hello or sit down by the table to chat.

For more than a year this bar, located in the center of Oslo, formed the nucleus of my fieldwork among older gay men.[2] Three or four days a week I spent several hours there, mostly in the afternoon and early evening when the chances were best of meeting the older crowd. Some of the men I befriended I later made repeated life-story interviews with in their homes. Others I never met anywhere else but in the bar. Although I never carried out formal interviews "on location," I participated in hundreds of informal conversations, which are documented in my field notes. These conversations and observations, along with the life-story interviews, form the empirical basis of my doctorate project on older gay men in Norway.[3]

The purpose of this paper is twofold. First, I want to identify and describe what I see as three sets of moral concerns that figure promi-nently in the lives of older gay men in Norway. In this respect, the focus is on their situation in the present, on how they experience them-selves and their social surroundings today. Second, I want to explore differences within the category of "older gay men," and particularly differences related to the men's respective relationship histories. How do differences in past life experience translate into differences in con-cerns in later life? One would expect the men to share some basic moral

---

[2]To date no ethnographic studies of gay bars have been published in Norway. My sources of inspiration have been American studies, such as Achilles (1967), Sage (1979), and Read (1980). All personal names used in this text are fictitious.

[3]The average and median age of the sample was (by January 1, 2000) 72 years, and most of the older gay men were retired by the time I interviewed them. The average age is thus considerably higher than in many recent American studies on "older gay men" and "gay aging," where the focus is on "middle age" rather than "old age" (see Herdt et al., 1997; Adams & Kimmel, 1997; Cohler et al., 1998; Beeler et al., 1999; Kertzner, 1999). With respect to age, my sample is more similar to the lesbian women studied by Kehoe (1989), who were all over age 60.

concerns and orientations because of their shared identity as gay men and because of their having come of age under more or less the same historical conditions. At the same time, the men differ greatly with respect to their individual life trajectories, and it is reasonable to assume that this should have an impact on their present-day situation and concerns. Some of the men married women when they were young adults and "discovered" their homosexuality relatively late in life. Others met a male lifetime partner in early adulthood and lived in a marriage-like union with their partner until "death did them part." Others yet remained single and had only short-term relationships or episodic sexual encounters with men.[4]

MORAL CONCERNS

Before I present the three relationship categories, it needs to be sorted out what I mean by "moral concerns." I use this concept in a broad and loose sense to describe a set of worries, complaints, and orientations that older gay men carry with them as they relate to each other and to the world (cf. Barth, 1993, p. 343). In contrast to concepts such as "culture" or "discourse," the concept of "concerns" orients research toward accounting for how people experience themselves and their everyday lives. The use I make of this concept is inspired by the call made by several social and cultural anthropologists for a more person-centered and experience–near ethnography (Cohen, 1995; Crapanzano, 1980; Herdt & Stoller, 1990; Okely, 1996; Rosaldo, 1989; Wikan, 1990, 1991; to mention only a few prominent names).

The concept of "concerns" differs somewhat from the concept of "needs" (Jacobs et al., 1999; Beeler et al., 1999). Assessing the needs of a person or a group of persons implies taking a point of view external to what might be called the horizon of concerns of that person or group. An implicit or explicit theory of "what is good for" the subjects under study is always already built into the concept of "needs." A brief example will illustrate this point. Although I state below that "discretion" is an important moral concern to older gay men in Norway, I would never label it a "need." Social workers and gay activists alike may even consider

---

[4]All except for two of the informants (who considered themselves bisexuals) saw themselves as homosexual at the time of the interview. In the following text, these two men will be included when I use the label "older gay men." Both of the self-identified bisexual men were previously married, and both stated that they at present related sexually only to other men.

older gay men's concern with discretion an obstacle to the fulfillment of their needs; for example, their need for increased social interaction with other gay people. However, greater understanding of concerns such as discretion may help us to explain the apparent paradox that older gay men may express wishes for more opportunities to socialize with other gay men, yet stay away from gay community activities (cf. Berger, 1982, p. 161; Beeler et al., 1999).

I will concentrate on what I perceive as three broadly shared moral concerns—or rather sets of concerns—among older gay men. I have chosen to call them *discretion, sexual dignity*, and *familial ties*. Some readers may feel uneasy about my use of the word *moral* in this context, and it should be emphasized that *moral* is used here in a very broad sense, inspired by the philosopher Charles Taylor. *Moral* comprises not only "our notions and reactions on such issues as justice and the respect of other people's life, well-being, and dignity," but also "our sense of what underlies our own dignity, or questions about what makes our lives meaningful or fulfilling" (Taylor, 1989, p. 4).[5] What I describe below as "moral concerns" is therefore not primarily concerns with "what it is right to do," but rather with "what it is good to be" (Taylor, 1989, p. 3). What takes center stage is the older gay men's perception of what it means to live a dignified and good life—in the phase of life where they presently find themselves. Thus, considerations of what affects their own well-being and happiness, such as concern with sexual dignity and with maintaining familial ties, are also included here, although such concerns would not qualify as "moral" in a more narrow sense of the term. Health concerns, however, and concerns of a purely existential kind—such as concern with aging or death—fall outside of the scope of this paper. But before turning to the concerns proper, I will comment briefly on the men's relationship histories and give a presentation of some of the older gay men I met during fieldwork.

THREE KINDS OF RELATIONSHIP HISTORIES

Only a few weeks into the fieldwork period, I realized that the older gay men I met in the Pub and in other contexts not only differed with

---

[5]Taylor continues: "These might be classed as moral questions on some broad definition, but some are too concerned with the self-regarding, or too much a matter of our ideals, to be classified as moral issues in most people's lexicon. They concern, rather, what makes life worth living" (Taylor, 1989, p. 4). Taylor criticizes different strands of naturalism for giving

respect to their age, social background, and present relationship status, but they could also be separated into three categories based on their relationship histories: (1) the formerly married men; (2) those who for the most part had remained single; and (3) those who had been engaged in long-term relationships to other men (lasting for 20 years or more). Of the 23 men in the interview sample, 11 were previously married, 8 were or had been in long-term partnerships, and 4 had been predominantly single.[6] It should be emphasized that his division of the sample is not based on the men's present relationship status, but on their main relationship status when they were in the age group of 25–50 years.[7] In this respect my approach differs from the typology of "lifestyles" developed by Bell and Weinberg (1978), which focuses on present relationship patterns. Much of the research literature on relationship status and mental well-being has focused on the difference between "single" and "coupled" gays and lesbians (Lipman, 1986; see Hostetler, this volume, for a review of the literature), and such categorizations are based on present relationship status.[8] One of the things that gets lost in such comparisons, however, is the distinction between those who have been married and those who have not, a distinction that I see as crucially important.

---

a very narrow focus to morality. "Morality is conceived purely as a guide to *action*. It is thought to be concerned purely with what it is right to do rather than with what it is good to be" (Taylor, 1989, p. 79).

[6]In a large survey of living conditions and quality of life among lesbian woman and gay men in Norway (n = 2987), one in three of the women and one in four of the men in the age group 50–59 were or had been married (Hegna et al., 1999). The percentage was even higher among the respondents over the age of 60: 43% of the women and 31% of the men were or had been married. In the younger age groups, the survey showed much lower percentages of men and women who had been married. In a questionnaire survey conducted in Chicago among 160 gay men and lesbian women and bisexuals over the age of 45, 40% of the respondents had been married to a member of the other sex (Herdt et al., 1997). Among the respondents in Berger's (1982) study, 29% of the gay men in the sample had been married to a woman.

[7]Two of the men were married only for a couple of years, and both were involved in long term couple relationships with other men when they were in their 20s, 30s, or 40s. Still, I have chosen to classify them with the "formerly married men" in this paper because they both have children and therefore seem to have more in common with this group than with the "partnered men."

[8]In the Norwegian survey of living conditions and quality of life among lesbian woman and gay men (Hegna et al., 1999), those who were in a stable relationship reported to be more satisfied with life in general than persons who were not in a stable relationship. They were also happier with their sexual life and had more frequent sex. These differences were a feature in all age groups.

The tripartite division of the sample into "formerly married," "formerly single," and "formerly partnered" will be reflected in the following discussion as I attempt to identify some of the men's common concerns. The following three examples are meant to exemplify each of these three categories. As Berger (1982) emphasized two decades ago, in order to do away with stereotypes about the older homosexual man, it is vital that we take into account the diversity within this group.

A Formerly Married Man: "Henry"

Henry is in his late 60s and lives alone in a small apartment in one of Oslo's suburbs. He meets his gay friends in the Pub once or twice a week but has practically no contact with other gay men outside of the bar context. He is presently retired, but has worked most of his life as an engineer. He has, however, a part-time manual job in a shop in downtown Oslo, "in order not to get bored to death sitting at home not knowing how to pass the days," he says. When Henry was in his late 20s, while studying in Oslo, he was involved in a love relationship with another man and was part of a homosexual friendship circle. In his early 30s, however, he got married to a woman and moved to a city in the northern part of Norway. There he fathered a daughter and a son and led what he himself describes as a "normal, but a bit uninteresting life." He divorced his wife after 15 years of marriage. Henry maintained that the reason for the divorce was not his homosexuality, but the fact that he and his wife did not get along. Gradually he resumed contact with his former gay friends, and after he retired from his job as an engineer a decade or so ago he moved back to Oslo, partly to assist his now-grown daughter with babysitting and child care. Several days a week he helps his daughter out by looking after his grandchildren. Although he suspects that his children know about his sexual orientation, he has never spoken to them about the topic.[9]

Henry's relationship to his daughter and grandchildren figured prominently in his everyday life. For one thing, he is one of the few in the group who is equipped with a mobile phone, as illustrated in the following excerpt from my field notes:

> I am sitting at the regular table in the Pub together with four other men, all of them in their late 60s or early 70s. Suddenly a mobile phone sounds, and

---

[9]He never told his parents nor other family members that he is gay.

after some confusion the man next to me, Henry, reaches for the right-hand pocket of his jacket. He lifts the phone to his ear, and I can hear a female voice in the other end. "Hi, I'm out having a beer with some friends," Henry says. He arranges to meet someone, and assures his interlocutor that it is "no problem at all." After terminating the phone call, he tells us that it was his daughter on the phone and that he has to go and pick up his grandchildren at the kindergarten. He says that it is for these kinds of eventualities that he has acquired the mobile phone. Henry empties his beer—he never drinks more than one glass—says goodbye, and leaves the bar.

A Lifetime Single Man: "Willy"

Willy, presently in his early 70s, lives in a middle-class neighborhood in Oslo, in the apartment that he shared with his mother until she died in the late 1970s. He was the only child, and his father died when he was still a teenager. In his early teens Willy started to interact sexually with men that he met in the city, among them German soldiers during World War II and American soldiers in the first postwar years. In the 1940s, 1950s, and 1960s he made numerous sexual contacts with other men, mostly in the public restrooms and parks in Oslo. He has been involved in three short-term love relationships with other men, but he has never lived together with his lovers. In contrast to many of the other men I interviewed, his mother knew that he was homosexual, and she had a very good relationship with his homosexual friends. For most of his professional career he worked as a receptionist in a hotel in Oslo. Although many of his older gay friends have died, he still has a couple of friends left—gay men he has known since his youth. They visit each other and call each other on the phone. Today Willy rarely visits gay bars or cruising areas, and he tends to see his sexual life as a past stage. This is what he answered when I asked him whether he frequents places like the Pub:

I've been there [at the Pub]. But I don't feel comfortable there for some reason. It frightens me. I was there once, and this guy made a pass at me, to use that expression. A large, tall guy winked at me and raised his glass, stuff like that. But I didn't respond—I simply didn't dare to. I wasn't interested anyway. Because—I don't know if it's due to diabetes or what else it might be, but the urge is gone. So I just want to live in peace. That's all that matters to me now. I don't have any desire. I might look at a pretty boy, just like I look at a flower. But I no longer run after him or try to make a pass at him. [. . .] No, that ended quite abruptly when I rounded 60, I think. I simply felt no need anymore. I didn't crave for it—the craving disappeared. They say that it might be due to diabetes. But I think it might be Nature itself. [. . .] Or maybe your hormones start failing, I don't know. But in a way I'm glad. It gives you more peace of mind. I often think that to go running around in the Frogner Park now that I'm 70 would look plain stupid. So I'm kind of glad I don't have to do that. You don't have that—Now I have to go out and get me something. But I think that it's Nature itself that does that to you, because otherwise you wouldn't be able to put up with it. I don't know.

A Formerly Partnered Man: "Alf"[10]

Alf is in his early 70s and has spent the last three years in a retirement home in Oslo. After his lifetime companion for 45 years died in 1993, he kept on living in the old apartment for a couple of years until he got ill and was hospitalized. Today he is dependent on a wheelchair and unable to live alone. All of their life together he and his lover were extremely careful not to let anyone know about their loving and sexual relationship, and to family and friends they always cloaked their relationship as a close friendship. For many years they shared an apartment with Alf's mother and aunt, and Alf and his partner slept in the maid's room, in bunk beds. They had exclusively heterosexual friends but were always invited together to parties and other social gatherings. In the course of his working career, he had several well-paid jobs within the area of accounting and personnel management. He has presently neither family nor gay friends in Oslo, but an older heterosexual couple—friends he has known since his youth—visits him occasionally. I got in touch with Alf through a young gay nurse who worked at the retirement home where Alf presently lives. This nurse, whom I met at the Pub, is one of the few people to whom Alf has confided that he is homosexual. The following excerpt from my field notes is from the first interview I made with Alf in the autumn of 1999:

> As I am about to leave Alf's small and narrow room after the interview, Alf signals to me that I shall come back inside and close the door once more. Then he carefully instructs me on what to say if—on my way out—a member of the staff should ask me about the purpose of my visit. He says that I should tell them that I am interested in antiques and that I had brought with me a

---

[10]Registered partnership has been a possibility for Norwegian lesbian and gay couples since 1993 and is, with the exception of the right to adopt children, equivalent to civil marriage (see Halvorsen, 1998; Hegna et al., 1999).

silver spoon that I wanted him to assess. "You can never know," he said. I nod, slightly embarrassed over this precaution more worthy of a secret lover than an anthropologist, and leave the room. Luckily I am not asked by the staff to explain my relationship with Mr. Andersen. He has already told me that he considers himself a "closet homosexual" and that he does not want the staff or anyone else to know that he is gay.

This last example leads directly into the first concern I want to address, namely, discretion.

DISCRETION

The following "advice to the young homosexual," quoted from the book entitled *We Who Feel Differently* (Grodal, 1957),[11] is probably representative of the attitudes toward discretion that prevailed among homosexual men in Norway in the period between 1940 and 1965: "First of all, there is one thing you should know: you have no reason to be ashamed of hiding your true face. You have chosen to do that because you feel that given the attitudes of society, you will have far better opportunities to realize your personality in this way than by laying yourself bare" (Grodal, 1957, p. 223, my translation). For many older gay men in Norway, Grodal's advise is still valid, and if I were to choose a name for the generation of men that I have studied, I think that "the discreet generation" would be a good alternative. The topic of discretion and being discreet is probably where the differences between gay men over the age of 60 and younger generations of gay men come most clearly into view, giving rise to a host of misunderstandings and misrepresentations. This is also where the historical changes in attitudes toward gay men and lesbian women are most evident (see Lee, 1989; Grube, 1991; Herdt, 1992; Herdt & Boxer, 1992, 1996; Rosenfeld, 1999; Cohler & Galatzer-Levy, 2000). My contention is that while the older generation's concern with discretion has been loudly condemned and ridiculed by the younger generations of gays and lesbians—and by the Gay Liberation movement from the 1970s onward—it has rarely been studied on its own terms.

---

[11]The book entitled "We who feel differently" (*Vi som føler annerledes*) from 1957 is one of the first books to be published on the subject of homosexuality in Norway. The name "Finn Grodal" is a pseudonym for the late Øivind Eckhoff (1916–2001), one of the pioneers in the Norwegian homophile movement, The Norwegian Association of 1948 (Kjaer, 2003).

The main reason I have chosen the term *discretion* is that this particular concern is easily misunderstood when rendered in the terminology of "being out" versus "being closeted." This terminology has become popular mainly because of the efforts of the Gay Liberation movement and the call for gay men and lesbians to "come out" (Sedgwick, 1990). While maintaining silence about one's sexual relationships and orientation was clearly seen as prudent and positive in the 1950s and 1960s, the Gay Liberation movement in the 1970s and onward has tended to see this concern with discretion as opportunistic and cowardly (Grube, 1991; Howard, 1999, p. 31; Rosenfeld, 1999; Friele, 1990).[12] The popularity of words such as *closet queen* over the last few decades attests to this change. Even though some of the older men I met during field work used terms such as *closet homosexual* or *being in the closet*, the opposition "being obvious" versus "being discreet" is much more prominent in their self-understanding than the opposition "open" versus "closeted." Being discreet is clearly seen as the positive side of the equation, while being obvious or indiscreet is associated with gender digression and public display of same-sex affections. Alf's interview clearly attests to this. This is how he answered when I asked him if he and his lifetime partner could be open in front of their heterosexual friends, for instance, by hugging or holding each other tight.

> No, we didn't do that. Maybe we could have, but we never did. The only time was on New Year's Eve at twelve p.m., then we gave each other a hug, but so did everybody else in the party, and it was a heterosexual party. No, the rest of the time we were very cautious about how we behaved, and we were never outrageous in any way. We were strict about that. Nor did any of us feel like it. I very much resent those who behave in an obvious manner.

In the opinion of people like Alf, being or acting in an obvious manner compromises the public reputation of homosexual men in general.[13] This was also the dominant view of the homophile organizations that

---

[12]The autobiography of Karen-Christine Friele (1990) is a good example of how the new generation of gay and lesbian liberationists who took control of the Norwegian Association of 1948 in the late 1960s condemn what they see as the secrecy and paranoia of the previous generation. Friele became chairperson of the Association in 1966 and maintained a leading position in the gay and lesbian movement in Norway until 1989.

[13]It is important to note, however, that concern with discretion and reluctance to disclose sexual identity are not necessarily a matter of shame about being homosexual (see Lee, 1989, p. 86). Alf, for instance, who was extremely concerned with discretion, saw his lifelong relationship to another man as the most wonderful thing that had happened to him in his life.

were founded in Europe and the United States in the late 1940s and 1950s (Grodal, 1957; Altman, 1971; D'Emilio, 1983; Meeker, 2001).

Older gay men's concern with discretion must be understood in relation to the specific historical circumstances under which they came of age (see Reid, 1995, p. 217). The men I have studied had their youth and early adulthood in the so-called Gerardsen era of Norwegian history, a period marked by the reconstruction after World War II and the consolidation of the welfare state. The social democratic Labor Party (*Arbeiderpartiet*) was the hegemonic party and reigned supreme from World War II until 1963 without interruption. This was an era characterized by great political stability and social homogeneity in Norway.[14] Male homosexuality was not officially decriminalized until 1972, and according to paragraph 213 in the Norwegian Penal Code of 1902, sexual acts between men could be punished with up to one year of imprisonment. It should be noted, however, that this paragraph was rarely applied to acts of voluntary homosexuality between adults (Halsos, 1999). It was specified in the text that prosecution would only take place if it was necessary for the sake of "public interest." The reason for this seems to have been concern on the part of those who made or enforced the law that prosecution would draw the public's attention to "crimes" that would otherwise simply remain hidden (Aarset, 2000, p. 147; Rian, 2001, p. 53). The principle of "mutual discretion" was thereby written into the letter of the law itself.[15]

Is the concern with discretion equally compelling to older gay men from all three relationship-history categories? In a recent article, sociologist Diana Rosenfeld points to the existence of two distinct identity cohorts of lesbian and gay elderly in the United States (Rosenfeld, 1999).[16] According to her, elderly (over the age of 65) who began to understand and identify themselves as gay or lesbian in the "pre-Stonewall era" understand themselves differently from those within the same age group who did so during the ascendance of Gay Liberation in

---

[14]The work of anthropologist Marianne Gullestad is a valuable source to understanding value changes in present-day Norway and the continued emphasis in Norwegian culture on equality conceived as sameness (Gullestad, 1984, 1996, 2002).

[15]Female homosexuality has never officially been a criminal offence in Norway and was not mentioned in paragraph 213 (Halvorsen, 1998). Sexual intercourse with animals, on the other hand, is mentioned side by side with sex between men. This indicates that the lawmakers still considered homosexuality on a par with bestiality and thus as deserving of strong moral condemnation (Aarset, 2000, p. 149).

[16]Rosenfeld's study is based on interviews with 17 self-identified gay men and 20 lesbians over the age of 65, living in the Los Angeles area.

the 1970s and 1980s. She links each of these identity cohorts to two historically specific "discourses of homosexuality": homosexuality as stigma and homosexuality as status. According to the first, which predominated from the 1920s to the 1970s, homosexuality was a discreditable aspect of self, and passing as heterosexual was essential to the competent understanding and enactment of homosexuality (p. 126). According to the second, which has prevailed from the 1970s to the present, homosexuality is an essential and accrediting part of self, and public proclamation of this identity is positively valued. Rosenfeld argues that membership in each of these "identity cohorts" may have more impact on a person's self-understanding as gay or lesbian than does absolute age. Even within the same generation of gay men, one would expect considerable differences with regard to the concern with discretion between members of the two "identity cohorts."

In view of this, one would expect the formerly married men in my study, most of whom "came out" in the 1970s and 1980s, to be less preoccupied with discretion than people like Alf, who identified as homosexual in the late 1940s and 1950s. Although some of the formerly married men in my sample were less concerned with discretion than most of the formerly partnered and single men, Rosenfeld's discussion of identity cohorts does not square with my Norwegian material. A careful reading of the life stories of the formerly married men shows that many of them were in touch with homosexual friendship networks and had sexual relationships with men even before they got married. Three of the men in this category had even been involved in couple relationships to men in the years preceding their marriages, relationships lasting 2, 8, and 12 years, respectively. It is therefore reasonable to assume that even many of the formerly married men belong to the "pre-Stonewall" identity cohort and share its concern with discretion. This is particularly clear in the case of Henry, who after his divorce in the 1970s resumed his relationship to his former gay friends.

Even the formerly married men who had not identified as homosexual prior to marriage tended to express views on discretion that were clearly in accord with those who identified as homosexual in the 1940s and 1950s. Ivar is a case in point. He had practically no prior sexual experience when he in his early 20s married a woman. After a long process of what he describes as self-discovery, he identified as homosexual in the early 1970s and got divorced a few years later. Despite his having "come out" during the heydays of Gay Liberation, he expressed concern with being around other gay men who might be seen as "behaving in an obvious manner":

I very much react to being seen in the city together with a person who is noticeably homosexual, or behaving in a homosexual manner in places where you could be seen, not so much by strangers—that doesn't matter much—but by people you know. Not long ago I had such a reaction. I must go back to the Pub, because down there I met a young man who clung to me. He insisted on coming home with me and this and that. And I think he came from Drammen[17] and was going back to Drammen, and I offered to accompany him to the train station. But both with respect to how he dressed and how he behaved—this was in the summer—he was so . . . He had mini-shorts like this or whatever it was, and I felt so bad going there next to him. He was outrageous, yes he was, and he had had a lot to drink, so he was very cuddly and stuff like that. So it was no pretty sight (laughs). And I remember well that I sighed with relief when I got rid of him.

The preoccupation of formerly married "late bloomers" like Ivar with living discreet lives might also be due to generation-specific characteristics transcending the heterosexual-homosexual divide. Besides, when considering why some of the formerly married men express less concern with discretion, one should bear in mind that it is much easier for these men to cover up their sexual identity simply by referring to their status as fathers, grandfathers, and (former) husbands. Despite some debate about lesbian and gay parenthood in recent years, being a father and, even more so, a grandfather is generally seen as incompatible with gayness in Norwegian society. Their status as divorced fathers and grandparents—and in two cases greatgrandparents—gives these men a safe shelter from suspicion of being gay and represents a resource they can use, for instance, in conversations with strangers whom they did not want to let in behind their veil of discretion.[18]

SEXUAL DIGNITY

The concept of sexual dignity is meant to sum up another set of concerns that features the moral horizon of older gay men in Norway. In contrast to "discretion," the men themselves would probably never use nor immediately understand the concept of "sexual dignity," and I will give a brief explanation of what is meant by this. "Dignity" refers to the

---

[17]Drammen is a city just outside Oslo.
[18]Of the 10 men in the interview sample who were fathers and had children (one of the married men was childless), 7 said that their children knew that they were gay. In most of these cases it had been brought up in connection with the divorce.

characteristics by which we think of ourselves as commanding (or failing to command) the respect of those around us, respect here meaning that others think well of us or even look up to us (Taylor, 1989, p. 15). A person's "sexual dignity" has to do with preserving "self-respect" or "self-worth" in interaction with others. Receiving some kind of recognition—primarily from other gay men—of sexual attractiveness or desirability is but one aspect of this concern. More importantly, maintaining sexual dignity involves behaving in what is considered a dignified way with respect to sexual matters, for example, by not too readily communicating sexual interest in men who may not reciprocate this interest. The concern with sexual dignity is primarily relevant in gay-defined contexts such as bars or bathhouses and should not be confused with a wish for recognition of one's sexual orientation by family and heterosexual colleges and friends.

The men's concern with sexual dignity comes most clearly to the fore in their dealings with younger gay men. The topic of love and sexual relationships surfaced on various occasions in the conversations at the bar table, generally in conversations between no more than two or three persons. It was also a topic much referred to in the interviews. What stands out from these conversations is a strong concern with upholding sexual dignity while at the same time being engaged in intimate relationships with younger men. Contrary to what has been reported by Berger (1984) and Kelly (1977), most of the men in my sample who still saw themselves as sexually active (14 of the 23) were primarily interested in men considerably younger than they were—men in their 20s to early 40s. Opinions differed, on the other hand, when it came to the question of accessibility. Some of the informants claimed that reaching maturity had actually made it easier for them to get erotic contact with younger men. Others gave examples of ageism and rejection by younger men.

Trygve, a self-identified bisexual in his early 70s who was married for 15 years and has three grown children, gave the following statement. "I have never in my life had more opportunity than after I rounded 60 and up till now. I still get off with them, no problem. And I used to think that it was weird, but I've learned that there are actually a whole lot who like grown-up, older men." This is echoed in the interview I made with Ola, a 62-year-old, formerly married man. "Despite me being a fat, old graybeard, there is evidently something about me which young boys find attractive."[19] Both of these men were involved in relationships

---

[19]Similar experiences were reported by some of the bisexual informants in Weinberg, Williams, & Pryor (2001, pp. 190–191).

with men who were 30 years their juniors at the time of the first interview, but none of them lived with their partners.

About one third (8) of the 23 men were involved in couple relationships or more loosely defined "liaisons" to men who were more than 30 years their juniors. Although some kind of economic transfer from the older to the younger man apparently took place in some of these relationships, for the most part the younger party seemed to be involved mainly for the emotional and/or sexual comfort that these relationships provided. For many years Vegar (one of the formerly married men who is presently in his mid 70s) had a young Pakistani-Norwegian lover visiting him. This is what he told me in one of the interviews:

Vegar: It has been 10 to 15 years now since I had a steady relationship. That is, there was a boy who came here from time to time. He used to come here when he got too hot and horny. But he has stopped doing that now because he got married [to a Pakistani girl]. He was a Muslim, strangely enough. But I could touch him and do whatever I wanted with him. And he accepted it in a way, and didn't turn me away. I was even allowed to touch his butt. The butt is holy for a Muslim, you know. So . . .

Hans: But how did you get in touch with him?

Vegar: I met him when he was 16 years old. So he has been in and out of my place for 16 years. And I met him over at the . . . there used to be a urinal in the wall by the *Hersleb* school, so that's where I met him when he was 16. It was last year or this year that he stopped coming, and then he was 32 years old.[20]

I only had the chance to meet three of these younger boyfriends face to face, but based on what the older men told me I was able to form a general picture of them. Mostly they seemed to be men who were in some way marginal in relation to the "out and open" gay community: Five of them were bisexual first- or second-generation immigrants from Asia or Southern Europe. Another was a married, bisexual man of Norwegian ancestry. The key to understanding such "liaisons" may be that these younger men shared the older gay men's concern with discretion. Gay and bisexual immigrants and bisexual, married Caucasians are probably just as hesitant about making use of the "out and

---

[20]Age of consent in Norway is 16 years, both for heterosexual and homosexual relationships.

open" gay environment as are most of the older men. The two remaining boyfriends were Caucasian gay men who preferred older men as sexual partners.

Relationships of this sort were the source of much concern among the older gay men that I befriended, and in my view this was primarily linked to what I call "sexual dignity." The problem was not so much ageism or exclusion from the "sexual marketplace"—although some of the men complained of this—as the men's fear of placing their own self-respect in jeopardy. Fear of being exploited by younger men with whom they got involved was an important ingredient in this concern. The worry seemed to be that younger men who expressed love and erotic interest for them did this mainly to gain some kind of economic benefit or—in some cases—inheritance. Clas, for instance, a formerly partnered man whose lifetime companion died some years ago, was involved in what seemed to be an on-and-off relationship with a man 30 years his junior. He often voiced his concerns about this relationship to me or to other interlocutors at the bar table. The following example of a conversation between Clas (early 70s), Trygve (early 70s), and myself may illustrate this.

> I sit down by the table with Clas and Trygve. The two men are at first so deeply immersed in conversation that they do not seem to notice me. I understand that Clas is telling Trygve about his relationship to Åge, a man in his 30s. Clas complains that he and Åge have only had sex a couple of times during the three years they have been together. (They live in separate apartments.) Trygve, who is already quite drunk, says that he is certain that it is Clas's money that Åge is after. Later the same night Clas tells me that he once helped Åge out by lending him a considerable amount of money, money that Åge has never returned to him. (Excerpt from field notes)

The older men in the Pub tended to group the younger gay men they met and interacted with into two distinct categories: those who *like* (i.e., are erotically aroused by) older gay men and those who *take advantage of* older gay men. The fact that these two categories could and probably often did overlap was a topic that the men hardly ever pursued. Falling into the latter category were young barflies, eager to sponge beer or small amounts of money from older gay men, as well as the more insidious con-men who tried to get at the older men's wallets by way of their hearts. The older gay men were faced with the quandary of seeking out men of the first category—those who *like* older gay men—while at the same time keeping men from the second category at arm's length. A saying often repeated in the pub, and always in connection with talk about relationships to younger men, reflects this anxiety: "When the prick stands up half of your brains are gone, and when your brains come back to you, half of your prick is gone." The meaning of this saying is of course that it is easy to do stupid things when sexually aroused. But it also seems to imply that loss of dignity and manhood may be the outcome of being carried away by sexual desire or feelings of affection for younger men.

The concern with sexual dignity also surfaced in statements that many of the older men made to the effect that they were now beyond sexuality. General cultural expectations of sexual abstinence in old age, combined with negative stereotypes of pathetic and unappetizing older homosexuals on the prowl for young men, seem to create strong normative pressures toward stepping out of the arena of sexuality. Willy's assertion that his sexual urge is gone and that he just wants to live in peace is one example of this. Another example is Sigurd, a former shop owner who is presently in his early 80s. When he divorced his wife at 45 he had practically no sexual experience with other men. This is how he summarizes his homosexual "career":

Sigurd: I was divorced when I was 45, and until then I hadn't lived a homosexual life at all. I was 45 years old and had maybe been sleeping with five persons. At the most. But now I've had my share. [. . .] I certainly have. It was easy for me to get [sexual partners]. My looks weren't so bad, and I was quite well-off. So I've had my share. But now I've given it all up. And I prayed to Our Lord for that, because I've always felt disgusted by those old homosexuals who hang out by the urinals and . . . like this (opens his mouth and stares out into the air with widely opened eyes). Yes. And I didn't want to become like that. So I've prayed for that every night. I started doing that when I passed 70, or at least at 75. And he has answered my prayers: I feel no [desire]. I have given it up.

Hans: So you don't go out anymore?

Sigurd: No, I never do. No, I don't want to do that anymore, because I think that if I did it today, then it is only to satisfy myself or to let myself be satisfied. And I don't want that. When there are no feelings involved anymore . . .

The way I interpret it, Sigurd's renunciation of sexuality has more to do with his self-presentation than with any real-life changes in his sexual habits. In the same interview he relates a sexual episode with a younger man that took place the preceding year. For men like Willy and Sigurd, maintaining sexual dignity seems to be tantamount to sexual resignation.

The bogey of the older homosexual man that Sigurd refers to brings to mind Berger's comments on the stereotypes of older gay men in American society: "Gay men supposedly become 'odd' and extremely effeminate as they age, repulsing the people around them. Finally, older gay men are said to have desperate unfulfilled sexual needs which are satisfied by preying on the young" (Berger 1982, p. 157; see Rawls, this volume). Because of such stereotypes, the parallel that is sometimes drawn between the exclusion from the sexual marketplace of older heterosexual women and older gay men (Grodal, 1957; Danielsen, 1992) is somewhat misleading. Although sexual dignity is clearly an issue for middle-aged and older heterosexual women, for older gay men the threats to sexual dignity are compounded by these negative stereotypes.

Although there were examples of this kind of renunciation of sex among men from all three relationship-history categories, it was more common among the formerly single and formerly partnered categories than among those men who had been married. The formerly married men seemed to be more willing to take the risk of getting erotically and/or emotionally involved with younger men, possibly because they felt that they had to make up for all of the "wasted years." It might also have to do with the fact that they had children, and therefore felt less vulnerable to attempts of economic exploitation. Since they would be expected to use most of their economic resources on their children and grandchildren—who will also inherit them when they die—the formerly married men were not exploitable to the same degree.

FAMILIAL TIES AND NETWORK DISRUPTION

The third and final set of concerns I want to address has to do with older gay men's ties to blood relatives, on the one hand, and gay friends and lovers, on the other. This is where the difference between men from the three relationship-history categories becomes most visible. It is also a field of great tension in the interaction between older gay men who have their own children and those who are childless. The concern with "familial ties" involves questions—not so much about what is good or what is bad—but about what is important and what is not, what has meaning and importance and what is trivial and secondary (Taylor, 1989, p. 28). This is why I feel justified in including it among the other moral concerns.

In conversations in the Pub, the men's relationship to blood relatives, and particularly children and grandchildren, was a somewhat suppressed topic. Gay grandparents like Henry seldom mentioned their children and grandchildren, unless they were explicitly asked. Neither did I ever see any of the formerly married men showing pictures of their children and grandchildren to other gay men in the pub (cf. Herdt et al., 1997, p. 241). Fear of hurting or disrespecting those among the men who were childless was probably the main reason for this conspicuous absence of talk about blood relatives. One evening when Henry and I were alone at the table in the Pub, he informed me that he is usually very hesitant about discussing his relationship to children and grandchildren in the presence of his gay friends. "It's a very tender spot, you know, to many of those who are alone and don't have anyone they are close with."

When the topic was brought up at the table, it was generally introduced by one of the men who did not have children. The following exchange between Karl—a formerly partnered man whose lifetime companion died a decade ago—and Henry may illustrate some of the soreness that this subject brought up.

Just like the last time I sat with them, Karl asks Henry if he is going to be babysitting this weekend. Henry says that it is not so much for the sake of babysitting, but more for the opportunity to be close to his grandchildren. He says that he is going to have his daughter and her family over for dinner on Sunday. "You're so lucky," says Karl half-jokingly, "I have no more than a red cat to cuddle with." (Excerpt from field notes)

In the interviews and in conversations I had face to face with the previously married men, they were far less hesitant about this topic, and many expressed that they saw themselves as more fortunate and better off than most of the men who did not have children of their own. In the interview I made with Henry in his home, I asked him what he saw as his greatest achievement in life. He answered without hesitation:

That I should get the chance—to put it that way—to experience being a dad. And now, even more, being a granddad and have a family who loves me and that I love and care about and all that. Here I can compare myself to others in the clique. Although one or two of them have a background similar to mine, most of them are alone and have no close relations. And to be totally honest, I have to say that they don't know—and thank God for that—what they are missing out on. Do you get my point? Because I will absolutely and unconditionally say that the greatest thing that has happened to me in my life, is to be allowed to have this little family of mine.

Generally the formerly married men expressed regret that they had married, and remarks like "I was stupid enough to marry" and "I should never have married" were often heard in the Pub and in the interviews. At the same time, practically all of the 10 men who had become fathers expressed that they had taken great joy in raising their kids and felt fortunate to have close blood relatives now that they were growing old.[21]

My impression is that many of the men who have lived single or partnered lives are concerned that they will have nothing to "fall back on" if their partner or close gay friends die. Since many of the homosexual friendship circles or cliques from the 1950s and 1960s were rather undifferentiated with respect to age, it was not uncommon to meet men in their 70s with almost no friends left. Especially for men like Willy, the withering away of friendship networks made them vulnerable to social isolation in their 70s and 80s. There seemed to be a general agreement among the older gay men I met that although friendships and friendship ties are valuable and rewarding, they can never muster the same degree of social support and intimacy that bonds to blood relatives can. For example, I did not hear older gay men using *family* with reference to *chosen families* in Weston's sense of the term (Weston, 1991), although such friendship families have been described among later generations of gay men in Norway (see Andersen, 1987).

Provided that the partner was still alive, older gay men who had lived in long-term partnerships enjoyed much of the same love and unconditional support as did men who had their own children and grandchildren. But especially the younger party in such unions was vulnerable to spending his last years in widowerhood and relative social isolation, as was the case with Alf and (although not so definitely) with Karl. Another informant, Ragnar, recently lost his partner of more than 40 years. His partner was 77 when he died, while Ragnar is still in his mid 60s. This was a concern to both the younger and the older party

---

[21]This is also in accord with what has been reported from focus group interviews with middle-aged gay fathers in Chicago (Herdt et al., 1997, p. 241).

in many of the long-term gay couples that I met.[22] The Norwegian state-run health care and retirement system secures every citizen a decent livelihood in older years. But to most senior citizens, spending one's last years at a retirement home is not considered an attractive alternative.

Familial ties are troublesome also in another respect. Such bonds are susceptible to disrupting gay friendship networks by drawing the formerly married men away from their gay friends. It appears that the formerly married men tend to be increasingly reclaimed by their blood family with old age. As the formerly married men "retire" to their blood relatives and retreat from the gay environment, the single men and the formerly partnered widowers risk further social isolation.

"Lars" (early 70s) may serve as a case in point. I got acquainted with him early on in the field work, and through our conversations in the bar I learned that he came from a small city in the southern part of Norway ("Southerntown"), where he had grown up and where most of his family still lives. He got married in his early 20s and stayed married for nearly 20 years. Since the late 1960s he has lived and worked in Oslo, in the restaurant business. I met him in fall 1999, and in December I made an interview with him in his home in the working-class neighborhood where he has lived for 30 years. In the interview he expressed that he felt good about living in Oslo and that he had no wish to move back to Southerntown:

> They [his children] say that they want me to come back to Southerntown. But—as I say—why should I go to Southerntown and stay indoors all day long? I will rather stay here so that I can go out and meet my friends. I have almost no friends left in Southerntown, except from my brothers and sisters and the like. And my friends from school—I wouldn't even recognize them if I met them on the street.

The following spring, Lars's health deteriorated and he was rarely seen in the Pub. I called him on the phone almost every week, and he told me he was suffering from low back pain (sciatica) and intestinal problems. Not until the end of March did he feel well enough to go through with the second interview. When we met I asked him if he had experienced any particular changes in his life as a result of growing

---

[22]There were also some cases of what seemed to be late-onset alcoholism (see Gorman & Nelson, this volume) among the formerly partnered widowers, apparently due to the combined effects of bereavement issues and the importance of bars in these men's attempts to reestablish contact with gay friendship networks.

older. He answered: "No, I've been waiting for that. But I can't say I have. The only problem is that I've been sick. It feels as if everything has been thrown upon me lately. If it's not this it is that. That's how I've experienced it."

When I talked to him again two months later (in May), he informed me that he had been on vacation for two weeks in Southerntown and that he was planning to move back there the upcoming summer. He was already making arrangements to sell his apartment. I asked him if it was because he had family and friends there, and he answered a bit hesitatingly: "You know, as one grows older." He also told me that his closest gay friend in Oslo, a single gay man in his mid 60s, and his next-door neighbor (another single gay man) were quite upset that he was leaving Oslo for good.

The point I am trying to make is that it seems as if bonds to blood relatives, especially to children and grandchildren, grow stronger for the formerly married men as they get older (see de Vries & Blando, this volume). This may potentially lead to a disruption of gay friendships and a retraction of these men from the gay environment. This is a field of inquiry that deserves more attention in studies of gay and lesbian aging.[23]

A CONCLUSION OF SORTS

In this paper I have pointed to three sets of moral concerns that I consider crucially important in the lives of older gay men in Norway. The list of concerns could of course be expanded and refined, and some of the concerns that I have treated as subsidiary might have deserved a more independent treatment.

Knowledge of what is at stake for older gay men may also be of use to health care and outreach workers who provide services to members of this group. For example, greater understanding of what discretion has meant and means to gay men of this generation may prevent researchers and service providers from applying ahistorical, psychological stage models to lesbian and gay elderly. Older gay men concerned with keeping their own and other homosexual men's identities from

---

[23]As Hostetler and Cohler (1997, p. 206) point out, very little is known about the relationships and relationship histories of heterosexually married gay men and lesbians, self-identified bisexual individuals, or those individuals who experience their sexuality as fluid.

becoming public knowledge should not be confounded with persons "functioning at the identity confusion stage" (Pope, 1997), although this might be an appropriate description in some isolated cases. The positive evaluation of "discretion" among older gay men may well provide some of the explanation for Rawls's (this volume) conclusion that lower levels of disclosure do not seem to be related with higher levels of depression among self-identified gay and homosexual men over the age of 60 years.

This paper has also provided an opportunity for me to think in terms of connections between older gay men's past lives and their situation in the present. Relationship history stands out as an important factor in differentiating older gay men with respect to moral concerns in later life. Seen from a life course perspective, it seems that the formerly married men, and in particular those among them who have children and grandchildren, experience adulthood very differently from gay men whose dominant relationship status has been either single life or same-sex partnership. Most of the formerly married men saw themselves as fortunate compared with the partnered and single men. They also seemed somewhat less concerned with discretion and more confident and less concerned about intimate relationships with younger gay men. The most important difference, however, seems to be related to father-hood and to the formerly married men's link to the next generation. The importance of considering heterosexual marriage and having children when mapping out differences and similarities between individuals in the larger population of older gay men has earlier been pointed out in a study by Herdt et al. (1997, p. 244).

Although this paper focuses primarily on concerns and lived experience, it may also have some relevance to the discussion about "successful aging." Several American studies have concluded or hypothesized that "discretion" (phrased as "passing" or "being in the closet") adversely affects the quality of social support, and that "being in the closet" isolates gay men from the support of others (Berger, 1992). According to Berger, this is because "passing" impedes development of close personal relationships, isolates the individual from other gay persons, and makes the covert gay man "unable to reciprocate in sharing of intimate details of his emotional life" (Berger, 1992, p. 89). This is consistent with Friend's (1991) theory of successful aging, according to which "those lesbian and gay people who will age successfully are those whose identities are formed in the affirmative direction" (Friend, 1991, p. 109). Other researchers, most notably Lee (1987, 1989), have come to the opposite conclusion, namely, that "successful aging involves being fortunate and/or skillful enough to avoid stressors, including the stress of 'coming out' " (Reid 1995, p. 225).

My material on older gay men in Norway does not fully support either of these positions. Successful aging for this generation of gay men seems to be related to other factors than self-disclosure and "coming out." The effect of self-disclosure should not be seen independently of factors such as relationship history and bonds to blood relatives. The group of men that seems most at risk—at least when it comes to social isolation in later years—are men like Alf, who have been the younger party in long-term partnerships and who at the same time have lived extremely discreet lives. Those who have remained single all or most of their lives seem to have been better at diversifying their social networks of friends than the formerly partnered men and are thus somewhat less at risk when it comes to social isolation.

To end on a more positive and thoughtful note, I will let one of the older gay men round off this paper. This is what Kristian said about his experiences of growing older:

> Sooner or later you get to that point in life where you realize that you don't have the same chances anymore, do you know what I mean? The opportunities are no longer there. That's when you learn to appreciate so much more the ones that do come along. It doesn't have to develop into a relationship or anything like that, but you are so much more thankful for the fleeting caresses you get on your way. That's how you notice it. And as you get older you try to gather your experience and pride yourself that you'll never commit the same stupidities again. But you always do.

REFERENCES

Aarset, A. H. (2000). *Rettslig regulering av homoseksuell praksis 1687–1902*. Oslo: Institutt for offentlig retts skriftserie nr. 2.

Achilles, N. (1967). The development of the homosexual bar as an institution. In J. Gagnon & W. Simon (Eds.), *Sexual deviance* (pp. 228–244). New York: Harper & Row.

Adams, C. L., Jr., & Kimmel, D. C. (1997). Exploring the lives of older African American gay men. In B. Green (Ed.), *Ethnic and cultural diversity among lesbians and gay men*. Thousand Oaks, CA: Sage Publications.

Altman, D. (1971). *Homosexuality: Oppression and liberation*. New York: Outerbridge & Dienstfrey.

Andersen, A. J. (1987). *Coming out—coming home. Vennskap som sosial strategi*. Hovedfagsoppgave i sosiologi, Universitetet i Oslo.

Barth, F. (1993). *Balinese worlds.* Chicago: University of Chicago Press.

Beeler, J. A., Rawls, T. W., Herdt, G., & Cohler, B. J. (1999). The needs of older lesbians and gay men in Chicago. *Journal of Gay and Lesbian Social Services,* 9(1), 31–49.

Bell, A. P., & Weinberg, M. S. (1978). *Homosexualities: A study of diversity among men and women.* New York: Simon & Schuster.

Berger, R. M. (1982). *Gay and gray. The older homosexual man.* Boston: Alyson Publications.

Berger, R. M. (1984). Realities of gay and lesbian aging. *Social Work,* 29(1), 57–61.

Berger, R. M. (1992). Passing and social support among gay men. *Journal of Homosexuality,* 23(3), 85–97.

Cohen, A. P. (1995). *Self consciousness: An alternative anthropology of identity.* London: Routledge.

Cohler, B. J., & Galatzer-Levy, R. M. (2000). *The course of gay and lesbian lives: Social and psychoanalytic perspectives.* Chicago: University of Chicago Press.

Cohler, B., Hostetler, A. J., & Boxer, A. M. (1998). Generativity, social context, and lived experience: Narratives of gay men in middle adulthood. In D. P. McAdams & E. D. St. Aubin (Eds.), *Generativity and adult development: How and why we care for the next generation.* Washington, DC: American Psychological Association.

Crapanzano, V. (1980). *Tuhami: Portrait of a Moroccan.* Chicago: University of Chicago Press.

Danielsen, K. (1992). *Slike gutter. Eldre menn forteller om sitt liv.* Oslo: Pax Forlag.

D'Emilio, J. (1983). *Sexual politics, sexual communities: The making of a homosexual minority in the United States 1940–1970.* Chicago: University of Chicago Press.

Friele, K. C. (1990). *Troll skal temmes.* Oslo: Scanbok.

Friend, R. A. (1991). Older lesbian and gay people: A theory of successful aging. In J. A. Lee (Ed.), *Gay midlife and maturity.* New York: Harrington Park Press.

Grodal, F. (1957). (Ed.). *Vi som føler annerledes. Homoseksualiteten og samfunnet.* Oslo: H. Aschehoug & Co.

Grube, J. (1991). Natives and settlers: An ethnographic note on early interaction of older homosexual men with younger gay liberationists. In J. A. Lee (Ed.), *Gay midlife and maturity.* New York: Harrington Park Press.

Gullestad, M. (1984). *Kitchen table society: A case study of the family life and friendships of young working-class mothers in urban Norway.* Oslo: Universitetsforlaget.

Gullestad, M. (1996). *Everyday life philosophers: Modernity, morality and autobiography in Norway.* Oslo: Scandinavian University Press.

Gullestad, M. (2002). Invisible fences: Egalitarianism, nationalism and racism. *Journal of the Royal Anthropological Institute,* 8(1), 45–63.

Halsos, M. (1999). *Almindelig borgerlig straffelov av 1902. Homoseksualitet i Norge og rettslige sanksjoner mot den fra slutten av 1800-tallet til 1972.* Hovedoppgave i historie. Universitetet i Oslo.

Halvorsen, R. (1998). The ambiguity of lesbian and gay marriages: Change and continuity in the symbolic order. In J. Löfström (Ed.), *Scandinavian homosexualities: Essays on gay and lesbian studies.* New York: Haworth Press.

Hegna, K., Kristiansen, H. W., & Moseng, B. U. (1999). *Levekår og livskvalitet blant lesbiske kvinner og homofile menn*. Oslo: NOVA.

Herdt, G. (1992). "Coming out" as a rite of passage: A Chicago study. In G. Herdt (Ed.), *Gay culture in America: Essays from the field*. Boston: Beacon Press.

Herdt, G., Beeler, J., & Rawls, T. W. (1997). Life course diversity among older lesbians and gay men: A study in Chicago. *Journal of Gay, Lesbian and Bisexual Identity, 2*(3/4), 231–246.

Herdt, G., & Boxer, A. M. (1992). Introduction: Culture, history, and life course of gay men. In G. Herdt (Ed.), *Gay culture in America: Essays from the field*. Boston: Beacon Press.

Herdt, G., & Boxer, A. M. (1996). *Children of Horizons: How gay and lesbian youth are leading a new way out of the closet*. Boston: Beacon Press.

Herdt, G., & Stoller, R. J. (1990). *Intimate communications: Erotics and the study of culture*. New York: Colombia University Press.

Hostetler, A. J., & Cohler, B. J. (1997). Partnership, singlehood, and the lesbian and gay life course: A research agenda. *Journal of Gay, Lesbian and Bisexual Identity, 2*(3/4), 199–230.

Howard, J. (1999). *Men like that: A southern queer history*. Chicago: University of Chicago Press.

Jacobs, R. J., Rasmissen, L. A., & Hohman, M. M. (1999). The social support needs of older lesbians, gay men, and bisexuals. *Journal of Gay and Lesbian Social Services, 9*(1), 1–30.

Kehoe, M. (1989). *Lesbians over 60 speak for themselves*. New York: Harrington Park Press.

Kelly, J. (1977). The aging male homosexual: Myth and reality. *The Gerontologist, 17*(4), 328–332.

Kertzner, R. (1999). Self-appraisal of life experience and psychological adjustment in midlife gay men. *Journal of Psychology and Human Sexuality, 11*(2).

Kjaer, R. (2003). Look to Norway? Gay issues and mental health across the Atlantic Ocean. *Journal of Gay and Lesbian Psychotherapy, 7*(1/2), 55–73.

Lee, J. A. (1987). What can homosexual aging studies contribute to theories of aging? *Journal of Homosexuality, 13*(3), 43–71.

Lee, J. A. (1989). Invisible men: Canada's aging homosexuals. Can they be assimilated into Canada's "liberated" gay communities? *Canadian Journal on Aging, 8*(1), 79–97.

Lipman, A. (1986). Homosexual relationships. *Generations*, Summer.

Meeker, M. (2001). Behind the mask of respectability: Reconsidering the Mattachine Society and male homophile practice, 1950s and 1960s. *Journal of the History of Sexuality, 10*(1), 78–116.

Okely, J. (1996). *Own or other culture*. London: Routledge.

Pope, M. (1997). Sexual issues for older lesbians and gays. *Topics in Geriatric Rehabilitation, 12*(4), 53–60.

Read, K. E. (1980). *Other voices: The style of a male homosexual tavern*. Novato, CA: Chandler & Sharp.

Reid, J. D. (1995). Development in late life: Older lesbian and gay lives. In A. R. Augelli & C. J. Patterson (Eds.), *Lesbian, gay and bisexual identities over the lifespan: Psychological perspectives*. New York: Oxford University Press.

Rian, Ø. (2001). Mellom straff og fortielse. Homoseksualitet i Norge fra vikingtiden til 1930-årene. In M. C. Brantsaeter, T. Eikvam, R. Kjaer, & K. O. Åmås (Eds.), *Norsk homoforskning*. Oslo: Universitetsforlaget.

Rosaldo, R. (1989). *Culture and truth: The remaking of social analysis*. Boston: Beacon Press.

Rosenfeld, D. (1999). Identity work among lesbian and gay elderly. *Journal of Aging Studies, 13*(2), 121–144.

Sage, W. (1979). Inside the colossal closet. In M. P. Levine (Ed.), *Gay men: The sociology of male homosexuality*. New York: Harper & Row.

Sedgewick, E. K. (Ed.). (1990). *Epistemology of the closet*. Berkeley: University of California Press.

Taylor, C. (1989). *Sources of the self: The making of the modern identity*. Cambridge: Cambridge University Press.

Weinberg, M. S., Williams, C. J., & Pryor, D. W. (2001). Bisexuals at midlife: Commitment, salience and identity. *Journal of Contemporary Ethnography, 30*(2), 180–208.

Weston, K. (1991). *Families we choose: Lesbians, gays, kinship*. New York: Columbia University Press.

Wikan, U. (1990). *Managing turbulent hearts*. Chicago: University of Chicago Press.

Wikan, U. (1991). Toward an experience-near anthropology. *Cultural Anthropology, 6*(3), 285–306.

SECTION 3

Future Directions

CHAPTER 10

Issues to Consider in Studies of Midlife and Older Sexual Minorities

Douglas C. Kimmel

here are many important reasons to study the process of aging among middle-aged and older gay men, lesbians, and bisexuals. It is useful to focus on why we want to study this phenomenon so as to understand better the questions we are asking and the methods we choose to use in our empirical research. We will use the term *sexual minorities* to include lesbians, gay men, bisexuals, and transgender persons.

WHY STUDY AGING SEXUAL MINORITIES?

One reason to study aging is to increase the intergenerational contact and knowledge within the lesbian, gay, and bisexual communities. This goal is important because most lesbians, gay men, and bisexuals do not have role models for aging within their family of origin, as most heterosexuals do. They may therefore fall into stereotypes about negative views of aging for sexual minorities. These stereotypes are not easily challenged in age-segregated communities, which is often the case for gay men especially, but also is frequently true for lesbians and bisexuals. The absence in the lives of many middle-aged sexual minorities of children and their grandparents can further reduce opportunities for intergenerational contact. Empirical studies of patterns of aging can provide insights into possible future life courses for middle-aged lesbians, gay men, bisexuals, and transgender persons. Research can also promote services for the social, emotional, and physical aspects of aging that can involve intergenerational organizations.

A second reason to study aging is to reduce the impact of ageism within sexual minority groups. Contemporary U.S. culture is noted for its ageism, manifested in an emphasis on youth, beauty, and physical strength. Many commentators have suggested that men, whether heterosexual or homosexual, may be more ageist in their emphasis on physical attractiveness than are women, especially women who are attracted to other women. Whether or not this is true, in general the potential exists for the gay male community to be strongly affected by ageism. Greater contact with older role models may reduce this potential risk for ageism.

Third, studies of aging can provide positive role models for the transitions into middle age and old age, which otherwise can be hidden or overlooked. Conversely, negative role models can provide examples of pitfalls to avoid, which can also be useful information for younger persons.

Fourth, studies of aging can point out problems, needs for services, and gaps in public policies that affect lesbians, gay men, and bisexuals in particular ways. For example, the lack of Social Security benefits for domestic partners, the frequent lack of health insurance coverage, and end-of-life medical or legal concerns raise important issues for future legislation regarding same-sex civil unions. Research has the potential to improve the quality of life for older sexual minorities now and in the future.

Finally, the study of older lesbians, gay men, bisexuals, and transgender persons broadens the focus of gerontology to include sexual orientation and gender identity in ways that are beneficial for the field. It raises questions, challenges assumptions, and highlights issues that otherwise are neglected, often as a result of ignorance rather than bias or conscious omission.

THEORIES AND MODELS FOR RESEARCH WITH OLDER SEXUAL MINORITIES

One of the problems with gerontological research is the frequent absence of theoretical perspectives for the study, especially with respect to social and psychological aspects. Often the studies are described as exploratory or descriptive. Although such research has merit, it does not advance the science of gerontology as much as theory-based research can.

There are five theoretical perspectives that have emerged from studies on sexual minorities or in gerontology that may be useful models to employ in studying older lesbians, gay men, bisexuals, and transgendered persons: (1) social psychological, (2) minority stress, (3) lifespan developmental, (4) strength and resilience, and (5) successful aging models.

Social Psychological Models

Three models grow out of previous research related to sexual minority issues and are rooted in social psychological theories. Each could provide a useful template for studies of older sexual minorities. It should be noted, however, that one general finding has been that older samples are more diverse than younger ones with respect to most variables. Moreover, it would be expected that outcome variables of interest often result from multiple pathways.

Disclosure of Sexual Minority Status

Considerable research has been conducted on the effects of disclosing one's sexual orientation to others and the generally beneficial effects it has on the recipient's attitudes toward sexual minorities and on the self-esteem of the person who discloses (Herek, 1991). The impact is not always positive in terms of employment and other forms of discrimination, however (Badgett, 1996). Views of the importance of disclosure also tend to reflect generational differences, with older persons being less likely than younger persons to value indiscriminate disclosure because of historical factors (Kimmel, 1995).

Commitment to or Involvement With the LGBT Community

Finding social support, peer group endorsement, and role models within a community of like-minded persons can provide an important foundation for positive identity development and maintenance. It is also likely that persons who are attracted to community involvement differ from those who prefer to avoid such involvement. Thus, both personality style and the impact of social support from the LGBT community interact to affect the outcome variables of interest (Grossman, D'Augelli, & O'Connell, 2001).

Multigenerational Family of Choice

It is widely thought that most older lesbians, gay men, bisexuals, and transgendered persons develop groups of friends who function as if they were kin; this has been termed a *family of choice* and is thought to provide more support, in many cases, than the individual's biological or legal "family." Therefore, variations in the degree and type of emotional, financial, practical, and intergenerational support may influence the outcome variables of interest.

Minority Stress Model

The concept of *minority stress* sheds considerable light on issues affecting lesbians, gay men, bisexuals, and transgendered persons by examining the stress that reflects their status as minorities. For example, Meyer (1995) found that three minority stressors independently predict psychological distress for gay men: internalized homophobia, perceived stigma, and actual prejudice events. This model provides parallels with other minorities in society. It also provides a theoretical basis for three related concepts that have been used in research.

Crisis Competence

Early work on older gay men found evidence that some respondents benefited from skills developed as a result of having to cope with their sexual minority status (Kimmel, 1978, 1995; Weinberg & Williams, 1974). This perspective was criticized by Lee (1991) as only applicable to a segment of the population—such as the more affluent—whereas others were devastated by the crises they experienced. Since older samples of sexual minorities are made up of survivors who are available for study, the samples may be biased in favor of those who did develop crisis competence.

Multiple Minorities

It is widely assumed that having more than one minority characteristic is more problematic than having a single minority status. For example, an older African American lesbian might be described as a "triple minority"; and the impact might be expected to be three times greater, or even more (Greene, 2000). It is also possible that developing competence with one minority status might provide skills in dealing with a second one. If physical or health disabilities are added, the compounding of issues might seem to be overwhelming, however. It would be useful to investigate the coping styles of persons with multiple minorities to determine whether coping skills transfer aid in dealing with additional stigmatized social characteristics and whether some types of minority characteristics are more detrimental or benign than others.

Survivorship

Few longitudinal studies have been conducted on social psychological aspects of aging, and none have considered sexual orientation to my knowledge. It would be of considerable interest to follow multiple cohorts through the aging process. It would also be very interesting to add sexual orientation questions to some of the ongoing biosocial and medical longitudinal studies currently under way.

Lifespan Developmental Models

Five models have emerged from lifespan developmental psychology that would seem to be well suited for the study of lesbian, gay, and bisexual midlife and aging. Each has been used in research on gerontology and provides a theoretical framework for developing methodology and recruiting an appropriate sample.

Convoy Model of Aging

This perspective views each generation, or cohort, of older persons as distinct groups moving along the lifespan with their collection of interpersonal attachments, social roles, and social support moving along with them (Kahn & Antonucci, 1980). In keeping with the idea of a convoy of trucks and other vehicles moving along a highway, each generational group carries unique "baggage" reflecting its historical period. In terms of lesbian, gay, and bisexual history, each generational group would be unique, building upon the previous generations, but also affected by historical circumstances. The support system for sexual minorities would typically differ from that of aging heterosexuals, however, consisting of more friends and fewer biological kin.

Social Exchange

The nature and type of social support differ across the lifespan (Kimmel, 1979). The pattern of social exchange varies in adulthood from a relative balance of mutual give and take in the various domains (services, financial aid, emotional support, and so forth) to a pattern where one may be receiving more in one or more domains and giving more in other domains. In some cases, the imbalance becomes difficult to reciprocate equitably, and some degree of interpersonal stress may result. Caregiving is an important example of this process. Studies on partners who cared for persons with AIDS may have useful insights for studies of caregiving issues for old persons.

Social Psychological Transitions

Many models of adult development incorporate some idea of transitions between one relatively stable period and the next one. It may be equally relevant to view adult development as a process of ceaseless change (Riegel, 1976) or of different periods marked off as if they were chapters in one's own life history (Kooden & Flowers, 2000). In general, social patterns mark off specific transitional periods, such as graduations, retirements, and family events (Neugarten, 1968). Many of the latter do not apply to lesbians, gay men, and bisexuals who do not marry or have children, however. Other idiosyncratic events may be important, such as coming out, coming into a LGBT community, or beginning a long-term relationship. Studies of adulthood and aging can benefit from an analysis of these transitions and the age at which they occur, especially when cross-cultural comparisons are being made or when different generations or regional groups are being compared.

Continuity Model

Although periods of change and instability often attract attention, many aspects of growing older reflect the continuity of life over time for each individual (Costa & McCrae, 1980). For example, some individuals tend to be *crisis-prone* throughout their lives—experiencing an unusual number and degree of crises during development (Chiriboga &

Cutler, 1980). Others are relatively adept at coping with changing circumstances. In part, these differences reflect personality variables—which have seldom been examined with regard to lesbians, gay men, and bisexuals. They may also reflect skills or styles that have been learned from role models. To compare and contrast the transitions and continuity models in qualitative studies would make an exploratory study of aging lesbians, gay men, bisexuals, and transgender persons much richer and interesting.

Generativity, Integrity, and the Life Review

Erikson (1976) emphasized the themes of late life as a dialectical struggle between a sense of generativity versus stagnation and a sense of integrity versus despair, with the awareness that death is the final theme of human development. In middle age one is dealing with earlier themes of intimacy versus isolation combined with generativity versus stagnation, according to Erikson. But when death becomes a conscious reality, in contrast to a distant possibility, the themes shift to the last two dialectical struggles and one searches for the belief that one's life was a worthwhile adventure. When death becomes imminent, the focus shifts to the last struggle of life: the sense of integrity versus despair in the face of death itself. Butler (1963) noted that the process of the *life review* was often helpful in resolving these struggles in a positive outcome. For sexual minorities, however, aging can be problematic since *intimacy* often involves same-gender relationships that are stigmatized by mainstream society; moreover, *generativity* is frequently not linked to one's offspring and alternate forms might not be valued as highly. The *life review* process also may be selective, except when conducted with sympathetic and understanding persons or members of the LGBT community. Therefore, it could be of interest to inquire about these developmental issues of intimacy, generativity, integrity, and the life review. It would also be useful to explore the extent to which social stigma of sexual minority aging interferes with the successful resolution of these dialectic struggles and the extent to which there is "unfinished business" that cannot be discussed with friends, family members, or others.

Strength and Resilience Models

When studying aging sexual minorities, it is useful to search for theoretical models that emphasize positive aspects of minority status, as noted above, and also positive aspects of aging. Four themes worth considering are briefly discussed in this section. The next section on successful aging expands this focus in more pragmatic dimensions than the theoretical ones noted here.

Sense of Purpose (Existential)

Based on his experiences in a Nazi concentration camp, Frankl (1992) described the importance of a search for meaning in life, especially when conditions are stressful and involve persecution and social stigma. Similar ideas were important in the existentialist movement in Europe and the United States (Barnes, 1959; May, 1958; Sartre, 1956). The essence of this perspective is that one creates a sense of purpose, meaning, and role in life; the ultimate meaning inherent in life is one's free choice to continue living or to commit suicide. The implication of this view is that questions about the individual's construction of a sense of meaning and purpose may be important for understanding the degree of satisfaction, adjustment, or despair in life as an aging sexual minority.

Optimism

Seligman and Csikszentmihalyi (2000) proposed a positive approach to psychology in which hopefulness, optimism, and positive reframing of negative events promote healthy outcomes. This perspective may also apply to aging in general, and to sexual minority aging in particular. The ideas are similar to the development of *crisis competence* discussed earlier; the difference is that this positive approach provides a model for understanding why similar crises may promote competence in some persons and are destructive for others. It would also be likely that this dimension of functioning would be reflected in measures of adjustment, satisfaction, and coping ability, so empirical studies should be cautious about the circularity of such variables, especially in samples of older persons who, having lived to an advanced age, are unique survivors.

Coping Skills

One important dimension on which persons differ is their array of coping skills—that is, their strategies for dealing with difficult issues and problems in living. Moreover, some coping skills are more successful than others, and their efficacy varies with different types of problems. In general, one's array of coping skills may be thought to increase with aging, and one key to *successful aging* is the ability to compensate for actual losses that occur with age and disease. Some coping skills are also much more likely to promote psychological and physical health than are others (e.g., exercise versus overeating, meditation versus aggression). Since sexual minority aging can involve more challenges than either condition alone, it may be helpful to look at the coping skills and their outcome for the individual, in addition to the problems with which individuals may be coping.

Stress and Hassles

Considerable literature in health psychology has focused on the role of stress, different types of stress, and the frequency of stress on the functioning of individuals. This literature differentiates between stressful events, such as moving, and "hassles," which are daily occurrences that are irritating (Chiriboga & Cutler, 1980). It would be likely that sexual minorities experience more daily hassles than those who are not socially stigmatized, whether the stigma is directed precisely at them or not—for example, the derogatory use of the term *faggot* is common in casual speech. Thus, when studying the effects of minority stress, it would be useful to think of both aging and sexual minority status as potential causes of daily hassles, as well as causes of stressful events. The resulting matrix of stressors, offset by coping skills, would give a view of the daily life of the aging lesbian, gay, bisexual, or transgender person that would be helpful for understanding them.

Successful Aging Model

Rowe and Kahn (1987) shifted the aging paradigm from one of losses and declines to a view of older persons who are aging with a high degree of social, psychological, and physical vitality. A parallel view of aging has been to focus on longevity as a positive goal and an attainable outcome for a growing segment of the population worldwide (Butler & Kiikuni, 1993). This emerging view of aging focuses on those characteristics and life patterns that increase the chance of living successfully into advanced old age, and the attributes that are associated with this state.

One outcome of this perspective has been to identify a number of risk factors and benefits that may increase the likelihood of aging with a minimum of impairment and a maximum of social, physical, and psychological vigor, independence, and involvement with meaningful activities. If we focus on aging sexual minorities, it is possible to propose a list of risk factors and benefits that would have a pragmatic effect on successful aging; eleven are briefly described here.

Openness Regarding Sexual Orientation

Maintaining secrecy regarding one's sexual minority status would be likely to have a negative effect on successful aging because it would increase the level of stress, impair communication between oneself and health care providers, and increase the chances of negative involvement with genetic family members. Conversely, openness could reduce the quality of care and increase the risk of discrimination in some health care settings.

Health Status

In general, chronological age is far less relevant to successful aging than is physical health. Self-care regarding diet, exercise, and appropriate medical services is probably the most important element in aging successfully. Some aspects of sexual minority status may increase self-care practices (e.g., focus on physical attractiveness for gay men), while others may decrease it (e.g., higher incidence of excessive weight for lesbians). Transgender health issues are seldom discussed and may affect longevity and successful aging (Donovan, 2001).

Risk Factors

Tobacco use, excessive alcohol use, and driving under the influence of any substance have clear effects on higher mortality and disability rates. In general, accidents and hazardous employment situations are also risk factors for unsuccessful aging. Sexual minorities are potentially at greater risk for tobacco, alcohol, and substance use in part because of the social stress of living with a concealable stigma (Gay and Lesbian Medical Association & Columbia University Center for LGBT Health, 2000). These factors may also increase the risk of accidents. To the extent that sexual minority status also affects occupational opportunities (e.g., due to discrimination against transgender persons or divorced lesbian mothers), there may be an increased risk of unsuccessful aging from dangerous, stressful, or unhealthy employment conditions.

Having a Partner

In general, being alone is associated with greater risk of unsuccessful aging—in part because persons who are alone may be alone because of other factors that are also related to mortality risk, such as alcoholism, antisocial personality, or inability to control anger. Moreover, it is likely that having a partner is associated with interpersonal skills that may be independently related to successful aging. A partner may also serve as a *buffer* against losses and someone who can aid with challenges of aging (Lowenthal, 1964). A partner may also be a caregiver, a reason for living, or a spiritual soul mate who promotes successful aging just by being around. Conversely, loss of a partner can be a severe blow and disrupt, at least for a time, an otherwise successful aging process. Loss of their domestic partner may produce different effects for sexual minorities than for typical heterosexual spouses. For example, same-sex couples have a similar life expectancy, whereas for other-sex couples the woman usually lives longer (and typically marries an older man); thus, sexual minorities, in general, may be less likely to spend a prolonged period alone as compared to heterosexual widows. Sexual minorities may also have multiple significant relationships that are long-lasting, so that even if the primary relationship ends, other relationships may persist (e.g., previous lesbian lovers, gay male friends, divorced spouses). Since sexual minorities typically create a "family" of choice for support and mutual aid, the relevant factor is the age of these persons; if one wishes to benefit from these support groups, it is necessary to develop multigenerational relationships that include younger people.

Living Alone

Regardless of one's partnership status or the presence of a self-chosen family of support, living alone can be a risk factor for successful aging, especially in old age. In some cases this risk is offset by shared housing, assisted living settings, or innovative arrangements (e.g., a small multigenerational apartment house where each resident is available for mutual aid). Sexual minorities may be at some risk for discrimination or harassment if their sexual orientation is known, but generally people assume that after a "certain age" sex is not important anymore. Of course, this assumption is not accurate. Sex is a private matter that is different from sexual orientation. There are situations in housing settings for the elderly where same-sex liaisons would cause problems for some staff, however. For this reason, housing alternatives for sexual minorities are being developed (e.g., openhouse, a grassroots project in San Francisco).

Social and Educational Background

It is often assumed that all sexual minorities are affluent, but this is not the case, especially for aging persons whose life circumstances reflect great diversity of educational and economic histories. Discrimination as a sexual minority, as a woman, or as an ethnic or racial minority, as well as individual hardship may have reduced income and savings, leading to financial hardship in old age. Economic and employment circumstances affect access to health care, housing options, and social resources. Educational background, likewise, varies among older sexual minorities, as well as across generations—with older generations generally having less chance for higher education than younger generations. These demographic variables may directly or indirectly affect the likelihood of successful aging for individuals. The lack of financial resources in old age among the pioneers of the LGBT movement—often as a result of their resultant lack of employment options—has been one reason for the development of retirement communities for sexual minorities.

HIV/AIDS

Progress in treating persons who are infected with the human immuno-deficiency virus (HIV positive) has made it possible for many to live for years with the virus relatively dormant. As a result of these medical advances, a greater number of older HIV-positive sexual minority persons, especially gay and bisexual men, are growing older (Allers, 1990). Some older people are also becoming infected through unprotected sex or IV drug use. The impact of HIV infection on older persons is not well understood, but it clearly is a factor that affects aging processes—in terms of self-esteem, acceptance, physical health risks, and the need for social support (Meris, 2001). Therefore, studies of aging sexual minorities should consider the possible impact of HIV/AIDS and include relevant variables in data collection.

Support System

Although the term sounds somewhat mechanical, its intent is to capture the complex interaction of mutual aid, financial support, caregiving, friendship, and interlocking obligations to significant others in times of need. One study of older sexual minorities found that participants were more satisfied with the support they received from persons who knew their sexual orientation than from persons who did not know it; the sexual orientation or age group of the person providing support did not matter, however (Grossman, D'Augelli, & O'Connell, 2001). The members of a support system, their connection to the individual, and the patterns of reciprocal aid and caregiving would be important to include in a study of aging sexual minorities. It would be interesting to know, not only who helps with what, but whether this aid is reciprocated and what the positive and negative effects of these support networks are.

Relations With Family

Often family ties are broken or minimized for older sexual minorities, especially when there is lack of acceptance by the family of origin for the person's sexual orientation or gender identity. This situation varies by cultural background, however, with African American families maintaining closer ties than most European American families; Asian American families also stress family ties, which often creates serious conflicts for sexual minority adults who do not marry or have children (Greene, 1997). Some sexual minorities do marry and have children; these relationships may be significant (cf. Kristiansen, this volume). Of course, some lesbians and gay men have children within the context of a committed relationship, or rear biological children, adopted children, or foster children (Patterson, 1997). Some adopt an adult as a son, daughter, or lover; and some are legal coparents of a child with a gay or lesbian partner. Since these relationships may provide significant social support in old age, they are important to include in studies of aging sexual minorities.

Advance Planning

In the United States, laws and customs give biological or married family relations greater power and entitlement than is given to domestic partners or intimate friends; this is especially important in the case of serious illness, incapacity, or death. For this reason, lesbian and gay relationships need to be documented in appropriate legal papers such as a *power of attorney* or *health care directives*. In addition, a *will* and *letter of last instructions* help ensure that matters are handled as the person would have wished following death. These documents require planning in advance for death and possible incapacity, illness, or emergency medical assistance. Of course, these steps are not limited to aging sexual minorities, since they are often important for many other persons. They do, however, force individuals to confront their mortality and, if appropriate, their sexual minority status and the impact that has on end-of-life decisions. Therefore, it may often be useful to inquire about such planning, to include it as a relevant variable in empirical studies, and to consider the importance of educating older sexual minorities about these issues.

Long-Term Friendships

In addition to domestic partners (i.e., lovers, long-term companions, intimate partners), many older sexual minorities have long-term friendships that may be overlooked because of the heterosexual model of marriage as between only two persons. It is possible that some sexual minorities have practiced *polyamory*, that is, have had intimate and possibly sexual relations with two or more significant partners at the same time (Rust, 1996). Moreover, some may have developed long-term relationships with past lovers that continued after the partners moved on to other lovers; this may be more often the case for lesbians than for gay men. Likewise, some older persons may have had multiple significant sexual partners who were never considered to be lovers but who were long-term intimate friends; this pattern may be more often the case for gay men. Bisexuals may have long-term intimate relationships with persons of both sexes, including former spouses. These points suggest that the *social network* or *domestic partner* themes should be amplified to include some inquiry as to the nature of the relationship and whether there were additional significant intimate relationships at the same time. It would be interesting to explore whether these multiple relationships play important roles in the older sexual minority person's successful aging.

ISSUES TO CONSIDER IN EMPIRICAL RESEARCH ON OLDER SEXUAL MINORITIES

In addition to finding useful theoretical models and developing an interesting set of variables, the researcher on topics related to older sexual minorities would be wise to consider a range of issues early in the project. Of course, when conducting and reporting empirical studies it is important to avoid ageist (Schaie, 1988) and heterosexist (Herek, Kimmel, Amaro, & Melton, 1991) research bias. Moreover, there are several useful points to think about in advance regarding each section of the written report of the study.

Discussion

Although the final section of the published report, it may be helpful to think about some key points in the discussion at the beginning of the research project and before writing the report. These points will help frame the literature review and design of the study. First, why is the study interesting? If there is no point in finding out the information, then it is not a useful exercise for either the researcher or the participants. A simple "fishing expedition" needs to be justified and should be limited to a pilot study. Use of some theoretical model is recommended, as has been discussed above.

Second, think about how the data will be used when they are reported. If there is a strong possibility they might be misused to stereotype or stigmatize older sexual minorities, the study might not be a good idea. For example, if the questions focused on the respondent's views on the "cause" of their homosexuality, or on their fantasies about unacceptable sexual practices, those who believe sexual minorities have chosen to be sexual deviates could easily misuse the data. Moreover, the researcher should consider the impact the study would have, if any, on ageism, homophobia, heterosexism, sexual prejudice, and on the lesbian, gay, bisexual, and transgender communities.

Third, the researcher would do well to reflect on what the study might add to what we already know in the fields of sexual minorities and in gerontology, and what research might follow from this study.

Methods

The method reflects the question being asked in the research project. In general, two types of methodology are useful in studies of midlife and older sexual minorities: matched samples and representative samples.

Matched samples are useful when representative samples are difficult or impossible to obtain. They do not describe the frequency of the phenomenon, but they can clarify the effect of a relevant variable. For example, a comparison of partnered versus nonpartnered groups would provide useful information, especially if the two groups were matched as closely as possible on a range of variables such as social class, education, age, income, and health status—or if these variables were taken into account in the analyses of the data.

Representative samples are more feasible than had been thought because of the use of telephone surveys that include sexual orientation; random samples in neighborhoods with a high density of sexual minorities; and voter surveys on election days that include sexual orientation questions. Such samples are especially helpful for needs assessment studies, such as for services that are required or the desire for retirement housing. Representative samples are also needed for accurate descriptive studies, such as on current emotional adjustment, frequency of sexual activity, or risk for HIV infection.

Sample

As with the method, the sample depends on the question asked in the research project. For example, one study might be concerned with self-identified sexual orientation as lesbians, gay men, bisexuals, or all of these groups. Another study might focus on sexual behavior—men who have sex with men or women who have sex with women—and these groups might be further refined by whether the behavior is in the present, in the past, or planned for in the future. Sampling decisions always need to consider whether bisexuals will be included, and if so how they will be described. Decisions about the sample also need to consider whether transgendered persons will be included. Of course, some studies might focus on bisexual or transgender persons exclusively.

It is also important to note that all samples are *survivors*, and this fact becomes more significant if older age groups are the focus of the study. This consideration implies that there may be some inherent bias in the samples obtained because an unknown portion did not live long enough to be included—for example, because of the AIDS epidemic—or are not available for sampling because they are in prison, lack telephones (for telephone sampling), are homeless, and so forth.

IMPLICATIONS

There are three implications from this discussion on the importance of studying older sexual minorities. First, there are many interesting questions that have not been explored at all, and very few that have received adequate attention to date. The eleven topics described above in terms of successful aging are each relevant and significant questions awaiting empirical research.

Second, sexual minority aging can best be described as a mosaic of diversity. In my view, it is important to keep the beauty of that diversity in mind as one delves into specific research topics. In research on aging, the people are often more interesting than the study and point out the inadequacy of our models and paradigms. They also remind us of the multiple pathways and the importance of diversity for successful aging patterns. As with autumn in Maine, if one focuses on counting types of tree bark, one might miss the beauty of the leaves.

Third, in so far as possible, barriers to successful aging for sexual minorities should be removed or, at least, reduced for this and future generations. Therefore, it may be helpful to keep in mind the potentially positive impact the research may have and to focus on those things that can be changed. Not all research needs to be applied to social problems, of course, but if one looks carefully, there may be nuggets that can be mined that will make some difference somewhere.

Finally, we must remember that *age* is not the only relevant variable in the study of aging; in fact, it may not even be the important one. I like to keep my childhood model trains in mind when I think of aging: the oldest, now 53 years old, runs the best and the fastest; the "middle-aged" one, about 45 years old, doesn't run at all anymore; the youngest one, about 40 years old, never ran as well as the others, but it is still going strong. To stretch this parable further, I have noticed that my Marx-brand trains run well on Lionel-brand tracks, but cannot negotiate the Lionel switches. Similarly, some sexual minorities may be able to manage the basic life issues as well as anyone, but can have trouble on heterosexual transition points, such as those that may come with aging.

REFERENCES

Allers, C. T. (1990). AIDS and the older adult. *The Gerontologist, 30*, 405–407.

Badgett, M. V. (1996). Employment and sexual orientation: Disclosure and discrimination in the work place. *Journal of Gay and Lesbian Social Services, 4*(3), 29–52.

Barnes, H. E. (1959). *Humanistic existentialism: The literature of possibility.* Lincoln: University of Nebraska Press.

Butler, R. N. (1963). The life review: An interpretation of reminiscence in the aged. *Psychiatry, 26*, 65–76.

Butler, R. N., & Kiikuni, K. (Eds.) (1993). *Who is responsible for my old age?* New York: Springer.

Chiriboga, D. A., & Cutler, L. (1980). Stress and adaptation: Life span perspectives. In L. W. Poon (Ed.), *Aging in the 1980s: Psychological issues* (pp. 347–362). Washington, DC: American Psychological Association.

Costa, P. T., Jr., & McCrae, R. R. (1980). Still stable after all these years: Personality as a key to some issues in adulthood and old age. In P. B. Baltes & O. G. Brim, Jr. (Eds.), *Life-span development and behavior* (Vol. 3, pp. 65–102). New York: Academic Press.

Donovan, T. (2001). Being transgender and older: A first-person account. *Journal of Gay and Lesbian Social Services, 13*(4), 19–22.

Erikson, E. H. (1976). Reflections on Dr. Borg's life cycle. *Daedalus, 105*, 1–28.

Frankl, V. E. (1992). *Man's search for meaning* (4th ed.). Boston: Beacon.

Gay and Lesbian Medical Association & Columbia University Center for LGBT Health. (2000). Lesbian, gay, bisexual, and transgender health: Findings and concerns. *Gay and Lesbian Medical Association Journal, 4*(3), 101–151.

Greene, B. (2000). Beyond heterosexism and across the cultural divide: Developing an inclusive lesbian, gay, and bisexual psychology: A look to the future. In B. Greene & G. L. Croom (Eds.), *Education, research, and practice in lesbian, gay, bisexual, and transgendered psychology* (pp. 1–45). Thousand Oaks, CA: Sage.

Greene, B. (Ed.). (1997). *Ethnic and cultural diversity among lesbians and gay men.* Thousand Oaks, CA: Sage.

Grossman, A., D'Augelli, A. E., & O'Connell, T. S. (2001). Being lesbian, gay, bisexual, and older in North America. *Journal of Gay and Lesbian Social Services, 13*(4), 23–40.

Herek, G. M. (1991). Stigma, prejudice, and violence against lesbians and gay men. In J. C. Gonsiorek & J. D. Weinrich (Eds.), *Homosexuality: Research findings for public policy* (pp. 60–80). Newbury Park, CA: Sage.

Herek, G. M., Kimmel, D. C., Amaro, H., & Melton, G. B. (1991). Avoiding heterosexist bias in psychological research. *American Psychologist, 46*, 957–963.

Kahn, R., & Antonucci, T. (1980). Convoys over the life course: Attachment, roles, and social support. In P. B. Baltes & O. G. Brim, Jr. (Eds.), *Life-span development and behavior* (Vol. 3, pp. 254–286). New York: Academic Press.

Kimmel, D. C. (1978). Adult development and aging: A gay perspective. *Journal of Social Issues, 34*(3), 113–130.

Kimmel, D. C. (1979). Relationship initiation and development: A lifespan developmental approach. In R. L. Burgess & T. L. Huston (Eds.), *Social exchange in developing relationships* (pp. 351–377). New York: Academic Press.

Kimmel, D. C. (1990). *Adulthood and aging: An interdisciplinary developmental view* (3rd ed.). New York: John Wiley & Sons.

Kimmel, D. C. (1995). Lesbians and gay men also grow old. In L. A. Bond, S. J. Cutler, & A. Grams (Eds.), *Promoting successful and productive aging* (pp. 289–303). Thousand Oaks, CA: Sage.

Kooden, H., & Flowers, C. (2000). *Golden men: The power of gay midlife.* New York: Harper-Collins.

Lee, J. A. (Ed.). (1991). Forward. *Journal of Homosexuality, 20*(3/4), xiii–xix.

Lowenthal, M. F. (1964). Social isolation and mental illness in old age. *American Sociological Review, 29,* 54–70.

May, R. (1958). Contributions of existential psychotherapy. In R. May, E. Angel, & H. F. Ellenberger (Eds.), *Existence: A new dimension in psychiatry and psychology* (pp. 37–91). New York: Basic Books.

Meris, D. (2001). Responding to mental health and grief of homeless HIV-infected gay men. *Journal of Gay and Lesbian Social Services, 13*(4), 103–111.

Meyer, I. (1995). Minority stress and the mental health in gay men. *Journal of Health and Social Behavior, 7,* 9–25.

Neugarten, B. L. (1968). Adult personality: Toward a psychology of the life cycle. In B. L. Neugarten (Ed.), *Middle age and aging* (pp. 137–147). Chicago: University of Chicago Press.

Patterson, C. J. (1997). Children of lesbian and gay parents. In T. H. Ollendick & R. J. Prinz (Eds.), *Advances in clinical child psychology* (pp. 235–282). New York: Plenum Press.

Riegel, K. F. (1976). The dialectic of human development. *American Psychologist, 31,* 689–700.

Rowe, J. W., & Kahn, R. L. (1987). Human aging: Usual and successful. *Science, 237,* 143–149.

Rust, P. C. (1996). Monogamy and polyamory. In B. A. Firestein (Ed.), *Bisexuality: The psychology and politics of an invisible minority* (pp. 127–148). Thousand Oaks, CA: Sage.

Sartre, J. P. (1956). *Being and nothingness.* New York: Philosophical Library.

Schaie, W. K. (1988). Ageism in psychological research. *American Psychologist, 43,* 179–183.

Seligman, M. E. P., & Csikszentmihalyi, M. (2000). Postive psychology: An introduction. *American Psychologist, 55,* 5–14.

Weinberg, M. S., & Williams, C. J. (1974). *Male homosexuals: Their problems and adaptations.* New York: Oxford University Press.

Index

accidents, mortality in sexual minority population from, 274–275
Acquired immune deficiency syndrome. *See* AIDS
Advance planning, 278
Affair, defined, 8
Age at which disclosure of homosexuality took place, 130–131
  depression and, 130–131
AIDS, 12–15, 21, 276–277
  bathhouse sexual interactions, 219, 230
  community, impact upon, 85–87
  demographics, 77–78
  depression, 83–84
  developmental perspectives, 87–89
  effect on psychological well-being, 100. *See also* Depression; Grief
  epidemiological statistics, 76–77
  grief reactions, 11–12, 15, 81, 85–87
  integrity, development of, 87–89
  isolation with, 81
  meaning, finding of in diagnosis, 84
  medications for, 83
    side effects of, 83
  mortality, heightened sense with, 83
  multiple losses, effect of, 81, 85–86
  political consequences, 80–81
  psychological impact of, 79–80
  social consequences of, 80–81
  spirituality, development of with, 84

  substance abuse, 84
  survivor guilt, 83
  transmission of through oral sex, 220
  World Health Organization data, 76–77
Alcohol abuse, in sexual minority population, 274–275
  in dealing with AIDS-related grief, 84–86
  living alone, 163, 275
Anger, inability to control, living alone because of, 163, 275
Antisocial personality, living alone because of, 163, 275
Arthritis, in aging women, 50–55

Bars, finding same-gendered relationships in, 212, 227
Bathhouses, aging and sociosexual interactions, 211–234
  age segregation in, 211–234
  cleanliness of, 224–225
  criminal sanctions, imposition of for homosexual activity, 212
  demonstrations of safer-sex practices, 218
  erection, importance of in attraction of partner, 214
  fear of HIV/AIDS in, 219, 230
  gesture as means of communication, 214